Engagements with Nar

Balancing key foundational topics with new developments and trends, *Engagements with Narrative* offers an accessible introduction to narratology. As new narrative forms and media emerge, the study of narrative and the ways people communicate through imagination, empathy, and storytelling is especially relevant for students of literature today. Janine Utell presents the foundational texts, key concepts, and big ideas that form narrative theory and practical criticism, engaging readers in the study of stories by telling the story of a field and its development.

Distinct features designed to initiate dialogue and debate include:

- Coverage of philosophical and historical contexts surrounding the study of narrative.
- An introduction to essential thinkers along with the tools to both use and interrogate their work.
- A survey of the most up-to-date currents, including mind theory and postmodern ethics, to stimulate conversations about how we read fiction, life writing, film, and digital media from a variety of perspectives.
- A selection of narrative texts, chosen to demonstrate critical practice and spark further reading and research.
- "Engagements" sections to encourage students to engage with narrative theory and practice through interviews with scholars.

This guide teaches the key concepts of narrative—time, space, character, perspective, setting—while facilitating conversations among different approaches and media, and opening paths to new inquiry. *Engagements with Narrative* is ideal for readers needing an introduction to the field, as well as for those seeking insight into both its historical developments and new directions.

Janine Utell is Professor and Chair of English at Widener University, USA.

Routledge Engagements with Literature

This series presents engagement as discovery. It aims to encourage ways to read seriously and to help readers hone and develop new habits of thinking critically and creatively about what they read—before, during, and after doing it. Each book in the series actively involves its readers by encouraging them to find their own insights, to develop their own judgments, and to inspire them to enter ongoing debates. Moreover, each *Engagements* volume:

- Provides essential information about its topic as well as alternative views and approaches;
- Covers the classic scholarship on its topic as well as the newest approaches and suggests new directions for study and research;
- Includes innovative "Engagements" sections that demonstrate practices for engaging with literature or that provide suggestions for further independent engagement;
- Provides an array of fresh, stimulating, and effective catalysts to reading, thinking, writing, and research.

Above all, *Routledge Engagements with Literature* shows that actively engaging with literature rewards the effort and that any reader can make new discoveries. My hope is the books in this series will help readers discover new, better, and more exciting and enjoyable ways of doing what we do when we read.

Series Editor
Daniel A. Robinson

Available in this series:

Engagements with Close Reading
Annette Federico

Engagements with Narrative
Janine Utell

Engagements with Narrative

Janine Utell

Routledge
Taylor & Francis Group

LONDON AND NEW YORK

First published 2016
by Routledge
2 Park Square, Milton Park, Abingdon, Oxon OX14 4RN

and by Routledge
711 Third Avenue, New York, NY 10017

Routledge is an imprint of the Taylor & Francis Group, an informa business

British Library Cataloguing-in-Publication Data
A catalogue record for this book is available from the British Library

Library of Congress Cataloging-in-Publication Data
Utell, Janine, 1975–
Engagements with narrative/Janine Utell.
pages cm.—(Routledge engagements with literature)
Includes bibliographical references and index.
1. Narration (Rhetoric) I. Title.
PN212.U84 2015
808'.036—dc23
2015015911

ISBN: 978-0-415-73244-4 (hbk)
ISBN: 978-0-415-73246-8 (pbk)
ISBN: 978-1-315-77905-8 (ebk)

Typeset in Sabon
by Book Now Ltd, London

FSC
www.fsc.org
MIX
Paper from
responsible sources
FSC® C013604

Printed and bound by CPI Group (UK) Ltd, Croydon, CR0 4YY

Contents

Illustrations

Figures

Tables

Acknowledgments

Thanks are due first and foremost to those with whom I have worked at Routledge, starting with thanks to my external readers for excellent suggestions on the initial proposal. I am grateful to Ruth Hilsdon for her patience and assistance in preparing the final manuscript. My colleague and series editor Daniel Robinson extended the invitation to write this book; he also made a number of helpful suggestions for improving it, for which I am exceedingly grateful.

I was inspired to pursue a project along these lines after participating in the 2011 Project Narrative Summer Institute at Ohio State University. James Phelan and Frederick Luis Aldama led PNSI that year, and I couldn't have asked for more supportive mentors. My fellow "narrative campers" were likewise supportive, and offered seemingly endless opportunities for good conversation and invaluable feedback. In particular, I would like to thank Jennifer Ho, for helpful initial feedback; Leah Anderst, for insight into narrative and film; and James Donahue, for guidance and support in the final days of completing the manuscript. Their friendship is a gift.

A highlight of this book is the interviews that were so generously granted by colleagues working in narrative studies: Leah Anderst, Sarah Copland, James Donahue, Jennifer Ho, Suzanne Keen, Sue Kim, Adam Zachary Newton, Anastasia Salter. I know readers will enjoy and learn from their contributions as much as I have. It has been a privilege to work with them to bring this component of the book to fruition.

Much gratitude is due to my students at Widener University, especially in my courses on film, graphic narrative, life writing, and the British novel. They have given me good ideas, given me good feedback on my bad ideas, and allowed me to test readings and analyses on them with patience and enthusiasm. Thanks also to my colleagues in the English Department at Widener for their collegiality and support. And of course this project would never have been possible without the herculean efforts of the Interlibrary Loan staff of Wolfgram Memorial Library.

Finally, I would like to acknowledge, with appreciation beyond words, the support of my family: John and Linda Utell, Susan Utell and Bill Groshelle, and Tracy, Glen, and Abigail Farber. Their patience as I was trying to get this project done, their good humor, their unending support, and their helpful ideas and suggestions as lovers of good stories all made this book possible. Special thanks are due to John-Paul Spiro, without whom a lot of this would simply not be possible. My sister Tracy and I have shared a lifetime of stories, and her daughter, my amazing niece Abigail, is quite a remarkable storyteller in her own right. (Abigail also sat through numerous readings of *This Is Not My Hat* with a great deal of forbearance.) I dedicate this book to them.

* * *

I am grateful to the following for granting permission to use material herein:

Chapter 2:

Graphic Novel Excerpt from *American Widow* by Alissa Torres, illustrated by Sungyoon Choi, © 2008 by E-Luminated Books, Inc. Used by permission of Villard Books, an imprint of Random House, a division of Penguin Random House LLC. All rights reserved. Any third party use of this material, outside of this publication, is prohibited. Interested parties must apply directly to Penguin Random House LLC for permission.

Chapter 3:

Illustration from *Jimmy Corrigan: The Smartest Kid on Earth* by Chris Ware, © 2000, 2003, by Chris Ware. Used by permission of Pantheon Books, an imprint of the Knopf Doubleday Publishing Group, a division of Penguin Random House LLC. All rights reserved. Any third party use of this material, outside of this publication, is prohibited. Interested parties must apply directly to Penguin Random House LLC for permission.

Illustration from *Relish: My Life in the Kitchen* © 2013 by Lucy Knisley. Reprinted by permission of First Second, an imprint of Roaring Brook Press, a division of Holtzbrinck Publishing Holdings Limited Partnership. All rights reserved.

Robert Berry and Chad Rutkowski for the screenshot from *Ulysses "Seen"* (© Robert Berry, 2011).

Rosamund Davies for the screenshot from *Index of Love* (*indexoflove*, © Rosamund Davies 2010).

Simon Flesser and Simogo for the screenshot from *Device 6* (© Simogo 2013).

Introduction
How to do things with narrative

Argo, Ben Affleck's 2012 film about the rescue of six Americans during the Iran hostage crisis of 1979–80, depends heavily on the importance of story. Not only is story, the making of story, essential to the plot: the CIA plans to rescue the six from the Canadian ambassador's home in Tehran, where they are hiding out, by creating a ruse wherein they are disguised as a film production team scouting locations for a fake science-fiction movie called *Argo*, complete with storyboards, script, and publicity materials. The film is also remarkably sensitive to cultural difference and bias—especially remarkably for a post-9/11 Hollywood film about hostage-taking in the Middle East—and one way it achieves this is through story. In several scenes where the Americans interact with Iranian revolutionaries, continuing with the ruse (and thereby avoiding arrest and torture) rests on the notion that the power of narrative is a universal, that there are some stories that speak to us as a human community. There are certain shared stories, and certain ways we share those stories, that facilitate human connection and empathy. In one instance, the fake film crew is taken to the bazaar by a member of the Ministry of Culture and Islamic Guidance; intrigued by their work, he asks if the film is a "foreign bride story," where a "foreign bride comes to Iran, and she doesn't know the language or the customs . . . and there are lots of laughs." In another, the six are about to get on the airplane to escape Iran, and the Revolutionary Guard stops them. To get themselves out of the situation, one of the six, who speaks Farsi, takes out the storyboards and convinces the revolutionaries that they are making a film about a group of poor farmers who seek to stand up to an evil and corrupt ruler and liberate their country. It sounds a lot like *Star Wars*, a major intertext for *Argo*, but it also sounds a lot like the Iranian revolution. In both cases, a presumption is made that stories are universal, that they provide a shared, collective language around our most basic human needs for love, freedom, community.

Stories are everywhere. They can be intensely private, and they can be shared. They form the bonds between friends and family members, and as they are told and retold those bonds can become stronger. They can also provide the foundation for grudges and hatreds, and as they are told and retold, wounds can become deeper. The telling of stories can be therapeutic: a visit to a counselor's office, blogging a breakup or posting on Facebook, complaining with friends. They can also be celebratory, the recounting of a triumph. Our most basic social interactions often involve stories; stories are told over meals, in houses of worship, as part of getting acquainted and as part of catching up. But they are also necessary to the workings of our minds, to the complex process of giving our lives meaning. To make a story out of my experience helps me to order my world, to give significance to seemingly insignificant events, to define goals and see connections and feel purpose.

We are storytelling creatures. Aristotle says that two qualities define human beings' relationship to "representation," to art and stories: "Imitation is natural to man from childhood" and "It is also natural for all to delight in works of imitation" (2318). A small child learns to tell a story even before she learns how to read. She perceives this is a way to connect with others, to join the conversation, to share her experience. Possibly she even sees that telling a story is a way to make sense of her experiences and her impressions. In the telling the world becomes hers; stories help her to understand time and memory, to situate herself in her own life. She notes that her stories get responses: laughter, affirmation, possibly bewilderment. The telling of stories goes beyond the written word. The earliest stories come from an oral culture, a time before the invention of the printing press, when stories were transmitted via the recitation of poems like *The Odyssey*. They come from drawings on the walls of caves like those at Lascaux. They come from sacred texts. The earliest writing that we might call "literary theory" comes from trying to figure out how stories work, how they make us laugh and cry, how we enter into relationship with entirely fictional beings.

The relationships we are able to create with fictional beings are fundamental to how narrative works. Think about the first line of a novel:

- "Call me Ishmael."
- "It was a bright cold day in April, and the clocks were striking thirteen."
- "Someone must have slandered Josef K., for one morning, without having done anything truly wrong, he was arrested."
- "Once upon a time and a very good time it was there was a moocow coming down along the road and this moocow that was coming down along the road met a nicens little boy named baby tuckoo."
- "This is the saddest story I have ever heard."

The first line of Herman Melville's *Moby-Dick* is both an invitation and an imperative; actually, *all* first lines are in some respects invitations and imperatives. They create a pathway for us into the story, into the world of the story. They offer a welcoming gesture, but they also call upon our desire to keep reading. They *insist* themselves upon us, the same way Ishmael tells us what to call him. Are we calling Ishmael "Ishmael" for a reason? Is that his name? The name seems resonant, possibly carrying with it a Biblical allusion; does that matter? Is Ishmael the main character, is he just the teller of the story? Both? What is the relationship between teller and tale?

What about the first line of George Orwell's *1984*? The invitation here consists of a fairly straightforward situating in time, with setting (English writers love to note the weather). Bright cold days in April are not unusual, and by noting the time of year, the season, the weather, he connects to his readers' experiences of such things. The story builds from the beginning on our familiarity with the world around us. But this is only the first half of the sentence, a sentence almost perfectly balanced between the ordinary and the strange: the clocks were striking thirteen. Clocks don't strike thirteen. For the superstitious among us, thirteen seems like a rather ominous number. Orwell seems to be creating a world that is simultaneously recognizable and not. He sets out to defamiliarize the world for us, something that a lot of art aims to do. We are willing to participate in what the narrative artist, the storyteller, has created, because it invites us—seduces us?—into a world that feels familiar, and then not.

Sometimes the world of the story is unintelligible even to the characters living in it. Sometimes someone is in charge of their story, and the gaps among what the character knows, what the narrator knows, and what the reader knows are what shape the story and its telling. Take the first line of Franz Kafka's *The Trial*: "Someone must have slandered Josef K., for one morning, without having done anything truly wrong, he was arrested." Who is the someone? Does the person telling the story, the narrator, know something that Josef K. doesn't? Is the speculation of slander actually the attempt of Josef K. to figure out what the heck is going on? Arrests often happen in detective novels or crime fiction; is that what this is? If so, are we going to find out what the crime is, perhaps in a flashback? Kafka's novel begins less with an invitation and more with an activation of our curiosity. One event sets the story in motion, and that move plays with our desire to know, to find out what happens next.

One of the most recognizable ways to begin a story, one of the cues that is universally recognized to signify storytelling, is "once upon a time." In some ways, the first line of any story is a version of "once upon a time." It is the key that unlocks the door to the world of the story. Even Homer begins the telling of *The Odyssey* with a "once upon a time" that his listeners would have instantly recognized: "Sing in me, O muse, and through me tell the story. . . ." When people first began studying stories in a more formal way, what we might call the science of stories, in the early twentieth century, they began with fairy tales. This seemed a good place to start, because fairy tales have patterns. Certain types of stories always have certain types of characters who do specific things. One character might be the one who goes on the quest. One character might be the one who gets in the way. Another character might be the one who helps the hero solve a problem. But even more complicated stories follow patterns, and once we figure out the patterns, we can have some idea of what kind of story we're in. Except when we can't. James Joyce's novel *Portrait of the Artist as a Young Man* begins with the completely familiar "once upon a time": "Once upon a time and a very good time it was there was a moocow coming down along the road and this moocow that was coming down along the road met a nicens little boy named baby tuckoo." And then it stops, and we see the little boy hearing the story, and thinking, as his father tells the tale, that *he* is baby tuckoo. The wholly recognizable cue of "once upon a time" doesn't prompt the telling of a fairy tale here; it prompts the small child to make a connection between the story and himself. We're not in a fairy tale after all; we're in the story of the development of an individual's mind.

"This is the saddest story I have ever heard." Who *wouldn't* want to keep reading after that line? With this first line, Ford Madox Ford in *The Good Soldier* gives us a narrator, a teller, who seems to want to share something with us, seems to be inviting us to sit down and listen. Perhaps we are being asked to listen, and then agree: yes, this is indeed the saddest story we have ever heard. What makes a story sad? Why did our narrator get to hear this story in the first place? Who told it to him? Did it actually *happen*, maybe to him? Stories are acts of imagination, but they are also acts of communication. Someone wants to tell us something, and they want you to have a response. They want you to cry. They want you to judge. They want you to change your mind. But stories don't communicate anything in an entirely straightforward way. What would be the fun in that? Perhaps you've noticed that my taking a closer look at these first lines has prompted more questions than answers. Stories work by making us ask questions, and then delaying the answer a little while, and then maybe answering the question with another question. Stories make gaps we have to fill, and often the first gaps are filled by figuring out who is talking and why they are telling us what they're telling us. That's narrative. Narrative is the stuff that makes stories work, and what makes stories work *on us*.

What is narrative and why does it matter?

People have made extravagant claims for narrative and its power. Myths are narratives. They are stories that follow patterns, explain the world, organize reality. We have grand historical or cultural narratives. Nations and peoples tell stories about themselves to themselves to help them understand their history, and competing or conflicting narratives can be matters of life and death. How do we tell the story of the founding of nations or the destruction of peoples? Does it matter who is telling the story? Can the story ever be changed once it's fixed? What is it about stories that help us understand who we are and shape our identity?

Narrative is no less than a way of being in the world, of organizing reality in such a way as to give it meaning (Kearney 12). Narrative depends on the communication of *who, what, where, when, why, how* to a reader or listener or viewer. It depends on our ability to recognize patterns and genres or types of stories. It depends on us being able to half-mistake imaginary people and situations for real. It depends on us being able to enter into the reality of real people we've never met. Narrative relies on complex workings in our minds. We process the cues provided to us by an author in order to make a world through our own imagination; then we go and live in it and take it for "real" for at least a little while. In the gap between art and reality lies story, and our ability to enter into that gap is a testament to our capacity for complex mental working and emotional response. Narrative is fiction and lies—and its own kind of truth.

How do we define narrative? According to H. Porter Abbott, "narrative is the representation of an event or a series of events" (13). Furthermore, these events happen over time, and they usually involve people doing things or having feelings or learning or changing. But how do the events come about? What is the relationship of one event to another—is it causal? Is it temporal? What if it's random? And what do we mean by "representation"? Who is doing the representing, and what are the components of that representation? There's lots of different kinds of "representation": can a painting be a narrative? Can a chart? Can a symphony tell a story? If representing means "telling"—we have the representation of the events because someone is telling it to us in the form of narrating—then who's doing the telling? Is it someone inside the story? Outside the story? A character? An all-knowing, all-seeing figment? A shopping cart? The study of narrative means asking and trying to answer some of these questions.

If I say, "I got up this morning at 6:30. I made coffee. I started writing. I worked until I was interrupted by a phone call," I think we would all agree that this is not "narrative." This is a series of events related in the order in which they occurred, but there is nothing narrative about it in the way we recognize "narrative" simply through common sense and world experience. There is no meaning. There is nothing that makes this worth telling. In other words, so what? So, then, narrative would seemingly also require meaning as part of its representation. How is this meaning generated? Robert Scholes and James Phelan, two important writers on the subject of stories and how narrative works, offer this answer:

> Meaning, in a work of narrative art, is a function of the relationship between two worlds: the fictional world created by the author and the "real" world, the apprehendable universe. When we say we "understand" a narrative we mean that we have found a satisfactory relationship or set of relationships between these two worlds.
>
> (Scholes *et al.* 82)

I like this formulation because it gets away from the idea that there is somehow "deeper meaning." Whenever we talk about "meaning," I worry that we are falling into the trap of "deeper meaning." There is no such thing as "deeper meaning." There is no magical password or hidden treasure in the novels we read and the movies we watch that somehow unlocks "deeper meaning." (There might be in the games we play, but that's a subject for later.) What there are, when we read novels or watch films, are a lot of different pieces—characters, setting, events, thoughts, description—that are designed to generate a response in you. These responses might be feelings, or judgment, or—yes—straight-up confusion. The pieces are meant to give you the information you need to live in the world of the story; they are meant to help you know the world and its characters more deeply; they are meant to get you to re-evaluate your judgments; they are meant to bring you to a satisfying ending, with a sense of closure ... except for when that doesn't happen.

Above all, though, and I think this is what Scholes and Phelan are getting at: we understand narrative because we understand the world, and narrative helps us understand the world better. There can't really be "deeper meaning" because narrative lives in and is part of the world. Our experience of living in the world and trying to make sense of it teaches us how to understand stories. We get what characters are feeling, we get their motivations or their struggles or their misperceptions because these things happen to us or people we know. We can build imaginary worlds in our minds even if all we have to go on are the descriptions of those worlds, because we live in spaces and we understand places. I believe we bring our common sense and experience of the world to bear on our living with and in stories. When we read the first line of a novel, we know what to do, and the more we read, the better we get at it. I also believe that living with and in stories helps us live better in the real world. I won't go so far as to suggest that reading Harry Potter books makes you a better person. I will say, though, that living in different worlds with different people teaches us new things about what it means to be human. Recognizing how narratives work to organize reality and make meaning helps us question whether the story we're being told is the *only* possible story, whether that story is the only way to organize reality. Thinking of our own lives as a process of storymaking and storytelling helps us be intentional about constructing our experience in meaningful ways. For lack of a better way of putting it, narrative helps us see whether and how our lives might have purpose. It helps us live with others because we have the equipment to understand them. It helps us see motivations, causes and effects, how to know and how to make judgments based on what we know. It helps us change our minds.

What this book is about

This book is about narrative: how it works, and the kinds of questions we ask to try to figure that out. The concept of "narrative" has a few different components at work, besides just whether or not something is a good story. In fact, some people who study narrative don't really care whether a story is a good story or not; all they care about is how it works. I do care about whether a story is good, and so I've tried to pick examples throughout of stories that are good, and that I like.

So how does narrative work, and what makes a good story? The first part of the question can be answered through analysis of the forms of narrative and the pieces that make up an individual narrative. To understand how narrative works, we have to look at characters and how they act and feel. We have to look at how events unfold over time, and how those events play out as important. We have to look at setting and description and the ways an author helps us visualize spaces and places. We have to look at how people (or animals, or things) are thinking. And we have to look at how all of this information is being communicated to us. How do we know what we know, and what do we do with it?

The second part of the question is trickier: what makes a good story? Everybody's answer might be a little different, especially if there are certain kinds of stories you particularly enjoy. I think this question can be answered at least in part by considering what happens in our minds when we experience a story. A good story prompts an emotional response, but I feel I want to put a caveat on that: I don't like feeling manipulated. I don't like feeling like my emotional responses are gotten on the cheap. I remember as a small child I was taken to see the Steven Spielberg movie *E.T.*, and it's the first time I think I ever cried in a movie theater. I remember this making me really angry: I didn't like that the director seemed to be trying to make me cry, and I could see how he was doing it, and even though I was aware I was being manipulated I cried anyway. At the same time, of course, sometimes you need a good cry. So how does a story generate a meaningful emotional response in us?

A good story makes you do a little work to figure out what's going on. I'm not saying a story should set out to be deliberately unintelligible— although sometimes that is certainly the point. Figuring out how to fill in gaps is actually essential to experiencing a story. So is being willing to delay gratification a little bit. We have to be willing to suffer through a little bit of deferral before we get to the good part, or before we're able to know what happens at the end. The exposition we get in stories, the early part where a narrator tries to give us background information, is often riddled with gaps and we have to keep reading or watching to fill in. And the end is the part where it all comes together and maybe gives us some satisfactory closure, but if we try to circumvent the middle part and skip to the end, the story might not work as well because we missed how we got there. The satisfying ending is perhaps an important part of a good story.

A good story calls upon our ability to enter into relationship with characters. We might have to be able to empathize with them. They have to seem "real." It often helps if a character is well-developed, multidimensional. In 1927, the novelist E. M. Forster published a collection of lectures under the title *Aspects of the Novel*, in which he offered the famous formula of "flat" versus "round" characters. Flat characters are often static and defined by one or two traits, whereas round characters are dynamic and complex, sometimes even surprising. Characters can come to seem almost as though they were our friends; we can also find ourselves sympathizing with characters who in every respect seem to be vicious and appalling. Thanks to our narrators providing us with unfettered access to characters' lives and minds, we can get to know them better than we know some actual people in our actual reality.

Sometimes for a story to be good, interesting stuff has to happen. These might be surprising and dramatic events that are out of the ordinary. They might be totally ordinary events told in an extraordinary way. What happens might be subject to the genre in which the story takes place: a romance has people falling in love, a crime story has one person committing a murder and another person trying to solve it. We get satisfaction from having our expectations activated and fulfilled, and from witnessing how events and characters play them out.

These are some ways of judging how a narrative works and whether a story is good; going into more depth will be the focus of the following chapters. But there are other things we can do with stories, too. We can use stories to explore the nature of community and identity. Issues related to gender, race, and ethnicity can shape our storytelling practices and how we read, and awareness of those issues can give us radically new ways of telling stories. Stories can be used to engage people through interactivity as digital media becomes just as important a mode of telling stories as books and film. And stories can fulfill an ethical purpose. They can demand that we exercise ethical judgment, that we view others through a lens of ethical wisdom, that we appreciate difference.

This book is organized around engaging with all of these concepts and purposes, while also attempting to provide an overview of important theories related to the study of narrative and how we might apply them. There is a story to the study of stories, and the result of that story is that we have many different approaches we can use to figure out how stories work. We can look at the parts that make a story work in relation to the whole of a narrative, which is the focus of Chapter 1. We can look at how stories engage with the reader in the world as well as with the world of the reader's mind, as we shall see in Chapter 2. We can look at stories beyond the page, stories that can be told in multiple different kinds of media like film, graphic narratives, and digital; we will emphasize this in Chapter 3. And finally we will look at the ethical implications of storytelling and why stories continue to matter in Chapter 4. I hope the ways stories and storytelling are essential to being human will be clear along the way.

Works cited

Abbott, H. Porter. *The Cambridge Introduction to Narrative.* 2nd ed. New York: Cambridge UP, 2008. Print.

Aristotle. *Poetics. The Complete Works of Aristotle.* Vol. 2. Trans. I. Bywater. Ed. Jonathan Barnes. Princeton, NJ: UP, 1984. 2316–2340. Print.

Kearney, Richard. *On Stories.* New York: Routledge, 2001. Print.

Scholes, Robert, Robert Kellogg, and James Phelan. *The Nature of Narrative.* Rev. ed. New York: Oxford UP, 2006. Print.

Exemplary texts

Argo. Dir. Ben Affleck. Perf. Ben Affleck, Alan Arkin, Bryan Cranston, John Goodman. Warner Bros., 2012. Film.

Ford, Ford Madox. *The Good Soldier.* New York: Penguin, 2007. Print.

Homer. *The Odyssey.* Trans. Robert Fitzgerald. 1961. New York: Farrar, Straus, and Giroux, 1998. Print.

Joyce, James. *A Portrait of the Artist as a Young Man.* New York: Penguin, 2003. Print.

Kafka, Franz. *The Trial.* New York: Schocken, 1999. Print.

Melville, Herman. *Moby-Dick.* New York: Penguin, 2009. Print.

Orwell, George. *1984.* New York: Signet, 1950. Print.

Recommended further reading

Fludernik, Monika. *An Introduction to Narratology.* New York: Routledge, 2009. Print.

Herman, David, ed. *The Cambridge Companion to Narrative.* New York: Cambridge UP, 2007. Print.

Herman, David, Manfred Jahn, and Marie-Laure Ryan, eds. *Routledge Encyclopedia of Narrative Theory.* New York: Routledge, 2005. Print.

Hühn, Peter, ed. *The Living Handbook of Narratology.* Hamburg University, 2015. Web. 11 April 2015.

Prince, Gerald. *Dictionary of Narratology.* 2nd ed. Lincoln: U of Nebraska P, 2003. Print.

The journals *Narrative, Journal of Narrative Theory, Style,* and *Poetics Today* are also important sources for new research in narrative.

1 Story parts and purpose

One way to think about how narrative works is to consider the parts of the story—characters, actions, time—and how they work together. We can also look at how they all work in the context of the whole narrative, and we can look at how one individual instance of narrative, one particular story, works in relationship to other stories. In this chapter, we will take a look at how knowing something about the parts of a narrative can help us come closer to figuring out what it's doing, why it's doing it, and how it's creating responses in us as readers.

Any discussion of how stories work and how they achieve their purpose should begin with Aristotle (384–322 BCE). Aristotle's writing on poetics, ethics, and rhetoric have all proven to be immensely influential for twentieth- and twenty-first century readers of narrative. These readers have taken his ideas on tragedy and epic poetry, and applied them to narrative, especially prose fiction. In this chapter, we will focus on how readers of narrative apply more formal methods derived from Aristotle's *Poetics*; this means studying stories from an objective perspective, focusing on form and structure. In Chapter 4, we will return to Aristotle, this time with a focus on his *Ethics* (the *Nicomachean Ethics*, to be precise) and his *Rhetoric*. The *Ethics* has had an influence on readers who see stories as developing in us a kind of "practical wisdom," the imaginative capacity to understand others, make good decisions, and live in the world with meaningful purpose taking right action. Reading and understanding stories, in this context, then becomes a way to apply ethical reasoning based on working through narrative situations. The *Rhetoric* has had a major influence on readers who are interested in how audiences respond to stories, particularly the ways stories activate ethical thinking around practical wisdom (as opposed to the more abstract concept of virtue, or the idea of goodwill, which is more aligned with friendship). Readers influenced by the *Ethics* or the *Rhetoric* are concerned less with the formal properties and structures of literary texts, more so with the social nature of texts and what they do in the world. All of Aristotle's texts are important to how we think about narrative, and I think an integration of the formal, the social, and the ethical is the best way to get at what stories do.

In the early and mid-twentieth century, readers who called themselves "formalists" and "structuralists" dedicated themselves to the study of the formal components of narrative: how the parts of a story work in relation to the whole, and how individual stories work in relation to "stories" in general. This impulse to classify and categorize comes from Aristotle's *Poetics*, which proposed to systematically analyze tragedy, comedy, and epic poetry. According to Aristotle, these art forms are meant to imitate life and the world around us; this is called *mimesis*. Aristotle breaks these literary forms down into the six components he saw as necessary for mimesis and the effects mimesis creates in us, like pity or wonder: plot, characters, diction (including dialogue), thought (or the representation of a character's thought), spectacle, and song.

For Aristotle, plot is the most important; in the 1920s, Russian Formalists would take this so seriously they would make every effort to catalog every kind of plot that appears in traditional Russian folk tales, or *skaz*. For Aristotle, plot is so important because

> tragedy is essentially an imitation not of persons but of action and life. All human happiness or misery takes the form of action; the end for which we live is a certain kind of activity, not a quality. Character gives us qualities, but it is in our actions that we are happy or the reverse.
>
> (2320)

The writer of a tragedy or a comedy or an epic poem must create persons with agency who are capable of choosing to perform actions. This writer is also responsible for conveying the thoughts of characters in the appropriate diction, and for positioning the characters in relation to the audience, whether superior, inferior, or on the same level. Characters themselves should be good, appropriate, consistent, and life-like (2327). For example, "the character before us may be, say, manly; but it is not appropriate in a female character to be manly, or clever" (2327). (It might be unfair for me to call Aristotle out on that one, but I couldn't resist.) Even a person who has spent only limited time around other human beings can see that Aristotle's ideas about character do not necessarily give us equipment for dealing with people in our lives, nor do they capture the infinite varieties of personhood. It's not that characters aren't important in the stories themselves; they are the agents choosing certain actions which make the plot "go," and they must have certain qualities in order to provoke the necessary response in the audience. It's more that Aristotle takes these elements of character for granted. Aristotle's privileging of plot over character would stay with us into the twentieth century. The authors of our novels often teach us how to read before our theories do, and it took a greater interest in depicting the inner life of characters, and a different understanding of psychology, to teach critics that character matters.

Plot, for Aristotle, has several constituent parts. It consists of reversals (changes in fortune) and recognitions (the gaining of knowledge), and the combination of reversals and recognitions can result in simple plots or complex plots. Complex plots have a good combination of both, whereas simple plots depend on one or the other. A well-constructed plot has a beginning, a middle, and an end. The actions of a plot should not appear to be random, and they should appear to have unity (2322–2324). Pitiable and terrifying events are also preferred, because these prompt emotional responses, or catharsis, in the audience. Plot can dwell in possibility; it can represent not what *has happened*, but what *could happen*. Aristotle's terms, as you can probably see, make a lot of sense when applied not only to drama and epic poetry but to prose fiction as well, and what occurs in narrative overall. These terms are an important part of the history of narrative, and of how we understand it. Aristotle's *Poetics* analyzes and categorizes the parts necessary for what we now call narrative, but it also makes some value judgments, determining that tragedies and epics that offer complex plots in a unified way with the right kinds of characters provoking the right kinds of responses are "good stories."

Defining "good stories," and the purpose of "good stories," has been a matter for debate for centuries. While we're focusing on Aristotle here because he defined a number of concepts necessary to the study of narrative that have stayed with us, readers in every era have tried to figure out what stories are supposed to do. For Aristotle, it was *catharsis*, the releasing of emotion like pity or wonder. For other writers, stories are meant to teach us something, a moral or political lesson. Another purpose might be the creation and sustaining of community, or the attempt to effect political change. Maybe stories exist to give us pleasure. Stories could take as their purpose the providing of an opportunity to enter into a different reality, or to transcend reality altogether. The purpose of stories could be the ways they allow us to reflect on our own experience and impressions.

For Russian Formalists in the early twentieth century, the purpose of stories is simply to *be* (see Box 1.1). Russian Formalists were drawn to the more objective study of literary texts in part as defined by Aristotle—first poetry, then novels—because they rejected the traditional ways of studying literature in Russia at the time. Formalists emerged from a context wherein literary study, at least in Russia, consisted of worshipping a select canon of authors, like Alexander Pushkin or Leo Tolstoy, and digging in the archives for details about their lives. Or, "study" was infused with a sort of mysticism, an otherworldly reaching beyond the work to something transcendent. The Russian Formalists were actually looking for a new way of doing literary study, a kind of science that would give their investigations a method (Erlich 87). A major writer within the Russian Formalist movement was Viktor Shklovsky. In his writing, particularly "Art as Technique" (1917) and *The Theory of Prose* (1925 and 1929), Shklovsky moved Formalism beyond mere classification to try to figure out how the examination of constituent parts, of elements, function to bring the literary work itself into being—including the responses on the part of the individual reader. Shklovsky argued that we read literature as having a value in and of itself, and that it presents a reality that exists alongside our own; formal elements like plot and perspective and description bring that reality into existence. Our understanding of the nature of literary texts is made plain to us in a process of "defamiliarization" (*ostraneniye*). Shklovsky writes of defamiliarization in "Art as Technique":

> Habitualization devours works, clothes, furniture, one's wife, and the fear of war . . . . Art exists that one may recover the sensation of life; it exists to make one feel things, to make the stone *stony*. The purpose of art is to impart the sensation of things as they are perceived and not as they are known. The technique of art is to make objects "unfamiliar," to make forms difficult, to increase the difficulty and length of perception because the process of perception is an aesthetic end in itself and must be prolonged. *Art is a way of experiencing the artfulness of an object; the object is not important.*
>
> (12, emphasis in original)

The goal of the Formalist method was to define what makes a literary text "literary," to identify the parts of the text that led to that judgment, and to look at how all those parts created a complete whole. To their mind, the purpose of a narrative was not to create an opportunity for catharsis, as Aristotle might say; nor was it to teach a moral, social, or political lesson, as their contemporaries in Russia might say. It was instead simply to exist as a work of art, and through its existence to defamiliarize the reader's apprehension of reality. Representing a world in narrative destabilizes our sense of the real world. Shklovsky saw this happening in stories that, as he put it, "lay bare the device" (*Theory* 147)—these kinds of stories exist like any other story, with a narrator communicating the events of plot to us, but while they are doing that they are also showing us how the narrative, the work of art, is put together in a very self-conscious way. We see this happening in movies or television shows, for example, whenever a character pauses the action and turns to talk directly to the camera. Such an action draws our attention to the ways art is made, and breaks the illusion of mimesis, breaks the illusion that the work of art is merely a version or imitation of reality and makes us see it *as art*. The Netflix series *House of Cards*, starring Kevin Spacey as politician Frank Underwood, makes excellent use of this to show us not only the inner workings of Underwood's mind but also the ways the show deliberately seeks to defamiliarize our understanding of the "real world," in this case, the cutthroat arena of D.C. politics and our relationship to those in power.

Box 1.1 Viktor Shklovsky, *Opojaz*, and Russian Formalism

In 1914, St. Petersburg was home to one of the leading, and largest, universities in the world. Russian academe in the years immediately preceding the 1917 Revolution was rife with tensions around the nature of the university itself. New universities were being created with private funds and concentrating on practical skills and vocational or professional training, and these institutions were met with resistance by those who believed the university should maintain a more traditional model based on scholarly research within classic disciplines and "pure learning" (Kassow 369). The Russian Formalists were an important—and interesting—part of this moment for a variety of reasons. First of all, they were young, barely twenty years old, and they wanted to take on not only their professors but the entire Russian literary tradition. The Formalists existed in healthy competition and alliance with the Futurists, led by the poet and playwright Vladimir Mayakovsky, and together they embodied a kind of modernism in early twentieth-century Russia, each taking aim at Realists and Symbolists and the literary establishment in general. They shared the belief that literary art is a kind of language that talks mostly about itself, and they sought to formulate a system that would account for poetic language, specifically how poetic language is a kind of communication that is primarily communicating about *itself*.

Russian Formalists were concerned with art and purely aesthetic questions, rather than with a social or political agenda. In an interview with Serena Vitale, Viktor Shklovsky, one of the founders of Russian Formalism and its most well-known writer (and most intriguing character) said:

> We were aggressive, very. We certainly weren't gentle with our elders . . . . It [Russian Formalism and its society, *Opojaz*] made the first, violent impact. An impact that *had* to be made, with all its extremes. Art, like a clock that's stopped ticking, has to be shaken up. We provided that jolt. We were attacked, the pressure was strong, very strong, but we planted many seeds.
>
> (Vitale 80, 98–99)

The Formalist group *Opojaz*, or The Society for the Investigation of Poetic Language, was founded originally as a student association in St. Petersburg around 1916, and Fernande Degeorge describes how the young scholars (or part gadflies, part scholars) targeted Realists and Symbolists, each for the same reason: both of those earlier, more establishment movements imagined that the purpose of literary art was to reach beyond the work itself (to the world or to something transcendent and mystical, respectively) (22). The members of *Opojaz*, on the other hand, saw the purpose of criticism to be the study of form itself, and the purpose of form to have no other purpose but the manifestation of literary art.

We can place *Opojaz* within the wider context of student organizations (*studenchestvo*) around 1914. Students were politicized in the decade between the 1905 Revolution and the First World War, but the tradition of student organizing transcended politics. As the student body became more heterogeneous between 1911 and 1914, with greater numbers of peasants joining the universities as well as more students entering the new technical and professional institutes, *studenchestvo* organizations became more important than ever. Samuel Kassow, in an important study of student life and academia during the final years of Tsarist Russia, writes, "Student organizations were showing unmistakable resilience and vitality" (371). This "vitality" was primarily around issues of political and moral commitment, as well as student professionalism—*not* art and poetry. Yet *Opojaz* took that impulse and turned it towards questions of aesthetics and culture.

We might look back at *Opojaz* as a watershed moment in literary and cultural history. At the same time, however, the association of students with a passionate interest in something shared, coming together in a spirit of debate and collaboration around ideas, was very much part of *studenchestvo* life.

What set *Opojaz* apart, what would get it into trouble again and again, and finally lead to its suppression, was its priorities. In its early years, the emphasis on aesthetic questions rather than political or economic ones made it suspect. Early on, and as the Marxist line hardened, *Opojaz* seemed misguided not only because it was taking up the wrong kinds of questions, but because it was also finding the wrong kinds of answers. Formalism demanded answers to aesthetic questions beyond sociopolitical dogma and ideological didacticism.

Once the 1917 Revolution was upon them, and in the years following which saw a hardening of the Marxist position and increasing encroachment on university life and governance by the Soviet state, this stance held by the Formalists became dangerous; literary study should take as its purpose the refinement and propagandizing of Marxism, and to imagine that form is the priority was ideologically questionable. The Formalists got away with this for about ten years, but by the mid-1920s into 1930, as Stalin's first Five-Year Plan (1928–33) got under way, they were increasingly victimized by Soviet repression. *Opojaz* was finally suppressed in the early 1930s and its members forced to recant for being essentially heretical, for holding "an erroneous critical doctrine" and a "'reactionary' social position" (Erlich 106).

Let's now take a closer look at those important parts of narrative and how to read them. We can start by following the lead of French literary theorist Roland Barthes, who tried to define the smallest units of narrative and how they work. Barthes considered himself, and is considered by many, to be a *structuralist*. A structuralist is one who studies a story by looking at its parts in the context of the whole and seeing how those parts all work together in relationship, and then thinking about how that individual story works within an entire system of all other narrative, especially whether or not that system has rules and what they might be—analogous to how individual words work in sentences, individual sentences work within the system of an entire language, and each individual language works within the system of languages as a whole (see Box 1.2). In his "An Introduction to the Structural Analysis of Narrative," Barthes defines the smallest units of narrative: the level of plot, the level of characters, and the level of narration (the part where what's happening gets told, and how it gets told).

Box 1.2 Ferdinand de Saussure, the *Course in General Linguistics*, and Structuralism

Ferdinand de Saussure was an unassuming specialist in Indo-European languages. His *Course in General Linguistics*, a book we now recognize as a foundational work of twentieth-century literary theory, was never meant to be published. Between 1907 and 1911, his students compiled years' worth of lecture notes and published them in 1916, three years after the death of their teacher and in the midst of the First World War. These notes outlined an entirely new way of thinking about linguistics by trying to define language as a system of signs. These signs can be combined and recombined to form individual utterances. The rules for how this happens are finite; individual utterances can only happen according to the rules of the system. But the possible combinations of utterances are infinite. People who study literary texts came to see this as applicable to poems, novels, short stories, films. The individual parts of the whole text could be seen as analogous to individual utterances in a language, and they got their meaning based on the role they were playing in the context of the whole. Likewise, an individual novel or short story or film could be seen as an individual utterance, and could be analyzed as representative, or not, of the whole system of narrative itself. It's like thinking of novels as a "language," and *Great Expectations* or *Beloved* or *The Hunger Games* as "utterances" of that language. According to this logic, novels as a form then would have a grammar, with things like nouns and verbs and adjectives that could be put into combinations (like sentences) according to rules. Individual novels are the results of these combinations, and they can be read as part of the system. The individual cases might change over time; novels look different in some ways now than they did when Cervantes wrote *Don Quixote*, considered to be one of the earliest "modern" novels, but those individual cases still follow the rules of the system. This way of reading is called *structuralism*, because it is concerned with the larger structures within which individual texts reside, and the ways those larger structures create meaning for individual works.

One of Saussure's students recalled his classroom demeanor at the University of Geneva, where he taught for most of his professional life after a time at the École des Hautes Études in Paris:

> The professor entered, and we were immediately captivated by his person. He hardly seemed "professorial"! He looked so young, so ordinary in his bearing, yet at the same time his air of exquisite distinction and finesse, with that slightly dreamy and distant look in his clear blue eyes, gave us a foretaste of his power and originality as a thinker.
>
> (Quoted in Joseph 375)

The taking (and keeping) of an academic position in Geneva marked a shift in Saussure's work that would turn out to make his thinking hospitable to literary studies. In fact, one of his interests was the disciplinary divide between the study of language and the study of letters (or literature). It might be worth remembering that in the latter part of the nineteenth century, the study of literature—the "English major"—was not a formal field. One could study linguistics, or philology, or Biblical hermeneutics, and all of these areas eventually informed the creation of literary study as a discipline in the first third of the twentieth century. Saussure's question about the relationship between language and letters prefigures these disciplinary changes. Furthermore, his beginning to ask *how* we study language (As a system? Through historical change? Understanding words and sound?) would lead to fundamental questions about the study of literature as well. Saussure's shift into *general* questions about the nature of language, rather than highly specialized investigations into, say, Sanskrit (which formed the basis of his earlier career), would open the way to thinking about how *literary* language functions. Finally, the changing nature of Saussure's career as a professor led to new directions in his thinking and writing. His students in Geneva were less well-prepared to study linguistics at a highly specialized level; he needed to develop lectures that would facilitate their understanding of the field, and this altered his own theoretical approach.

Plot

Plot is a series of events presented in a sequence defined by causality and temporality, arranged and linked in a unified and nonrandom way: this happened because this happened, or first this happened then this happened. There are infinite permutations by which an author can arrange—or disarrange—the sequences and strands of a story. An assortment of episodes can be strung together, or several different plot lines can be interwoven. Within this infinite variety, however, we must have, of course, a beginning, a middle, and an end.

Events can be situations wherein characters have conflicts or tensions, and then those conflicts are resolved. Events might move other events forward, or fulfill promised or anticipated events. Certain events within the plot are necessary to move the plot forward, and many of these revolve around change. A character changes; the world changes; what someone knows changes. We might think an event isn't important at first glance, or that a moment in the story exists purely to provide information or establish a state, only to realize as we continue to read (or watch) that the event we believed to be insignificant is in fact transformative. We change our minds about the importance of events as the plot unfolds.

Different types of plot might involve a change in state (Aristotle's reversal) or a change in knowledge (Aristotle's recognition). Seymour Chatman, an important writer on narrative from whom we'll be hearing quite a bit in this chapter, offers two other ways of thinking about plot. The first is the *plot of resolution*, structured around the classic model of exposition, rising action, climax, falling action, and, of course, resolution. The second is the *plot of revelation*, stories that depend on readers learning about characters, having time to contemplate the characters and engage with their psychology or personality, and seeing them in different situations or with other characters. Secondary characters can be particularly important in this regard: they often serve to reveal quite a bit about a main character or characters, providing opportunities for a main character to interact with others or get into situations, and thereby allowing us to learn more.

Plot is the guiding framework for narrative, but plot itself is made up of smaller parts, including events but also hinges and pivots and set pieces that create connections or do a kind of stage-setting; description often works this way, and so does dialogue, or commentary from the narrator. Chatman has suggested ways to think about combinations and linkages among events: a "logic of connection" and a "logic of hierarchy" (53). The logic of hierarchy depends on differentiating between major and minor events. Major events are *kernels*, and minor events are *satellites*. Kernels are necessary to create nodes of narrative logic, instances where a direction must be taken that is clearly defined. Satellites are not essential to the narrative logic but might be considered important to the aesthetic effect of the novel, or for the opportunity they provide to make connections or let us witness the working-out of choices or the consequences of events. The event of Alvy Singer and Annie breaking up in Woody Allen's film *Annie Hall* is a kernel; the scene of the two of them sitting in the park making up funny stories about passers-by is a satellite. The former is essential to the plot of the film, the latter is an event that reveals something about their relationship but could be removed without destroying the narrative logic.

Engagements: Exemplary text

We could consider a fairly basic plot, the modern-day equivalent of a *skaz*, for an example: the long-running television series *Law & Order*. Part of what goes into our appreciation of *Law & Order* is the utter predictability of every episode as it follows the same plot, represents the same kinds of situations arranged in more or less the same pattern. An episode begins with an ordinary New Yorker going about his or her business, or, often, arguing with someone. The ordinary business is interrupted by the discovery of a body in a dumpster, an alley, a parked car, what have you. The discovery of the body is a kernel: we need it for the rest of the story to unfold. It also establishes a state: a state wherein a crime needs to be solved, and order needs to be restored. After the opening credits, we join the detectives either just arriving on the scene or in the middle of their investigation. This allows for exposition and rising action; it also allows for recognition as the detectives begin to gain knowledge of the crime and piece together the preliminaries of their investigation. The episode then proceeds with individual situations linked together, often situations involving discussion of the case, revealing of character, or more exposition. This network of linkages helps us arrange the events in a meaningful way, and facilitates the filling in of gaps related to what we know and how we know it. Then, another kernel: the arrest of the suspect. Depending on when in the episode this event occurs, a steadfast watcher well-acquainted with the *Law & Order* pattern will be able to tell whether the detectives have arrested the right "perp"; too early in the episode and it's probably a mistake, in which case we have recognition *and* reversal, and a resolution of tension. The trial is another kernel, and is also composed of a number of smaller situations: more knowledge is revealed, conflicts are presented and resolved, there may be reversals and recognitions. Ultimately, the trial functions as the climax of the episode as "order" is reaffirmed, followed by the falling action of the prosecutors and the cops wrapping up the day (often by walking down a hall, having a solemn late-night conversation in a darkened office, or entering an elevator as the doors are closing). There are as many ways to write an episode of *Law & Order* as there are to die horribly in New York, but there are only so many ways to arrange and link up the events to make a recognizable—and, for fans, an enjoyable—pattern.

Another writer on narrative who has defined the elements of plot and the ways they might be combined is Tzvetan Todorov. He was an early contributor to defining *how* stories are told, not just *what* gets told in them. Todorov is also responsible for coining the term "narratology" (*la narratologie*), or the science of narrative, in his *Grammar of the Decameron* in 1969. For Todorov, narrative is all about change, and in his *Poetics of Prose* he looks at the ways the formal elements of narrative can be combined to generate change in situation, or event, as well as how the story gets told. His idea of "transformation" accounts for multiple elements of narration, because it shows how change unfolds over the course of a story through a variety of means, including the passage of time, the representation of thought, and the suggestion of possibility. We might think of the job of a narrator, among other things, as combining plot elements in order to direct and communicate transformations. A possibility might be presented that may or not be fulfilled. Characters might exhibit the intention to do something, and then act on it or not. The plot might be moved forward by a character accomplishing an action, and the manner in which that action is accomplished might bear some significance. All of this is occurring over time, and may be of short or long duration. Time might even be suspended. Finally, Todorov's transformations account for mental activity on the part of the characters. Characters might gain consciousness, gain knowledge, believe or think, plan or lie.

Engagements: Exemplary text

A very short story by Harold Pinter, called "Girls," might work to illustrate Todorov's ideas of transformation, and how pieces of plot can be combined and connected together. Much of the story depends on the representation of mental activity, of failed action, of gaining and losing of knowledge, and so it serves nicely as an example for a concept that is attempting to define states of being, knowing, and acting (or not). "Girls" has a first-person narrator, a narrator who reaches out and engages us very explicitly, or overtly, from the start. (We'll see more about overt narrators in a moment.) First-person narrators often make their presence known through the assertion of an "I," a clearly defined subjectivity. This narrator has a deliberate way of going about interrogating the workings of his own mind and sharing them with us.

The story begins: "I read this short story in a magazine where a girl student goes into her professor's office and sits at his desk and passes him a note which he opens and which reads: 'Girls like to be spanked.'" The narrator then reveals he has lost the magazine and will never know how the story ends. What follows is question upon question, the questions presenting possibilities for what the story might hold, or might have held: "Did it happen? Did it happen in the professor's office, on the professor's desk?" The questions also attempt to probe who this girl might have been: "She may just have been talking about other girls, girls she didn't even know." The questions further seem to be attempting to get at some kind of deeper truth about women: is it, in fact, the case that girls like to be spanked? Does this have some kind of truth value? Thus Pinter's narrator effects trans-formation of mode, presenting possibility (we may one day know what happened in the story), along with impossibility (we can never know, the story has been lost, and we don't understand what women want anyway), and necessity (the narrator must know, he must know how the story ends, but cannot). We can see Pinter's narrator effecting transformations of man-ner, the manner in which the story is told, by going from asking multiple questions to offering speculation on the girl with the note, and girls as a species. Finally, we can see the narrator performing a transformation of subjectivation, wherein he presents himself in an attitude of thinking. In fact, it would be safe to say that the entire story, much like Virginia Woolf's "The Mark on the Wall" (discussed in Chapter 4), proceeds via a series of transformations related to thinking, the attitude of thinking and asking oneself questions of one's own mind.

Then what are we to make of the end, which reads, in its entirety:

> I love her. I love her so much. I think she's a wonderful woman. I saw her once. She turned and smiled. She looked at me and smiled. Then she wiggled to a cab in the cab rank. She gave instructions to the cab driver, opened the door, got in, closed the door, glanced at me for the last time through the window and the cab drove off and I never saw her again.

Whereas the first 650 words of the story represent a narrator struggling with his own desire to know how a story ends, thinking "I can't remember what happened next . . . . I've no idea how the story developed," asking questions to fill in gaps that can never be filled; the final 74 words deliber-ately thwart our own desire to understand how this particular story ends. Who is the wonderful woman? How could the narrator possibly love her, or think she's wonderful? We are left to ask the same kinds of questions our narrator was asking of his own story, his own reading. We also see the narrator inserting himself into the story; he represents himself having a revelatory moment upon the sight of the mystery woman. We might read Pinter's story as deliberately transgressing some of Todorov's categories. Perhaps this is a transgression of the transformation of description: actions are described, the woman getting into the cab for instance, but this type of transformation is supposed to provide knowledge through the mode of description, and we know even less than we did before. Pinter's story plays with our need, as readers, to know, to have closure, and the major situations of the story are questions that are never answered, the dominant attitude one of not knowing.

Character

In our example of *Law & Order*, we saw a clear instance of a plot of resolution; it depends heavily, in fact, on resolution being achieved by the end of the episode. What would a plot of revelation look like? For this, we'll turn now to character, because plots of revelation require extensive attention to character.

Characters have to demonstrate qualities of being and of acting. In other words, characters in a story have to seem like they could be real, and they have to have some kind of ability to make choices and take action, and maybe even have thoughts and be able to communicate them, as in thinking reported by a narrator or in dialogue. Without characters who can act, the plot—the kinds of deliberate events and changes described above—would be hard to pull off. Chatman writes,

> A viable theory of character should preserve openness and treat char-
> acters as autonomous beings, not as mere plot functions. It should
> argue that character is reconstructed by the audience from evidence
> announced or implicit in an original construction and communicated
> by the discourse, through whatever medium.
>
> (119)

For Chatman this means "a paradigm of traits," where personal qualities and plot intersect (126). Characters can be flat or round, static or dynamic, to use E. M. Forster's terms from *Aspects of the Novel*—defined by a singular trait, or three-dimensional; staying more or less the same or continuing to change, grow, develop, surprise. It helps if characters remind us of actual humans we have encountered; if not, it helps if they exhibit reasonably famil-iar mental activities, actions, motivations, feelings. We might spend only one day with a character, as we do in Virginia Woolf's novel *Mrs. Dalloway*, which takes place over the course of one day in London; we might spend an entire life, or a good part of it, as we do in Daniel Defoe's *Moll Flanders*. Either way, we learn about a character through observing her interactions with other characters both major and minor, the actions she takes or does not take, and through having her thoughts, dreams, desires, and intentions communicated or reported to us via a narrator.

A note about character and "truthiness" (to borrow a word from noted television satirist Stephen Colbert): are characters real? Can we, for instance, talk about how much Hamlet weighs? One answer might be, Hamlet weighs nothing, because he's not real. A more interesting answer might be: we *could* talk about it, if Shakespeare offered that information, because if Shakespeare *had* offered that information, it would be part of the bundle of stuff that makes up Hamlet as a character, and *Hamlet* as a play. Barring that, however, talking about how much Hamlet weighs is what we might call a category mistake: we're asking the wrong kind of question of a fictional character. We're attributing physical properties to something for which such attribution doesn't make any sense, doesn't hold any truth value, unless we're given the information. We can only know about a character whatever an author wants us to know. (At the same time, we often know more about literary characters than we do about people in our own lives; is there anyone in your life to whom you have unfettered mental access, such as we get in Hamlet's famous "to be or not to be" soliloquy?) To say that Hamlet visits Chik-Fil-A every Wednesday is decidedly not true; if someone wanted to make a movie version of *Hamlet* wherein that happens, it might become true, but until that happens, it's not. Hamlet killing Polonius is not "real," as in it doesn't take place in the actual world—but it is *true*, because we can say that the actions and thoughts of characters, within the context of the fiction in which they exist, carry with them a kind of truth that comes from being part of a story.

Engagements: Exemplary text

The novel *Nervous Conditions* by Tsitsi Dangarembga tells the story of a young girl, Tambu, growing up in colonial Rhodesia (now Zimbabwe) in the 1960s. It is a coming of age novel, and this genre often seems to prefer plots of revelation as a character is revealed, changes, and develops over time. Of course, change and development are also often the result of conflict, so moments of tension and resolution are present too, but these serve more to show us qualities of a character. Dangarembga's novel, like many coming of age novels, follows a narrative arc shaped by the main character's life, rather than conventional patterns of rising action, climax, and falling action. (We will look at another coming of age novel, Edna Ferber's *Fanny Herself*, in Chapters 2 and 4.)

The character of Tambu is revealed through the use of a first-person narrator, one we can designate as Tambu herself, and she seems to be telling her story retrospectively, from the position of adulthood. We'll see when we talk about narration that this is also known as a *homodiegetic* narrator: the *diegesis* is the story, and the person communicating the story is the same (*homo-*) as the person the story is about. Thus her mental activity is revealed as she reports to us her thoughts and her participation in important events as a subject with agency, a person capable of action. Early in the novel, she describes wanting to go to school so badly she works in the fields to earn the fees; she characterizes herself as "obstinate," "tenacious," strong and sturdy (17–20). Tambu's character, and her development, are further revealed through her relationships with her brother, her parents, and her cousin Nyasha, with whom she has a close connection despite their deep differences. As the two girls get older, Nyasha becomes a foil to Tambu, not only in her attitudes towards gender, family, and work, but also in her attitudes towards colonialism. Nyasha, disrespectful to her elders out of anger at her powerlessness as a woman in Rhodesian society, and full of rage at the oppression of colonialism, develops anorexia, while Tambu continues to achieve in school, seeing it as a way out of her similar feelings of powerlessness. While Tambu rejects Nyasha's choices, she also regards the way of her cousin as a path not taken. The relationship is essential to revealing Tambu's character, as is the representation of possibilities. The point of the story is not to resolve conflict or tension between Tambu and her parents or Tambu and Nyasha; the point is to represent Tambu's character and the development of her subjectivity.

Narrator and narration

The sequence of events in a plot is communicated (narrated) by a teller (narrator). There are many different types of narrator, and the ways we categorize and describe those types have to do with who is seeing what is happening, how he or she or it talks about it, and where in the story the narrator's presence is made known. Our definitions of narrator revolve around how present a narrator is, how visible, what it knows and how it chooses to share that knowledge with us. We can also think about a narrator in terms of voice, mood, and point of view, as we will see below. These categories allow us to consider how a narrator seems to feel about the story that is being told, and whether we can tell how the narrator feels—or if the narrator feels anything at all. Figuring this out helps us, as readers, understand how *we* are supposed to feel, whether our responses are aligned with the narrator's, and if not, why not. It helps us perceive what we know, how we might judge what we know, whether we need to know more, and what we should do with our knowledge.

Categories of narration also help us understand the relationships among characters and the narrator. Can the narrator access all the characters' mental states? Does the narrator move back and forth between and among different characters? Does the narrator sound like one of the characters, or does it have its own voice? How do certain choices about narrator and narration enlighten us as to the representation in stories of personhood, subjectivity, human nature and activity? All of these questions mean to get at *what* the narrator sees, *how much* the narrator sees, *how* the narrator communicates to us what it is perceiving, from *where* or aligned with *whom* in the story. Working on this level of the story, or *diegesis*, is referred to as working with *narrative discourse*.

The first way we might think about a narrator is to ask whether or not we can perceive that narrator at work: in its talking directly to us, or its commenting on the action, or possibly even its managing the action and our responses to it, telling us what to think. Or, the narrator might seem to be invisible in the telling. Chatman defines two types of narration: covert narration, where the narrator seems to be doing its work indirectly, present but not drawing attention to itself; and overt narration, where the narrator is clearly communicating, sometimes not only story but also delivering interpretation, commentary, and judgment. (The narrators of both "Girls" and *Nervous Conditions* are overt narrators, as we have seen.) A narrator can also operate on a few different levels; if there is more than one storyline happening, if multiple stories are embedded in one big narrative, each of those levels will have a narrator. Likewise, a narrator can reach out of one level to another—or reach out to the reader. If this sounds like an instance of a narrator being overt, it is. It's also known as *metalepsis*. We can look at an example of how these levels, and the breaching of levels, work in Ian McEwan's novel *Atonement*.

Engagements: Exemplary text

Ian McEwan's novel *Atonement* takes advantage of the interplay of narrative across levels. The narrative in *Atonement* occurs on multiple levels, each with its own narrator, until the end, when a surprising breach, or metalepsis, occurs. Throughout the novel, we come to perceive that the teller exists outside the story; by the end, we are not so sure. There are three embedded stories within the narrative as a whole. The first level, or embedded story, is the story of a young girl, Briony Tallis, in the years between the First and Second World Wars in England. She witnesses a passionate moment between her older sister, Cecilia, and a family friend, Robbie, and misconstrues this as a kind of assault; on the same day, a young cousin disappears from the house and then is found later that evening, traumatized. Briony, putting the two things together in a moment of semi-willful misinterpretation, accuses Robbie of rape. This level of the story is defined both by the time period—1935—and by access to multiple perspectives; at different points in this part of the story, we see the events from Briony's, Cecilia's, and Robbie's perspectives, and have access to their mental workings and how they see the events unfold. The second level moves forward in time and shifts location: Dunkirk, during the Second World War. This level is presented from Robbie's perspective; he has been released from prison to fight in the war, and is part of the evacuation of British troops from Dunkirk. Although the narrator does not make its presence felt explicitly, is more covert rather than less in other words, it does filter the events of the story through a point of view that is clearly Robbie's. The third level returns us to England after the war, with Cecilia and Robbie reunited and Cecilia and Briony reconciled; here, Briony's perspective dominates.

Then, the novel has a postscript, where the shift or breach occurs. The postscript of the novel radically alters the ways narration has been used throughout the text, and thereby alters our understanding of what has occurred up to that point. The postscript of the novel switches to an overt character-narrator: Briony herself, as a 77-year-old successful author suffering from dementia. Here, she ruptures all of the carefully laid narrative levels by confessing to her readers that everything they had been reading up to that point was a fiction constructed by herself. In fact, Robbie died at Dunkirk, Cecilia died in the London Blitz, and Briony was never reconciled with her sister. The overt narration provided by Briony at the end, in her own voice, serves to redirect her readers' interpretations, insisting they go back and re-evaluate what they thought they knew, and revealing—"laying bare," as Shklovsky might say—the workings of the narrative layers of the story.

Mood and voice

Mood is the attitude that comes through towards the story as it is being told, and the way that attitude determines responses on the part of the reader. Story happens not only through changes in situation but changes in aspect or attitude as well. A narrator can talk about desired states that don't exist; it can present things a character or reader is obligated to do; it can issue commands (including to the reader); it can present possibilities, hypotheticals, and conditionals; it can bear witness. If we take, for instance, Jonathan Safran Foer's memoir *Eating Animals*, in which he narrates learning about the factory farm industry and being so affected by the treatment of animals abused by that industry that he becomes a vegetarian, we can characterize the mood of his narration as one of testimony. We might further define it as ideological, and we might suggest that this mood is created in order to oblige us to do something—namely, re-evaluate our willingness to remain meat-eaters in the face of the moral questions raised by modern food production.

The voice of the narrator is what we use to think about who is *speaking*. The narrator can be speaking from within the story, as a character participating in the events; this would be *homodiegetic*, as we saw with *Nervous Conditions*. The narrator might also be speaking from outside the story; this would be *heterodiegetic*, or someone different (*hetero-*) from the story (*diegesis*). The narrator(s) of most of *Atonement* are heterodiegetic, except for that shifting at the end when Briony takes over in her own voice, at which point we would consider the narrator homodiegetic. When we talk below about *In Cold Blood*, by Truman Capote, we will see that the narrator of that book is a covert, heterodiegetic narrator: a figure existing outside the story who doesn't quite make its presence visible, but is clearly communicating in a particular way defined by mood, how much it knows and how it shares that knowledge, access to characters' actions and thoughts, and so on. In still other cases, the narrator can also be aligned with the author: we can trust that the narrator and the author are the same person. This is known as an *autodiegetic* narrator. Charles Dickens' novel *David Copperfield* would be an example of a narrator speaking from within the story—the main character or protagonist and the narrator are the same person—but we would not say that Charles Dickens and David Copperfield are the same person. The narrating "I" of *David Copperfield* is not Charles Dickens. On the other hand, the narrating "I" of *Narrative of the Life of Frederick Douglass* could be aligned with the author Frederick Douglass, and the power of this memoir and its argument against slavery probably depends on our being able to ally the author "I" and the narrator "I." (One text can have many voices; see Box 1.3.).

A narrator speaking from outside the story, a heterodiegetic narrator, can speak as though it knows everything about what's going on with all the characters (known as omniscient), or it can speak as though it only knows what's going on with one of the characters (known as limited). It can also take on the voice, the speaking or thinking style, of an individual character in order to show that the story is now interested in representing that particular character's subjectivity, what that particular character perceives. This idea overlaps with focalization, as we shall see. Perspective and focalization help us understand what the narrator *sees*, especially if what is seen is being filtered through the lens of a particular character's consciousness; voice helps us understand how the narrator *speaks* about what it sees. Both are important to the representation of subjectivity, the mind, and personhood—as well as to figuring out how we know what we know.

Engagements: Exemplary text

One of my favorite narrators in all of literature is the narrator of George Eliot's novel of provincial nineteenth-century English life—*Middlemarch*. Part of what I like about this narrator is her capacity for both sympathy and judgment. The narrator of *Middlemarch* is not part of the story. She (I can't help thinking of her as a she) does not seem to live in the town of Middlemarch, but knows everything about it. She is not a character. She occasionally refers to herself in the first person, she occasionally addresses the reader directly, and she often attempts to manage the reader's responses and judgments. She is separate from the world of the story, so we would consider her heterodiegetic, and she is most certainly overt. The reason this matters is her separateness allows her some critical distance on her characters; it's entirely possible she knows more about the world and about human nature than they do, and can judge them accordingly (and does, out loud, hence the overtness). Here is an example: the narrator has just finished reporting an incident between one of the main characters, Dorothea Brooke, and her much older husband, Casaubon, wherein husband and wife have misunderstood each other (one of many such incidents):

> We are all of us born in moral stupidity, taking the world as an udder to feed our supreme selves: Dorothea had early begun to emerge from that stupidity, but yet it had been easier to her to imagine how she would devote herself to Mr. Casaubon, and become wise and strong in his strength and wisdom, than to conceive with that distinctness which is no longer reflection but feeling—an idea wrought back to the directness of sense, like the solidity of objects—that he had an equivalent center of self, whence the lights and shadows must always fall with a certain difference.

> (211)

The narrator begins the paragraph by reaching out to the reader, trying to create a kind of solidarity with the use of "we." She then offers a reflection on the events that have just preceded, the misunderstanding and quarrel between husband and wife. This pause for direct commentary communicates the thoughts of the narrator to the reader, but it also serves as a unit related to subjectivation: we learn something about Dorothea, and we perhaps have changes in the status of her relationship with Casaubon prefigured to us.

This is also an instance of the narrator offering sympathetic thoughts regarding Casaubon's situation. He is not an especially sympathetic character, a fusty old pedant who exhibits an increasingly destructive possessiveness towards his young wife. We have very limited access to Casaubon's thoughts, furthermore, which does make it hard to sympathize with him; the more access we have to a character's mind, the more opportunities we have to generate sympathy with that character (much the same as we do with people). Most of the text of the novel is instead devoted to Dorothea's consciousness and perspective. Yet our narrator will occasionally intervene with gentle imperatives that we sympathize with Casaubon; the result is not that we *do* in fact sympathize with Casaubon, but rather that we develop certain perceptions of our narrator. We appreciate her insight into human nature, her generosity in considering people's flaws, and we accept taking her as a guide for our own judgment—even if we fall short of her expectations.

Box 1.3 Mikhail Bakhtin and heteroglossia

We can consider the Russian philosopher and literary critic Mikhail Bakhtin an outlier for two reasons. The first is quite literal: he spent a good part of his adult life in professional and personal exile. The second is more relevant to our purposes here: Bakhtin offered a great deal to the study of narrative, but he was never really connected with the Russian Formalists (though he was at university in St. Petersburg from 1913 to 1918), nor were his priorities the creation of any formal system. His ideas were considered politically suspect during the Stalinist period and he was sent into exile in Kazakhstan. His ideas on the French early modern author François Rabelais were considered "aberrant" by Russian academics and he was refused a doctorate (Holquist xxv). Bakhtin labored in obscurity, his manuscripts destroyed during the Second World War and the Nazi invasion, or lost in the chaos of the Soviet archive, in what his translator Michael Holquist has called "a vicious pattern that was to repeat itself throughout his life" (xxiii). Yet, with the rediscovery of his work in the 1960s, Bakhtin has given us some of the most powerful concepts in literary study in the twentieth century.

Holquist points out the core problem Bakhtin had with the ways language- or linguistically-based analyses of the novel proceed about their work: "The novel cannot be studied with the same set of ideas about the relation of language to style that we bring to bear on other genres" (xxix). According to Bakhtin—and the sympathetic Holquist—the results of attempting to study novels the same way some formalists study folk tales and "primitive narratives" are "inadequate" and "lugubrious" (xxx). It is precisely the difference between analyzing *skaz* and more complex texts that Bakhtin set out to examine in his studies of Fyodor Dostoyevsky and Rabelais. We will focus here on his essay "Discourse in the Novel," from 1934–35; this piece gives us the important term *heteroglossia*.

The concept of heteroglossia emerges from Bakhtin's understanding of the novel as a multilayered, infinitely diverse manifestation of how we use language in the world. According to Bakhtin:

> The novel as a whole is a phenomenon multiform in style and variform in speech and voice. In it the investigator is confronted with several heterogenous stylistic unities, often located on different linguistic levels and subject to different stylistic controls . . . . These heterogenous stylistic unities [letters, speech, narration, etc.], upon entering the novel, combine to form a structured artistic system, and are subordinated to the higher stylistic unity of the work as a whole.
>
> (261–62)

These different uses of language, the variety of speech types, and all of the ways such uses capture the "totality of the world of objects and ideas depicted and expressed in it" is heteroglossia (263). Bakhtin's understanding of the discourse of the novel is that it depends on a relationship between individual utterances and the multiform combination of different languages, speech forms, and texts that constitutes the structure as a totality. Thus the working of the novel cannot be reduced to thinking of it as a single utterance. Instances of singular utterance in the novel fulfill the narrative and aesthetic requirements of both the heteroglossic whole and the individual speech act (272). This movement has an effect on the reader as well, wherein the dialogism of the novel moves the reader towards evaluating beliefs and values expressed through the "heteroglot socio-verbal consciousness" (282).

Bakhtin's concept of heteroglossia demands that we read each instance of language use on its own terms. This is important for narrative because each instance creates its own world, each with its own rules and values. The use of a particular "heteroglot" points to a world and a consciousness. For Bakhtin, this manifests itself clearly in the comic novel—like Tobias Smollett's *Humphry Clinker*, which tells

(Continued)

(Continued)

the story through a series of letters of a servant who discovers his true father during a rather absurd tour of Scotland—but a more contemporary instance where the concept is highly relevant might be Junot Diaz's *The Brief Wondrous Life of Oscar Wao*. This novel exemplifies the notion of double-voicedness, where the narrator slips into Spanish inflected by living in both the Dominican Republic and New York; and where the text of the novel moves around among the story of an immigrant boy, the history of the Dominican Republic, and discourse drawn from sci-fi and manga—including explanatory footnotes written with a distinct satirical cast. The case also illustrates the three ways Bakhtin saw novels creating language: hybridizations, dialogized interrelations of languages, and pure dialogue (358). In this more contemporary case, different languages slide in and out of one another to signify hybridized consciousnesses and complicated relationships between self and other.

Time

Time is vital to the telling of a story in a few ways. Stories take place over time. Events happen in time. But the ways that time is presented, and the ways we can experience time, chronology, and order in narrative, is complicated. Events must occur in a particular order, but as long as that order is discernible to a reader or viewer, those events can occur in any order, not necessarily chronologically.

In narrative, time can really only progress in one direction, but we can disrupt the chronology of events through flashbacks (*analepsis*) or flashforwards (*prolepsis*). (We'll take a look at a good example of achronology, or events happening out of order in a story, when we consider the Quentin Tarantino film *Pulp Fiction* in Chapter 4.) We can perceive the deferral of a key piece of information until later in a story, way past the moment when to have that information would have made sense. Time can feel compressed, or it can feel lengthened; a moment can seem to go on forever, or a great deal of information can be packed into a short time. Events can occur with different kinds of frequency, singularly or multiple times; they can also be told once or multiple times. And, narrative can also manipulate duration. Chatman sees five ways in which this can occur: (1) *summary*, where a narrator summarizes several years' worth of action and experience in a single paragraph; (2) *ellipses*, where a narrator leaves out a chunk of time; (3) *scene*, where an event is being narrated as it is occurring, in "real time"; (4) *stretch*, where a narrator extends the telling of an event well past the amount of time the event took to occur; and (5) *pause*, where a narrator pauses the telling of an event to offer a description or a reflection or a tangent (68–74). We see the manipulation of order and progression over time, or the compression of time, in many instances, from novels with flashbacks to films with montage sequences.

Engagements: Exemplary text

Truman Capote's true crime "nonfiction novel" *In Cold Blood*, about the brutal murder of a prosperous Kansas family, exhibits a number of the techniques a narrative can use to manipulate time, and it does so to remarkable effect. The narrative is structured using several embedded plots, all told by a covert heterodiegetic narrator. There is the narrative layer dealing with the Clutter family, their hometown of Holcomb, and the effect the crime has on the town; the layer dealing with the murderers, Dick Hickock and Perry Smith, and their planning of the crime, their background, and their flight; and the layer dealing with the investigation and trial. This narrator also records many voices telling their versions of the story through numerous instances of reported dialogue as well as text from official reports (a good example of Bakhtin's heteroglossia—Box 1.3).

The narrative leading up to the murder of the Clutter family early in the book is prolonged, stretched out; one of the ways Capote does this is through pause, many moments where the narrative is stopped in order to describe aspects of the town of Holcomb, or provide description or exposition on the Clutters or their murderers. The representation of the murder itself is elided, and then told much later in the book via flashback in the form of reported dialogue, a confession during the trial period, from one of the killers. The arrest of the killers takes place six weeks after the murders, yet the time it takes to tell the story—Capote's use of "stretch"—makes it feel much longer. This has at least three effects. The first is to create an awful suspense in the reader: we await the representation of the horrifying event, we are provided with extensive detail about the town of Holcomb, the Clutter family, and the planning of Dick Hickock and Perry Smith—and then Capote thwarts our (possibly perverse) desire to actually *witness* the killings. The second effect is to render the representation of the murders more gruesome; by the time we read about it, we have begun to suspect that the narrator will never tell us, and then we are reminded, within the context of the trial, how horrible the crime is. The third effect of the withholding of the actual event of the murder until later in the book, thus disrupting the chronology by eliding the act and then showing it later, is that it forces the murderers, Dick and Perry, to confess. Much of *In Cold Blood* is devoted to complicating our relationship with and our sympathy for Dick and Perry, and the duration of the narrative includes a number of flashbacks, as well as multiple voices accounting for the two men, their background, and their motives. Making the two men tell the story, in their own words, at the end of the book complicates even further how we perceive them.

Thus, Capote creates in us a feeling that we are experiencing a disjunct between the amount of time the narrative covers and the amount of time devoted to the telling of its events. Time is stretched in order to fully render the world of the Clutters and their community, and to juxtapose that world with the seedy criminal underbelly of American society in which Dick and Perry move. The night over which the murders take place is elided. Capote describes Dick and Perry arriving at the Clutters' farm—"Presently the car crept forward" (57)—and then jumps to the next morning with a neighbor girl finding the bodies (59). Chronology is manipulated to create suspense, thwart our desire to see the representation of horror for its own sake, and then resituate us in a position of judgment and pity, not for the criminals but for their victims. As we shall see in Chapter 4, the ways a narrative can play with the progression of events over time has profound implications for our ethical judgment, and I think activating that ethical judgment is very much what Capote is trying to do with his choices related to time in *In Cold Blood*.

Perspective and focalization

If mood, voice, and attitude are what we use to talk about who is speaking in a narrative, perspective and focalization are what we use to talk about who is seeing, and what they are seeing, and from which point of view they are seeing. We've already seen a bit of how this works in our discussion of *Atonement* above; there, how the story works, how we assess our knowledge and judgment in reading, depends heavily on McEwan's manipulation of perspective. Perspective asks whose "point of view" is filtering the narrative, and from where in the text they are seeing the action unfold. Focalization is the part of perspective that helps us understand *how* a narrator knows things. Sometimes our narrator seems to know more, and sometimes our narrator seems to know less. Focalization and voice are allied concepts, because voice—especially whether a narrator takes on the voice of a character—is one of the ways we can tell when a narrative is being focalized.

Engagements: Exemplary text

Let's take an example to bring all of these different components together and illustrate them: a short story by Tessa Hadley called "Sunstroke," from her collection of the same name. In the story, two couples—Rachel and Sam, Janie and Vince—go to the seaside with their children. The women take the children to the beach while the men stay behind at the house, supposedly so Sam can write. Rachel spends much of the time confiding in Janie about her feelings for a mutual friend Kieran, whom she suspects desires her; she is trying to decide whether to have an affair. About half-way through the story, Rachel speaks on the phone to Sam to say she and Janie will take the children out to dinner, and Sam tells Rachel that Kieran has arrived unexpectedly to visit. The scene then shifts to the house and we see the men hanging out, smoking pot and talking. The two levels meet after dinner; one of Rachel's children gets sunstroke and throws up, so she stays home with the kids while the other adults go to the pub. We then, again, follow two different levels, one with Rachel at the house and the other with Kieran and Janie walking home, drunk, from the pub. They kiss. Everyone returns home and goes to bed. The final scenes of the story are (1) Janie thinking that no harm has been done by kissing Kieran, and her husband probably "owes" her; (2) Rachel deciding not to have an affair; (3) Kieran reflecting on whether or not domestic life is all it's cracked up to be.

This would seem to be a plot of revelation. The events reveal aspects of character, and we learn about the characters through the unfolding of the situation. The plot also depends on complex transformation, or combinations of different kinds of plot elements: characters learning new forms of knowledge about themselves and others, and relying on switching subjectivities. In a story such as this, where little happens except the revelation of character, it seems as though everything is a kernel. Take, for instance, the kiss between Kieran and Janie. The kiss could be a kernel—although if you deleted the kiss, the end of the story would be much the same, especially since Rachel decides not to have an affair without knowing her best friend kissed the object of her desire. On the other hand, right after the kiss, Janie and Kieran realize that all of the stimulation made Janie expel milk (she is in the midst of breastfeeding). In her version of the final scene, Janie finishes breastfeeding, feels "herself hollowed out from her old life" (22), and seems to decide to pursue the affair. In Kieran's version, "He finds himself longing for the perfect silence of his own room" (23); does he once again crave solitude because of the jarring disconnect between sexual desire and the reality of the women's lives as mothers? If we judge the decisions and responses of these characters to rest not upon the seemingly major event of the kiss but on the seemingly less major event of Janie's response, we might come to different conclusions.

The story-time of "Sunstroke" follows the arc of the day, but we spend more discourse-time with the women than we do with the men, and more discourse-time during the day than we do during the evening and night. We also have iteration, as the first part of the day is told with the narrator depicting the women, and then the same part of the day is told again, first with summary (many of the details of Sam's and Vince's morning are left out until Kieran arrives, and are simply summarized), and then with scene. Kieran's entire day is an ellipsis, except for his arrival at the seaside cottage and his final thoughts at night at the end of the story. Much of the story takes place in scene—the long sequences of dialogue between the women, for instance—but time seems to be manipulated during the kiss, in the form of stretch. The kiss does not take up much story-time, but in terms of discourse-time it goes on for an extended period of time, achieved through description and the representation of mental activity: "His mouth is hot and liquid. His lips feel swollen and thin-skinned . . . . She thinks of the many parties at Sam and Rachel's where she has stayed dumb while Kieran has spoken out eloquently on some subject . . . . It's marvelously simplifying that there's no time for this to become anything more than a kiss" (20). Even the marker of time—"there's no time"—indicates here that story-time and discourse-time are not synchronized.

To simply note that the narrator of "Sunstroke" is separate from the story and its characters is necessary but not sufficient. It would also not be entirely accurate to suggest that the narrator is focalizing any of the characters, although we do have access to the subjectivity—perspective— of each of the characters at one point or another in the story. Chatman's idea of the overt narrator is here quite helpful. The style of the narration draws attention to its telling, and occasionally even comments, such as here: In communicating to us the women's pleasure at being able to spend the morning at the seaside with no real obligation except to indulge their children a little, the narrator says, "In order to earn this day in the sun-shine with their beautiful children running around them, how many toiling domesticated days haven't these young mothers put in?" (4). The narrator here is observing and commenting on the perception of the women, as well as suggesting that perhaps it has some insight into the motivations that will lead to the choices the women make later. Is the narrator being sympathetic? Ironic? Judgmental? It does seem to raise the question of what these women "earn": sexual fulfillment? Pleasure? Freedom? This is a key question for the rest of the narrative.

I hope this chapter has given a preliminary sense of how narrative works, as well as a kind of "toolkit" of concepts we can use to analyze the different parts of stories and their relationship to each other. Going forward, I think it's important to bear in mind that these concepts are only helpful inso-far as we see them functioning in relationship with each other, all working together, to make the world of a story. It's the making of that world, and our place in it, to which we will now turn.

Works cited

Aristotle. *Poetics. The Complete Works of Aristotle*. Vol. 2. Trans. I. Bywater. Ed. Jonathan Barnes. Princeton, NJ: UP, 1984. 2316–2340. Print.

Bakhtin, Mikhail. *The Dialogic Imagination: Four Essays by M. M. Bakhtin*. Trans. Caryl Emerson and Michael Holquist. Ed. Michael Holquist. Austin U of Texas P, 1981. Print.

Barthes, Roland. "An Introduction to the Structural Analysis of Narrative." *New Literary History* 6 (1975): 237–272. Print.

Chatman, Seymour. *Story and Discourse: Narrative Structure in Fiction and Film.* Ithaca, NY: Cornell UP, 1978. Print.

Degeorge, Fernande. *The Structuralists from Marx to Lévi-Strauss.* New York: Doubleday, 1972. Print.

Erlich, Victor. *Russian Formalism.* The Hague: Mouton, 1955. Print.

Holquist, Michael. Introduction. In *The Dialogic Imagination: Four Essays by M. M. Bakhtin.* Trans. Caryl Emerson and Michael Holquist. Ed. Michael Holquist. Austin: U of Texas P, 1981. Print.

Joseph, John E. *Saussure.* New York: Oxford UP, 2012. Print.

Kassow, Samuel D. *Students, Professors, and the State in Tsarist Russia.* Berkeley: U of California P, 1989. Print.

Shklovsky, Viktor. "Art as Technique." *Russian Formalist Criticism: Four Essays.* Ed. Lee T. Lemon and Marion J. Reis. Lincoln: U of Nebraska P, 1965. 3–24. Print.

——. *Theory of Prose.* Trans. Benjamin Sher. Champaign, IL: Dalkey Archive P, 1990. Print.

Todorov, Tzevtan. *The Poetics of Prose.* Trans. Richard Howard. Ithaca, NY: Cornell UP, 1978. Print.

Vitale, Serena and Viktor Shklovsky. *Shklovsky: Witness to an Era.* Champaign, IL: Dalkey Archive P, 2012. Print.

Exemplary texts

Annie Hall. Dir. Woody Allen. Perf. Woody Allen and Diane Keaton. MGM, 1977. Film.

Capote, Truman. *In Cold Blood.* New York: Vintage, 1994. Print.

Dangarembga, Tsitsi. *Nervous Conditions.* Emeryville, CA: Seal Press, 2004. Print.

Diaz, Junot. *The Brief Wondrous Life of Oscar Wao.* New York: Riverhead Books, 2008. Print.

Eliot, George. *Middlemarch.* New York: Penguin, 2003. Print.

Foer, Jonathan Safran. *Eating Animals.* New York: Back Bay Books, 2010. Print.

Hadley, Tessa. *Sunstroke.* New York: Picador, 2007. Print.

Law & Order. Prod. Dick Wolf. Perf. George Dzundza, Chris Noth, Dann Florek, Michael Moriarty, Richard Brooks, Steven Hill, Jerry Orbach, Paul Sorvino. NBCUniversal, 1990–2010. Television series.

McEwan, Ian. *Atonement.* New York: Anchor, 2003. Print.

Pinter, Harold. "Girls." *Granta* 51 (2008). 22 December 2008. Web. 5 May 2015.

Recommended further reading

Bal, Mieke. *Narratology: Introduction to the Theory of Narrative.* Toronto: U of Toronto P, 1997. Print.

Barthes, Roland. *S/Z.* Trans. Richard Miller. New York: Hill & Wang, 1974. Print.

Culler, Jonathan. *Structuralist Poetics.* Ithaca, NY: Cornell UP, 1975. Print.

Genette, Gérard. *Narrative Discourse: An Essay on Method.* Trans. Jane E. Lewin. Ithaca, NY: Cornell UP, 1980. Print.

Rimmon-Kenan, Shlomith. *Narrative Fiction: Contemporary Poetics.* 2nd ed. New York: Routledge, 2002. Print.

Engagements: Interview with Sue J. Kim

Sue J. Kim is Professor of English and Co-Director of the Center for Asian American Studies at the University of Massachusetts, Lowell. She is the author of *On Anger: Race, Cognition, Narrative* (U of Texas P, 2013), *Critiquing Postmodernism in Contemporary Discourses of Race* (Palgrave, 2009), and essays in *Modern Fiction Studies, Narrative,* and the *Journal of Asian American Studies.* She is coeditor (with Meghan M. Hammond) of *Rethinking Empathy Through Literature* (Routledge, 2014) and guest editor for "Decolonizing Narrative Theory," a special issue of the *Journal of Narrative Theory* (Fall 2012).

How would you describe your approach to narrative
studies and/or narrative theory?

Generally, my approach to narrative studies is both historical-contextualist and formalist. While these two approaches have often been seen as opposed to one another, I don't really see how we can understand narratives in all forms—literary, cinematic, folk, digital—unless we understand *both* context and form, or what's been referred to as "external" and "internal." Gérard Genette informs my work just as much as Karl Marx and/or Frantz Fanon.

My scholarly work has focused specifically on issues around race—our narratives about race; how those narratives about race may shape how we read, say, narratives written by people of color (as well as white people); how sometimes the formal elements of narratives by people of color may complicate expectations about those narratives. In other words, I'm usually arguing that we have to think about race in as many ways as we think about narrative, and vice versa.

Describe your most recent project. What prompted your interest?
What were you hoping to achieve? What questions or ideas in
the field do you see it responding to?

My most recent project was the book *On Anger: Race, Cognition, and Narrative,* and its basic arguments are that anger is culturally, historically, and narratively constructed (particular in terms of race and gender); it's not as individualistic as we usually think it is; and fictional narratives about anger have a lot to teach us about the specific mechanics of anger. I became interested in it primarily because my sense was that both popular and academic conceptions of anger could be very narrow and/or problematic. I was also interested in the parallel but rarely intersecting genealogies of scholarly work on anger and emotion in, on the one hand, cognitive studies and, on the other hand, women's, ethnic, and cultural studies. One of my goals was to help bridge these two areas, although I'm not sure to what extent I succeeded.

I certainly think the recent developments in cognitive studies should be brought into more rigorous engagement with what we might call cultural studies (although that's too general a term). Particularly in terms of emotions and affect, we want neither to be ahistorical nor to completely dismiss possible biological and cognitive commonalities. We have a long way to go in terms of understanding emotion, which I find exciting.

What scholars and texts have influenced your approach?

For me, the most formative scholars and texts have been Marxist: Marx's *Capital*, Frantz Fanon's *oeuvre*, later Jean-Paul Sartre, Simone de Beauvoir, Angela Davis, Manning Marable, Raymond Williams. I've also been fundamentally shaped by Asian American studies historians like Gary Okihiro and Michael Omi, who have a keen sense of how history is narrative.

In narratology specifically, I've always loved the work of Mikhail Bakhtin and Tzvetan Todorov, plus I had the opportunity to attend the first Project Narrative Summer Institute at the Ohio State University in 2010, led by Jim Phelan and Robyn Warhol. That summer I had the chance to read more deeply in Gérard Genette, Wayne Booth, Susan S. Lanser, Brian Richardson, and others. In cognitive narrative studies in particular, David Herman, Frederick Luis Aldama, and Patrick Colm Hogan have influenced my work; I love that these critics are both invested in social justice while exploring our potentially shared capacities of mind.

What do you see as big questions confronting the field?
Where's the cutting edge? What are the trends?

Narrative theory has yet to really incorporate race and ethnicity in a substantive way. While narrative theorists have been talking more about postcolonial narratology, there's still a very large swath of ethnic and postcolonial studies scholars who fundamentally distrust narratology as Eurocentric and too-quickly universalizing, and I can't say this distrust is entirely unfounded. Just as narrative theory has made gender central to a large extent—thanks to the work of scholars such as Susan S. Lanser and Robyn Warhol—it needs a more fundamental reckoning with race and ethnicity. I don't mean just applying existing narrative theory to literary works by people of color. Rather, *how might ethnic studies transform the field of narrative theory itself?* I don't know the answers, but I think several people are working on exciting projects that may lead to some.

Similarly, narrative theory has yet to really grapple with queer theory.

At the same time, I do think narratology has a lot to offer all fields interested in systematic analyses of form and narrative. The general distrust of structuralism underlies some skepticism of narrative theory, and I think that's unwarranted for a variety of reasons, but that would take another 10 pages.

What are you working on next?

Someday—way in the future—my dream is to write a text that helps bridge Marxism, Asian American studies, and narratology, each of which has had an often fitful relationship to one another.

Engagements: Interview with James J. Donahue

James J. Donahue is Associate Professor of Literature for the English and Communication Department at SUNY Potsdam. He is the author of *Failed Frontiersmen: White Men and Myth in the Post Sixties American Historical Romance* and editor (with Derek C. Maus) of *Post-Soul Satire: Black Identity after Civil Rights*. His current research addresses the intersection of narrative theories and the study of race in prose fiction. This interest has produced the article "Focalization, Ethics, and Cosmopolitanism in James Welch's *Fools Crow*" and a collection of essays currently being revised for press, "Race, Ethnicity, and Narrative in the Americas" (co-edited with Jennifer Ho and Shaun Morgan).

How would you describe your approach to narrative studies and/or narrative theory?

I am always interested in exploring the ways that theories and methodologies can productively work together, so my approach to narrative theory is always "narrative theory and …." Narrative theory—that is, the variety of narrative theories—begins by asking a number of very important questions about the nature, use, and reception of narratives, so it's a fantastic place to begin any scholarly project focused on the variety of narratives in literature, film, television, etc. So for me, narrative theory provides the starting point from which I begin my projects.

Describe your most recent project. What prompted your interest? What were you hoping to achieve? What questions or ideas in the field do you see it responding to?

I am currently co-editing a collection of essays titled "Race, Ethnicity, and Narrative in the Americas," with Jennifer Ho (UNC-Chapel Hill) and Shaun Morgan (Tennessee Wesleyan). This book collects essays that explore the means by which narrative theory and ethnic literary studies (including Critical Race Studies, postcolonial theory, and other approaches engaged in racial and ethnic identity) can productively work together to provide better tools to understand the racial and ethnic dimensions of narrative. When we first discussed this project, we were initially concerned with what we saw as the lack of such work in narrative theory. However, as we have discovered, quite a few scholars have been developing connections among these various theoretical approaches; ideally, this collection will provide a number of interesting models for scholars to draw from and engage with.

What scholars and texts have influenced your approach?

At my core, I am drawn to the structuralist dimensions of narrative theory, so topping the list of influences is Gérard Genette. However, I have also found much inspiration from the work of Mikhail Bakhtin, especially as it's been used to analyze Native American fiction. More recently, my work—particularly the project described above—has been influenced by the work of feminist narratology, and so is deeply indebted to the work of Susan Lanser. Although these theorists engage a relatively diverse range of concerns, from formalist studies to cultural studies, all three scholars developed their theoretical approaches by combining and refining theories and methodologies that were current at the time. Given my own interest in exploring connections between schools of thought, I am most drawn to those scholars who cast their intellectual nets widely.

What do you see as big questions confronting the field?
Where's the cutting edge? What are the trends?

Narrative studies is a rich and diverse field, with scholars engaged in a variety of exciting approaches. Right now, I think the most important questions being asked by the field as a whole revolve around the ways that narrative theory can be broadened and strengthened by other areas of academic inquiry. For instance, there is a great deal of interesting work being done right now in cognitive approaches to narrative, and narrative theorists are working side by side with cognitive neuroscientists, psychologists, philosophers of the mind, and others whose research explores the functioning of the brain and the nature of the mind. Such work is part of the trend (as I see it) of moving away from purely literary texts and approaches, recognizing the ubiquitous status of narrative in all aspects of human communication and self-definition.

What are you working on next?

Although I have not begun any formal work on it yet, my next project will be a study of experimental narratives and the ways such narratives force us to reconsider the function of the Ideal/Implied Reader. In short, I believe that some authors are currently constructing narratives that, by design, do not (perhaps even cannot) have an Ideal Reader. Although the Ideal Reader is an abstract concept, it is (like many other abstract narrative constructs) dependent upon a humanized figure. Further, readers are often compelled (through classroom instruction and professional training) to accept the potential of "getting it all," of knowing how all parts of the narrative work together to produce meaning. Some texts, I argue, frustrate this desire and force readers into an uncomfortable—but intellectually rewarding—incompleteness of understanding.

2   The reader in the (story) world

Narrative is a way of understanding the world, its knowledge, its structures, and its meaning. Paying attention not only to the form of narrative but also to how we *experience* narrative can help us understand what it means to be human in the world; it can help us to comprehend our own minds and the minds of others. As human beings, we have identities that are shaped by our relationships with our families, our origins, and our pasts. We are influenced by our race, our gender, our class, our ethnicity. We are social beings, living in a social world; narrative is a social act, situated in that world, emerging from it and shaped by it. Yet we also have highly individuated minds that can recognize patterns and respond to the ways stories attempt to touch us. In this chapter, we'll take a look at how we engage with narrative from two different perspectives. First, we'll consider the reader in the *real world*, and how identity as well as social, historical, and political contexts affect the ways we engage with narrative. Second, we'll consider the reader in the *storyworld*, and how the mind of the reader allows for each of us to immerse ourselves in a narrative universe.

The reader in the real world: Narrative and identity

So what about the reader in the world? To what extent does context defined by gender, race, or ethnicity play a role in how we engage with narrative? We can answer this question in at least two ways to start. The first answer has to do with *canon*. The "literary canon" is how people who study literature refer to works that a community of readers has determined are culturally and artistically significant. We study these works and their authors in school, they show up often in film adaptations, or on totebags, wall calendars, and mugs; and you can probably think of a few examples: the plays of William Shakespeare, the novels of Jane Austen. For decades, the idea of canon determined what we read, and how we studied literature. But what happens if some of how we understand how narrative works is defined solely by texts that come from this "canon"? It would be like trying to figure out everything there is to know about fish by only looking at salmon. A more diverse set of authors and texts are continually making their way into our reading repertoire, and this means we have many different kinds of stories that shape our understanding of narrative, and our understanding of people besides ourselves. Furthermore, recognizing that stories can tell us a lot about differences among people as well as about more universal things, like love and family, means we can start developing the equipment to ask, and possibly answer, difficult questions about race, gender, ethnicity, identity, history.

Stories can communicate these issues to us in a variety of ways, through a variety of techniques, which leads me to the second way we might think about how context and identity play a role in our engagements with narrative: through *communication*. Narrative can do a lot of things, and one of those things is communicate. An author tries to communicate with his or her audience; a narrator tries to communicate with the reader. Telling is a form of communication, and it has an effect on us. Ross Chambers points to the political implications of thinking about narrative this way: "The study of narrative as [communicative] transaction must open eventually onto ideological and cultural analysis" (9). If we think of narrative in terms of a teller telling us something, we might want to think about what the message is, how that message is shaped by the teller's identity, and how our own identity affects our ability to hear.

Stories that take as their subject matter the nature of identity as shaped by gender, race, or ethnicity might also take up particular themes. Different ways of reading informed by feminist literary theory, postcolonial literary theory, and ethnic studies help us see these themes at work, and how specific narrative techniques bring forth these themes. These ways of reading can also help us see that maybe methods of studying narrative that *don't* account for identity and context might be missing something. Margaret Homans, for instance, has suggested that feminist narrative studies might not only elucidate themes pertinent to feminism but might also critique and transform reading methods founded on conventional, linear, male-centric fictions (Box 2.1).

Box 2.1 Feminist literary theory

Feminist theory is dedicated to defining, analyzing, and exposing the ways patriarchal structures have shaped the experiences of both men and women. This area of study has developed over time, beginning in the late eighteenth century, with Mary Wollstonecraft's *Vindication of the Rights of Women* in 1792. Identity is an important concept for feminist theory, because it is interested in the ways gender shapes identity, and the ways identity is defined in terms of power and dominance. When applied to the study of literature, feminist theory is used to examine how literary form, technique, genre, character, and theme is influenced by gender. It has also been used to draw attention

(Continued)

(Continued)

to the ways the literary canon—the works some readers accept to be
of cultural and artistic significance—has privileged male writers, and
critics and scholars who work with feminist theory have used the
position to argue for opening up the canon to more women writers.
Feminist literary theorists make the claim that we cannot say that
the experience of literature and language is universal or the same for
everyone, because so much of that experience has been defined by
men via their dominant position in art, culture, society, and politics.

In an important article published in the scholarly journal *Style* in 1986, a
founding writer on feminist narrative studies, Susan Lanser, calls for the study
of narrative to pay more attention to writing by women; she also suggests
that the more we attend to how women tell stories, the more we might understand how the many forms of narrative can capture many different kinds
of experiences ("Toward" 342). According to Lanser, we have to revise
our cultural values that say some stories are more important than others.
Furthermore, we have to consider the possibility that some of the techniques
we examined in Chapter 1, like point of view, might be used differently to tell
women's stories than they would be in telling men's stories. We might have to
rethink these techniques entirely. As Lanser puts it, "Point of view in the fictional narrative, then, is a product of the same ideological systems and modes
of production that govern communication as a social act" (*Narrative* 106).
Like other feminist literary critics, Lanser sees a real need to rethink how we
talk about narrative as communicating "universal" themes and ideas. At the
very least, how can we begin to suggest that there are narrative "universals"
when all of the texts used to define such categories have been written by men?

Readers who approach narrative from a feminist perspective consider the
representation of character to be of the utmost importance. This is because
they believe that stories should capture lived experience; stories should tell
us what it is like to be a woman, to live in a woman's body, to see and know
the world through the eyes and mind of a woman. For Lanser, in this way
narrative can tell us something about the real world, and influence how we
think about it ("Toward" 344). Not only should narrative, then, speak back
to how we live in the world; it should also effect real-world change. The
representation of identity has political implications, calling upon readers to
engage with narrative as a way of engaging with the world, resulting in a
consciousness of how damaging structures of power can be. This position
is important for engaging with narrative through the lenses of postcolonial
theory and ethnic studies, as well.

Engaging with narrative through feminism, for Lanser and another
important critic, Robyn Warhol, lets us think about different kinds of techniques we see in women's writing. We might see a tension between public

and private writing, women expressing that certain stories or parts of a story cannot or should not be told. Our relationship to the narrator might be different, more engaged or more distant, or perhaps showing some ambivalence about how engaged or how distant the narrator should be. There might also be multiple layers, embedded stories that ultimately go unfulfilled. As we saw in Chapter 1, a narrative can consist of several layers, and it can suggest possible actions or wishes that never transpire. Each of these techniques can be linked to important themes in women's writing: the tension women experience between their public and private selves; the ways women construct personal relationships and the ways they communicate within those relationships; the ways women can feel thwarted in their lives, unable to take action or achieve their dreams.

Engagements: Exemplary text

Doris Lessing's short story "To Room Nineteen" exhibits many of the qualities we see in women's narrative. We find a tension between the public and the private, one the narrator seems committed to both representing and facilitating by giving us total access to every vagary of the protagonist's increasingly distressed mind while showing how others in the story do not understand her. We also see an emphasis on what can or cannot be told, what must remain silenced in the narrating of women's experiences. We find instances of faulty communication, dialogue that is reported and misunderstood, as well as conflicts between what is communicated outwardly to others and what is communicated inwardly to the self (or reported to the reader). Finally, we see numerous possibilities presented and thwarted, numerous actions suggested and not taken; the suggestion and then nonfulfillment of events creates the impression that the woman's plot, and thus her life, has stalled and cannot move forward. Failed plot possibilities here seem to point to the limited options a woman has to make the plot of her own life, to generate a meaningful story arc for herself.

The story is about a woman named Susan. She is approaching middle age, a stay-at-home mother who gave up a career in advertising to raise four young children; she has a seemingly successful and affectionate husband, and a large, luxurious home in a wealthy London suburb. Once all her children are old enough to be in school all day and "off her hands," as everyone around her says, her mind starts to unravel. She fills her days with little chores like baking and sewing, but even these appear to be pointless because she has household help. Her husband behaves in a sympathetic manner, but becomes increasingly distant as he perceives her to be "difficult," and begins having an affair. Susan's way of coping with what she feels to be a growing sense of purposelessness coupled with a desperate and inexplicable need to be alone is to start taking the train into London and renting a room at a seedy hotel (in a kind of reversal of the Charlotte Perkins Gilman story "The Yellow Wallpaper"), where she sits in a chair for eight hours a day. Finally, her husband suspects she is having an affair, because to simply go to a hotel and sit for eight hours seems so implausible that he can't believe that's what she's doing. She's so disgusted by how he perceives her, and so horrified that her private refuge has been discovered, that she goes to the hotel for one last time, and commits suicide.

The story is told by an overt—a very present—narrator, who comments on everything, who offers information and then qualifies it, who seems to know all the inner workings of Susan's mind and her marriage and is sympathetic but ultimately resigned to the inevitability of how this woman's story had to end: *it's sad but it all had to turn out this way, didn't it.* Susan is described as "sensible" and "intelligent" until the restlessness of a mind trapped in a life with no purpose makes her "irrational." Everything is presented as balanced—Susan even managed to give birth to an even number of boys and girls—until her feelings become excessive, and then Susan seems to overflow into the narrator; at the same time, the narrator takes on Susan's thoughts in a kind of sympathy. We can see this here, when Susan finds out that her husband has had a one-night stand:

> Except, thought Susan, unaccountably bad-tempered, she was (is?) the first. In ten years. So either the ten years' fidelity was not important, or she isn't. (No, no, there is something wrong with this way of thinking, there must be.) But if she isn't important, presumably it wasn't important either when Matthew and I first went to bed with each other that afternoon whose delight even now (like a very long shadow at sundown) lays a long, wandlike finger over us. (Why did I say sundown?) Well, if what we felt that afternoon was not important, nothing is important, because if it hadn't been for what we felt, we wouldn't be Mr. and Mrs. Rawlings with four children, et cetera, et cetera. The whole thing is *absurd*—for him to have come home and told me was absurd. For him not to have told me was absurd. For me to care, or for that matter, not to care, is absurd.
>
> (400)

The boundary between Susan's consciousness and our narrator's consciousness here becomes somewhat porous. The narrator seems to think that Susan has every right to be "bad-tempered" about her husband's infidelity, yet she reports Susan's attempts to talk herself out of it. We see a sliding into first-person as the narrator takes on Susan's "I," but at the same time would Susan have created a little literary moment as she's thinking through this difficulty—"a long, wandlike finger"—and would she have paused to process through figurative language—"like a very long shadow at sundown"—and then questioned herself as to her choice, which is thus transformed into a potential symbol for decline: "sundown." Finally, Susan realizes the whole thing is "absurd," because she sees how she is caught in a cliché plot: the middle-aged woman trapped in her home and family obligations watching her husband be free, and express that freedom through philandering. Our narrator, on the other hand, suspects that plot is in fact the very thing that traps women, because there are only so many stories, and only so many ways for those stories to end, when one's sense of autonomy is compromised by one's gender.

This lack of autonomy is captured by plot nonstarters, by possibilities that are not fulfilled and actions not taken. Susan has her destructive and desperate thoughts, thinks about talking to her husband, and does not: "No, clearly this conversation should not take place" (404). There are a number of instances where Susan is depicted as simply sitting, deliberately not doing anything: not going into the garden, not getting a cup of tea. Scenes where her husband tries to talk to her are truncated by Susan's vague responses; while we have access to her mental activity, while we have Susan's inner life communicated to us, her husband is shut out. We learn about Susan's feelings through an assortment of direct and indirect reporting techniques, as communication with her husband fails.

When she gets her room in London, the narrator asks, "What did she *do* in the room? Why, nothing at all" (419). To redress a lack of autonomy, Susan simply stops acting. If to take action is to commit to moving one's life (and one's story) forward, and all one sees with that forward vision is more pointlessness, then she simply pushes the pause button, until the final action of suicide—the only action to take that ultimately stops all action, ending the story irrevocably. This is, in the end, the only way the protagonist can take control of the story.

Multiple identities and intercultural intersections are very much at play in postcolonial and ethnic narrative studies. So far we have been talking about the ability to tell stories as a kind of ability to organize the world. I have been suggesting that such organizing is indeed possible, and that it might even be part of an assumption that our notion of the self is that of a unified entity. But what of stories that seem to be told from the perspective of a fragmented self? What if one's experience of the world is such that "organizing" it through narrative cannot be taken for granted? What if the telling of such stories relies not on the communicating of actual, achieved events, but of possibilities and actions that go unfulfilled? These are all qualities of narratives that come from a postcolonial context (Box 2.2).

Box 2.2 Postcolonial literary theory

"Postcolonial" refers to what has happened culturally, socially, politically, and economically in nations that are former colonies; for our purposes, it also refers to the kind of literary art that was produced in response to and in the context of decolonization and the postcolonial

(Continued)

(Continued)

period. Thinkers and writers started attempting to define the conditions of colonialism and postcolonialism beginning in the 1950s and 1960s, as decolonization emerged after World War Two. The literature of postcolonialism does not have to be defined only as that which has been produced in former colonies, such as India and Pakistan, or African and Caribbean nations. It is also defined as literature of *diaspora*, literary works created by and about those who have had to leave homelands that have been affected by the troubles of globalization, struggles for independence, political strife, and trauma. In addition to taking *identity* as a core concept (much like feminist theory), postcolonial theory is interested in the idea of *hybridity*—the notion that one's identity can have multiple facets which are not always entirely integrated with each other into a coherent self. Postcolonial theory also explores what kinds of stories get told; who is allowed the voice to tell them; what happens when historical narratives are erased or silenced; and how the stories of those who have been traumatized by colonialism, both historically and in our own time, can be told.

Gerald Prince claims that reading narratives from a postcolonial perspective might help us see new ways of understanding space because of the importance to those stories of boundaries and crossings ("On a Postcolonial" 375). Such a perspective might also give new insight into character, because postcolonial fiction is interested in hybridity, in characters with multifaceted identities trying to bridge multiple cultural experiences—or who are resisting traditional, Euro-centric models of the coherent self. Brian Richardson has noted a number of common features shared by postcolonial fiction: the use of a "we" narrator, plots that resist closure and linearity and expand our sense of time, characterization that calls notions of autonomy into question, an exploding of the concept of the individual reader in favor of the collective; all of this suggests the creation of an alternative way of telling and reading stories ("U.S. Ethnic and Postcolonial Fiction" 15–16). We might think of these narratives as being essential for working through historical and global forces beyond the agency of the individual; for trying to comprehend the ways pasts, traditions, and origins are disrupted by colonial oppression; for reclaiming stories and voices, identities and collective experiences that have been erased and silenced.

Engagements: Exemplary text

One quality we find in much postcolonial fiction is the positioning of individual stories against the backdrop of national narratives; through this manipulation of foreground and background, these individual stories play out across a vista of historical transformation, social upheaval, and political trauma. The narrative essentially operates on two levels: the individual and the global. The effect is to elevate the individual stories while also maximizing the horror of history because we don't always see the big picture in its entirety—only hints of the roiling of nations and the trauma of peoples. In the details chosen for the impact they have on individuals we come to realize the violence done to people through historical and political forces. For readers coming from a context not directly affected by colonialism and decolonization, this can be a destabilizing experience; knowledge of these pasts is presumed that such readers might not possess, and the not-knowing becomes a kind of indictment.

As we saw in Chapter 1, knowing and not-knowing in any story is made possible by a narrator, and one of the functions of the narrator in postcolonial fiction is to draw our attention not only to our knowledge of the world of the story and its characters, but to our knowledge—or lack thereof—of the colonial context. Making sense of a story depends on what we do with the hints that, taken together, generate historical and political understanding. Salman Rushdie uses this to great effect; here we'll focus on his short story "The Free Radio," which was published in the collection *East, West* and draws on his experience in Bombay (now Mumbai) before and after India gained independence from the United Kingdom in 1947. This story seems, at first, to tell of a rickshaw driver in India who gets involved with a thief's widow and allows himself to be talked into getting sterilized because she doesn't want any more children. This would be one level, the individual level. Yet as the story unfolds, we realize that a mysterious white caravan and the appearance of thuggish youth wearing armbands are part of an increasingly oppressive post-independence government pursuing a policy of enforced sterilization. This is the second, global/historical level; it is only hinted at, which also suggests that there are certain historical and political realities which are unspeakable.

The narrator gestures towards a collective by using "we," a characteristic of postcolonial fiction noted by Brian Richardson as mentioned above. The story begins, "We all knew nothing good would happen to him while the thief's widow had her claws dug into his flesh, but the boy was an innocent, a real donkey's child, you can't teach such people" (19). In addition to suggesting a communal telling with "we," the narrator also makes a gesture of solidarity with the reader: "you." Other suggestions that the narrator is entering into relationship with the reader are made through positioning the reader alongside the narrator in space, as in: "They met right here" (20). This implies that the narrator is leading the reader through his actual physical space, bridging the space between the actual world of the reader and the textual world of the narrator. The boundary between real and fiction is thus collapsed, and the story is rendered multidimensional. As noted above, the playing around with space is a quality we see throughout postcolonial fiction.

The narrator also presumes knowledge on the part of the reader, imagining a reader who is part of his world and historical moment. As the rickshaw boy, Ramani, gets mixed up with government thugs along with his liaison with the widow, the narrator says, "I knew those cronies of his. They all wore the arm-bands of the new Youth Movement. This was the time of the State of Emergency, and these friends were not peaceful persons" (22). The combination of under-statement and elision (What Youth Movement? What State of Emergency?) means our narrator is not filling in details he believes we know, and not telling things he believes shouldn't be told explicitly. He doesn't have to tell, because we know, and it's probably for the best, because such things shouldn't be spoken of.

"The Free Radio" progresses via the meddling of our narrator, an interven-tionist person as well as an overt teller. Yet when it comes to the political unrest and potential for violence that surrounds the story of Ramani, he absents him-self: "I sat quiet under my tree" (22); "I did not care to be in the vicinity … so I took my hookah and sat in another place. I heard rumors …" (24). Then the narrator conveys that Ramani believes the government will give him a free radio for voluntarily sterilizing himself; this fantasy takes over the poor boy's life, and he wanders the streets pretending to hold a radio up to his ear and singing. When he returns to the mystery caravan to, he believes, collect his prize, he is beaten and thrown into the street. This dramatic and terrible event, however, is reported indirectly. The narrator tells us that the story was told to him by an entirely different entity:

> Ram went into the caravan gaily, waving at his armbanded cronies who were guarding it against the anger of the people, and *I am told*—for I had left the scene to spare myself the pain—that his hair was well-oiled and his clothes were freshly starched …. And still—*they tell me*—the thief's black widow did not move from her place in the rickshaw, although they dumped her husband in the dust.
>
> (29–30; italics mine)

The narrator relinquishes his position as witness. At the same time, we have not been given any indication that we should not trust this narrator. Even though the story of Ramani's humiliation is coming from "they"—a mysterious social collective we don't see, existing outside the story we do see—and even though we have seen our narrator absent himself from painful scenes before, we do not distrust his recounting. The world of the story as presented up to this point makes something so awful seem entirely plausible, as well as dangerous to witness. It is the kind of event that might recede into the realm of rumor; but for all the ways our narrator presents himself as a gossip, he is in actuality telling a version of history.

The importance of race and ethnicity in defining identity also makes it important for studying narrative (Box 2.3). At the very least, we should be asking how we define our literary categories, how we define how narrative works, and just how far we can go with the assumption that all forms of storytelling are universal. To borrow an example from scholar of narrative

James J. Donahue, why is something like Nathaniel Hawthorne's novel *The Scarlet Letter* an important "American" novel, rather than an important "white" novel? Why do novels by African American writers, or by writers from a background explicitly defined as "ethnic," have to be marked as such? Narrative is one of the ways we explore and question identity; and it is just as necessary to consider how these make us different, and result in different stories, as it is to think about how they create opportunities for sharing and community. Greater awareness of how these stories work, how to read them, and how they contribute as well as speak back to and resist the construction of wider cultural, historical, and literary narratives is also essential.

Box 2.3 Ethnic studies

The study of race and ethnicity has its roots in the work of African American thinkers and writers of the nineteenth and early twentieth centuries; today it includes the study of Chicano/a, Latino/a, and Hispanic writers, Asian American writers, and Native American writers. Much of the focus in this area is on identity; and the ways language as well as political, social, economic, and cultural factors determine identity and how these determining forces might be subverted. Those working in these areas are also committed to making visible how race and ethnicity have an impact on the ways we read and write—something that has gone ignored in the construction of a literary canon constituted by authors of white European descent.

Engagements: Exemplary text

Percival Everett is one of the most prolific authors writing today, and an important voice in contemporary American literature. He takes as a regular topic of interest the challenges of narrating the African American experience in the context of history and through the forms of storytelling available to represent that experience. The results are novels that are wildly experimental, especially in terms of structure and voice, and that try to break through the constraints of familiar forms. The narrative of Everett's novel *Percival Everett by Virgil Russell* consists of several levels, with a frame that tells the story of a man, an author, Percival Everett, visiting his father in a nursing home. This level is conveyed mostly through scenes of dialogue; the dialogue is unmarked, so we can't always tell who is speaking to whom and how, and one of the speakers might be dead. The father wants his son to write the story of his life, and as the son begins to tell the story, that story is interrupted by a number of seemingly unrelated other stories. There are multiple narrators, I-narrators which may be different for each story, but which may all be originating from the subjective position of Percival Everett as character-narrator (author-narrator?).

Some of the narrative is marked by narrators whom a reader might identify as African American; some of it is not. Some of it appears to be told by
Nat Turner as constructed by William Styron in the controversial 1967 *The
Confessions of Nat Turner* (a fictitious memoir of the leader of a slave rebellion
by a white author), thereby reaching out beyond the world of the novel to a
signal moment in African American cultural and political history, and making
that ideologically and artistically problematic moment part of the world of the
novel. This also points to the ideological and artistic problems with certain forms
of first-person narration in general, particularly around issues of identity. At
other points, however, the narrator describes attending a costume party dressed
as Nat Turner, thereby drawing attention both to the perceptions formed by the
reader *and* to the public nature of racial performance (which is also a comment
on what it means to be an African American author and subject).

Thus the narrating-I—Percival Everett—comments on the authorial figure—
Percival Everett—and resists the assumption that they are not the same. Is this
experimental text, framed with dialogue whose subject is the father request-
ing that the son *write* his story, implicitly refusing oral or traditional forms of
storytelling? Is the breaking down of the barrier between narrator and author
speaking back to conceptions of the narrator that may have developed from
a position of white privilege—from a position that does not have to be conscious of cultural, artistic, political identities defined by race? Likewise, the
reliance on rupturing narrative levels as a narrative strategy (metalepsis, as
we learned in Chapter 1) would seem to suggest the insistence that past and
present, history and fiction, are not concretely defined categories. Everett uses
narrative to question the nature of fiction and history, to question how stories
are put together, and to subvert conventions of how we represent subjectivity.

Narrative doesn't only give us ways of thinking about being in the world;
the study of narrative also helps us see how our sense of ourselves is constructed through stories of identity. Stories show us how we embody or
perform identity; how identity is culturally scripted; how storytelling is
socially situated. Now let's turn to how the study of narrative helps us think
about our own minds. The rest of this chapter is concerned not only with
the reader in the real world, but with the reader in the storyworld. We'll be
looking at how a reader immerses herself in a story, using imagination and
other mental processes to engage with narrative universes.

The reader in the worlds of the story: Narrative and the mind

A major thinker in the world of narrative studies over the last two decades—
putting narrative in conversation with the rise of virtual reality and media
studies—has been Marie-Laure Ryan. We will return to her groundbreaking
work in these other areas when we get to Chapter 3, but first we'll consider
one of her earlier contributions: possible worlds theory (see Box 2.4).

Box 2.4 Ontology and epistemology

Ontology refers to the nature of *being*. When we say that a narrative world has its own ontology, we mean that it has its own existence that is separate from the "real" world but just as true; things *are* within that narrative world, and they function according to the rules that world has established. The things within the narrative world might not be "real," but they do exist.

Epistemology refers to the nature of *knowledge*. When we ask ourselves how we know what we know in a narrative world; how a narrator communicates to us what it knows; and what we do with that knowledge, we are working our way through a set of epistemological problems.

Possible worlds theory helps us see how a narrative universe can be made up of many embedded worlds; these worlds include the actual world of the text as well as the private worlds of the characters. Plot generates a set of ontological boundaries by setting in motion the creation of a series of worlds which, embedded within each other, become the narrative universe (Ryan 175). Analyzing all the possible worlds that make up a narrative universe helps us see how characters think, how they experience their own being within the world of the story, and how the combinations of different worlds help a story create themes. This process also helps us understand how we ourselves experience a narrative universe, how we enter into it, take all the different imaginative parts, and make them into a whole.

Figure 2.1 shows a model of possible worlds. On the outside is the *actual* world. This is the world in which we actually live, where authors create and readers read. There is only one actual world, and we're living in it. On the other hand, the *textual actual world* can consist of many embedded worlds, as the model shows. The *textual actual world* is the world of the story. It resembles the actual world enough that we can enter it and understand what's going on. Even a science fiction novel or movie has enough within its textual actual world to make us feel like we can access it from our own actual, real world and get how it works; perhaps it presents recognizable human-like figures doing recognizable things for intelligible reasons. The *textual reference world* is the world the narrator creates by telling us about the textual actual world. The textual reference world refers to the textual actual world; it's the narrated, told world. "How can we have a textual reference world that is separate from the textual actual world?", you might be asking. Think about what might be happening in the world of the story that is *not* narrated, but which happens nevertheless. For instance, in *Wuthering Heights*, Heathcliff disappearing for three years is part of the textual actual world, and there are possibilities related to his actions embedded in that

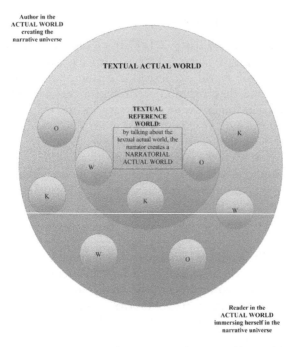

Figure 2.1 A model for understanding possible worlds. (O = obligation-world; K = knowledge-world; W = wish-world.)

textual actual world; but whatever *actually* happened while he was gone is *not* part of the textual reference world because it's not narrated to us. This example shows us that within a plot are embedded many possible worlds, some actualized, some not.

The narrator inhabits both the textual reference world—so it can tell the story of the textual actual world—and the *narratorial actual world*. This is the world the narrator lives in that is part of the textual actual world, but not necessarily part of the textual reference world, because it's not part of telling the story. Consider the narrator of Joseph Conrad's novel *Heart of Darkness*, an unnamed "I" who frames the story, appearing briefly at the beginning, to introduce Marlow, the teller of the tale of the downfall of Kurtz, and at the end. This unnamed "I" inhabits a narratorial actual world, about which we learn very little ("The Director of Companies was our captain and our host," he says, for example, indicating that he holds some kind of position in a trading company, and is for some reason on the ship on the Thames with Marlow). Nevertheless, cues appear within the story that point to a world, one inhabited by the narrator that is part of the textual actual world but not exactly part of the telling and therefore not part of the textual reference world.

Within both the textual actual world and the textual reference world are other worlds called *textual alternative possible worlds*, which would appear in the form of the mental life of the characters. These are the worlds designated with letters on our model: the K-world is the knowledge-world, which deals with knowledge, ignorance, and belief; the O-world is the obligation-world, which deals with obligations and prohibitions; and the W-world is the wish-world, which deals with goodness and badness. These make up the private worlds of the characters, and can be used to define different kinds of conflict; the types of world generate theme, and the conflicts lead to plot, which leads to the creation of more possible worlds. Conflicts can be created among the textual actual world and the private worlds, between different private worlds in one character, within one private world (different wishes, for instance), and between different private worlds between different characters. Plot happens when the relations among these different worlds is altered (Ryan 126). One example might be drawn from George Eliot's *Middlemarch*, a novel we've considered previously in Chapter 1. The main character, Dorothea Brooke, experiences conflict in all three of her private worlds: her O-world, in which she must remain loyal to her aged and failed husband Casaubon; her W-world, in which she desires both to pursue a relationship with the young and handsome Will Ladislaw and to abandon her promise to continue the scholarly work of Casaubon after his death in favor of her own work with the poor; and her K-world, in which her own perceived ignorance of history, philosophy, and literature led her to marry a man whom she imagined be intellectually superior only to discover his mental and emotional shortcomings. The work of the novel, among other things, is to resolve each of these conflicts within each of these private worlds, and to present the events that result from those conflicts.

Engagements: Exemplary text

Here's another example: take *Anchorman: The Legend of Ron Burgundy*, starring Will Ferrell as Ron Burgundy. The textual actual world of *Anchorman* represents Ron Burgundy working as a newsman at a local television station in San Diego; in this world he imagines himself to be, as he says, "kind of a big deal." The textual reference world presents situations wherein this would seem to be the case. Ron's news team has the highest ratings in San Diego, he goes to cool parties, he has fans. Yet the narratorial actual world, telling of Ron's story, presents an alternative. Ron is also depicted as an entirely un-self-aware buffoon; even as he is shown at a cool party, he says, "We've been coming to the same party for 12 years, and in no way is that depressing." When he tries to make a move on Veronica Corningstone, an ambitious up-and-coming TV journalist played by Christina Applegate (channeling Faye Dunaway from *Network*), she walks away in disgust, leaving him wearing a half-open bathrobe and holding a ludicrous umbrella drink. The dynamic between the textual reference world and the narratorial actual world generates further alternative possible worlds. Ron's K-world is defined by a near-total ignorance of how ridiculous he is, and part of the work of the plot is to put him in situations that allow him to gain this knowledge and change his behavior. We might also perceive Ron's W-world as one defined by sexist attitudes towards women, which lead him to become infatuated with Veronica while also rejecting the notion that she could ever be a news anchor. This goes along with his O-world, which says that because women are inferior, they are prohibited from being anchors. Of course, Ron's W-world and O-world are real, but they are completely wrong, and the narratorial actual world makes this clear. The incorrectness of these mental worlds brings him into conflict not only with Veronica but with his society; as Rocky the bartender says during one of Ron's benders, "Ladies can do stuff now, and you're going to have learn to deal with it." The work of the plot of the film, then, is to resolve the conflicts among these worlds, creating a new world for Ron; he gets over his sexism, saves the day, and is promoted to network anchor.

Each world embedded within any story has its own ontology, or version of reality, that is plausible within the fiction as a whole. In other words, even the possible worlds are true, their reality governed by rules. When we enter into a fiction, we agree to participate and accept the rules. This also means that fiction *can* refer to something "real"; it's real in the context of the possible worlds. It is the nature of stories that they create what must be considered an actual world, that has within it embedded many other possible worlds, which we as readers enter into when we accept the invitation to participate in a narrative.

Ryan makes the claim for the textual actual world that it is "epistemically accessible from the real world" because it has properties we recognize, inventory, or "furniture" we recognize as resembling the "furniture" of the actual world, time, space, and other physical properties of the world that we can understand, and that it makes truth claims that are analyzable and has a logic that does not seem to be contradicting itself (32–34). If we as readers do not get what we need to accept that the fictional world is "true," and if we're not given what we need to navigate that world effectively, we will not be able to live in that world, and the story will fail. When we recognize a fiction for what it is, and we think we have figured out the rules, we will be able to play the game.

As we read, we also look for certain kinds of coherence and credibility: historical coherence, psychological credibility, logical relationships that make sense. This is why character is so important, so unjustly neglected by formalist critics (as we have seen), and so integral to thinking about narrative through the lens of cognitive psychology (as we shall see). We can make judgments about characters when we are given information about them that resembles information we might have about a real-life person (Ryan 41). Readers will work to make allowances for characters, and to empathize with them, because of experience and expectations they have with actual people in the actual world; however, such willingness to participate will only go so far if a character is perceived to be incoherent or inconsistent. (Although, as Aristotle says, if an inconsistent character is at least consistently inconsistent, we can manage it.) Likewise, if a textual universe seems to be riddled with gaps of missing information, a reader will either get frustrated, or come to grips with the possibility that information is being held back for a good reason.

Engagements: Exemplary text

For an example, I want to suggest that we can apply possible worlds theory to analyze the narrativity of life writing, specifically memoirs of widowhood; my case here is the graphic memoir *American Widow*. (We will look more closely at graphic narrative as a medium in Chapter 3.) *American Widow*, by Alissa Torres with art by Sungyoon Choi, explores the chaos of grief and anger wrought in one woman's life by 9/11. In focusing, with painful detail, on the deeply personal nature of loss and trauma within the context of what was constructed as a "national tragedy," Torres offers both a memoir of her spouse and a subversive counternarrative to the story of September 11th. Torres' narrative proceeds by juxtaposing the unfolding events of 9/11 and her attempts to cope with its aftermath, alongside flashbacks of her courtship and marriage as well as the life of her husband, Eddie Torres, prior to their union: his childhood in Colombia, his arrival in the United States, the trajectory of his career to a position in finance with the ill-fated firm Cantor Fitzgerald, from whose floors he leapt to his death. The use of flashbacks as a key element of the narrative, combined with Choi's art, make Eddie a spectral yet physical presence; he is memorialized, and then further embodied in the birth of their son (with whom Torres was seven months pregnant at the time of her husband's death).

By considering this mode of life writing through possible worlds theory, the ontological stakes of what it means to lose a beloved person, and how that story is told, are made visible. Possible worlds theory here provides a means for understanding how narratives of loss perform the radical ontological shift in the actual world that occurs when someone loses a loved one. It also permits the exploration of theme through the semantic domain of elegy and the performance of mourning. The narrators in memoirs of widowhood are in fact the persons experiencing the loss; they create a series of textual possible worlds along with their textual actual world, which refers not only to the textual reference world but to the actual world, in order to narrate their loss. The textual actual world is composed of textual alternative possible worlds, each with its own ontological status, wherein the narrators narrate other versions of the story that seek to capture the radical destabilization of those narrators' own ontological status. In this case, those possible worlds relate to the death of the husband.

By conjuring possible alternative worlds, by making the deaths of the husbands—deaths they may not witness, deaths in which they do not participate, deaths for which they might not be present—part of the textual actual world, these narrators are seeking to make those possible worlds real, thereby sharing those final intimate moments with their husbands. By dying, especially alone and suddenly as Eddie Torres does, the husband closes off an entire world to the wife; not only is his life over but so is the life of the "we" of which he was such an integral part. The wife/widow-narrator conjures possible worlds as part of her narratorial actual world in order to access the experience of the husband's death, and maintain the ontological viability of the "we," and her own self.

The advantage of the graphic narrative medium as used by Torres and Choi is that we can see Alissa attempting to visualize her husband's final moments, and thus conjure the necessary textual possible world (Figure 2.2).

Figure 2.2 American Widow. (Graphic novel excerpt from *American Widow* by Alissa Torres, illustrated by Sungyoon Choi, © 2008 by E-Luminated Books, Inc. Used by permission of Villard Books, an imprint of Random House, a division of Penguin Random House LLC. All rights reserved.)

Throughout the book she also tries to visualize Eddie's past: his child-hood in Colombia, his migration to the United States. In those instances, these are parts of his story we might presume he had shared with her in order to facilitate the creation of a "we": each individual story becomes a shared story, part of the couple's history and intimacy. The past as narrated in flashback has its own ontology. In the case of Eddie's death, however, Alissa is confronted with an utter failure of knowing: she can never know what his final moments entailed. To conjure a possible world in which she witnesses his death, maybe even participates, at the very least sees his face, hears his words, knows what he might be thinking, is essential for the narratorial actual world to function ontologically in the ways the widow-narrator requires—because what the narrator is trying to tell us is what she can never know, and that lack is essential to the story and state of widowhood. The conjuring of possible worlds is the attempt to repair an epistemological and ontological wound.

The mind of the reader

Cognitive science is another way to think about how the mind works in relation to narrative. The intersection of narrative studies and cognitive science draws on the concepts of schemas and scripts first formulated in research around artificial intelligence (see Box 2.5). There are several components of cognitive science as applied to the study of narrative. We might use it to understand a reader's experience of a story: how the reader understands that she is in fact experiencing a story, rather than reality, or how the reader recognizes her emotional responses as she reads or perhaps determines the intentions of characters and responds accordingly. We might use cognitive theory to describe or analyze the specific processes used to figure out what's going on in a narrative: gap filling, mind changing, activation of memory. Cognitive theory may be used to describe, analyze, and interpret both readers' responses and how narrative works.

Box 2.5 **Cognitive science**

Cognitive science is the study of how our minds work. One of the questions it is most interested in is how our minds process information, and how they organize that information into something meaningful upon which we can act. The first step is to recognize *schemas*: these are collections of information that are recognizable based on real-world experience. So, for example, let's say I get invited to a wedding. My schema for this tells me a wedding is a special occasion for two people who want to get married, and I am among numerous others who have been invited to celebrate. This schema then activates a *script*:

(Continued)

(Continued)

the script is the progression of mental activities I follow based on my understanding of the schema. I understand the nature of the special occasion, so I think about what to wear. I'm not sure about how formal the wedding will be, so I ask, look at the time on the invitation and think evening means more formal based on my experience, etc. I realize I need a new dress, so I go to the department store. Thus another schema is activated: I know a department store is where they keep the dresses, I try some on, pick one out, pay for it—I more or less know how to navigate this situation. My arrival at the department store results in the deploying of another script, and so on, until hopefully I am suitably attired for a nice wedding. Experiencing a narrative works much the same way: I have a schema that tells me what a narrative is, and when I encounter one, my mind activates a script that tells me what to do with it.

Approaches to narrative that focus on the mind are not new, although it is only recently that they have come to draw explicitly on cognitive research in order to concentrate attention on the reader. For instance, in her *Transparent Minds*, Dorrit Cohn defines "psycho-narration," or the narration of what goes on in an individual psyche: thoughts, mental processes, "self communion" (15). Minds are rendered "transparent" in fiction in ways that are simply impossible in real life; we usually have no idea what another person is really thinking, even if they tell us. Cohn suggests that the narrating of the mind is a kind of realism, and it has the potential to place the narrator in a position of "cognitive privilege," superior to the characters she or he is telling about (29). Inner life and the working of the mind can be represented through monologues, either quoted monologue or narrated monologue. The narrator can also summarize thoughts for us. (We saw instances of this in our discussion of Doris Lessing's "To Room Nineteen.") For Cohn, the use of different modes of representing consciousness has stylistic and ethical implications; they indicate to us whether we should experience sympathy for a character, whether we should accept a seemingly ironic stance that might be occupied by a narrator, whether we should understand a self to be coherent.

Engagements: Exemplary text

The work of Jane Austen might be helpful in thinking about literature and the mind both in terms of how mental life is represented and in terms of how our own mental activity is affected by narrative. *Pride and Prejudice* has numerous examples of the mind being rendered "transparent." In fact, having the mental activity of Elizabeth Bennet represented to the reader is essential for making sense of the plot: we need to see how she thinks in order to see how it comes about that she changes her mind about Mr. Darcy enough to fall in love with and marry him at the end of the novel. Volume II, Chapter 13 has the remarkable scene of Elizabeth receiving, reading, and comprehending a letter from Mr. Darcy in which he explains his relationship to the rogue Wickham, why he thwarted her sister Jane's romance with Mr. Bingley, and how he feels about her inappropriate family. The chapter is full of words related to the work of the mind as Elizabeth realizes her errors in judgment. Austen uses a combination of summary and quoting to get at Elizabeth's state of mind. Some of her thoughts are summarized, as in here:

> It may be well *supposed* how eagerly she went through them [the contents of Mr. Darcy's letter], and what a *contrariety of emotion* they excited. Her *feelings* as she read them were scarcely to be defined. With *amazement* did she first *understand* that he believed any apology to be in his power; and steadfastly was she *persuaded* that he could have no explanation to give, which a just sense of shame would not conceal. With a strong *prejudice* against everything he might say, she began his account of what had happened at Netherfield.
>
> (198; italics mine)

Our narrator here reports to us Elizabeth's mental activity, signified by the italics in the passage, without directly showing it us via quotation. In this moment, Elizabeth is imagining herself to be impervious to anything Mr. Darcy might say: she is convinced she has judged him rightly. When the narrator does quote Elizabeth's interior monologue, in Elizabeth's own words, it is when she has realized that she has been wrong, that she misjudged. It is a very powerful moment, saved until the end of the chapter, because we hear the results of Elizabeth's self-reflection in her voice, and this becomes a turning point in the novel. She thinks:

> "How despicably have I acted!" she cried.—"I, who have prided myself on my *discernment*!—I, who have valued myself on my abilities! who have often disdained the generous candour of my sister, and gratified my vanity, in useless or blameable distrust.—How humiliating in this discovery!—Yet, how just a humiliation!—Had I been in love, I could not have been more wretchedly *blind*. But vanity, not love, has been my *folly* … I have courted prepossession and *ignorance*, and driven *reason* away …. Till this moment, *I never knew myself.*"
>
> (201–202, ellipses and italics mine)

The trajectory of this passage moves from a reflection on action to a realization that wrong action has revealed a lack of self-knowledge. The pain of reading and comprehending Mr. Darcy's letter results from Elizabeth's own delusions, her own ignorance not only of events but of herself. This moment is a pivot upon which the plot turns; the rest of the narrative takes on the consequences of Elizabeth's newfound self-knowledge, which make her love for Mr. Darcy possible. But in order for that to be intelligible, our narrator needed to make the mind of her protagonist transparent.

Perhaps it is the attention that Austen pays throughout her fiction to the working of the mind that leads many people interested in cognition and narrative to perform studies of "reading Jane Austen makes you a better person" or "reading Jane Austen makes you smarter." In recent years, articles on "your brain on Jane Austen" have appeared in *NPR* (Thompson and Vedantam) and in *Salon* (Miller), among numerous other outlets. These all picked up the same study done at the Center for Cognitive and Neurobiological Imaging at Stanford University in 2012. The data show that we read differently when we are immersed in a novel for pleasure as opposed to subjecting the text to critical analysis. We pay attention in different ways depending on how we are reading. The popular media grabbed on to the possible conclusion that reading Jane Austen makes you "smarter." Whether this is true or not, it is certainly the case that Austen is interested in the ways being attentive to their own mental processes makes her heroines smarter, and possibly more mature and empathetic as well.

When we are confronted with a narrative text, we mentally manage narrative elements and techniques in order to perceive and create a storyworld. This is different from what we saw in our discussion of possible worlds. There, the plot of a narrative generates a number of possible worlds which we navigate as we read. Here, the storyworld is generated by *us* as we read. We take what we are given as we read, and we project a world into which we immerse ourselves. The more the narrative gives us to work with, the richer the storyworld. As we work our way through the storyworld, we mind-read, or we attempt to understand the working of the minds of characters, as well as the characters' attempts to understand the working of the minds of the figures around them. Finally, we consider the social mind, the collective group mind of the people in the story. We'll take a look at each of these in what's to come.

One of the most productive attempts to think about narrative through the lens of cognitive theory has come from David Herman. He rightly points out that limiting our understanding of how narrative functions to a purely formal model, as we saw in Chapter 1, is limiting precisely because the work done by our minds when we interpret narrative is more complicated than that. Herman writes, "Narrative . . . furnishes a forgiving, flexible cognitive frame for constructing, communicating, and reconstructing mentally projected worlds— the only worlds, arguable, that any of us can ever know" (*Story Logic* 49). Describing and analyzing narrative should help us do the important work of understanding how and why stories have the effects they do.

The making of storyworlds

Drawing on a number of key concepts in cognitive theory, such as schemas and scripts, Herman says that as we experience a narrative, we make judgments about what each part of a story might be doing. Let's take the opening of the film *The Shawshank Redemption*. The film opens with the protagonist, Andy DuFrayne, sitting in a car with a bottle of bourbon and a gun; he takes a few swallows from the bottle, looks increasingly distraught and angry, and proceeds to load the gun. As the opening credits are shown, the film cuts between this scene and another, Andy on trial attempting to recount the events of the evening leading up to his wife's murder after she was discovered having an affair. The opening of the film hinges on us trying to figure out if the event of the wife's murder is indeed a reaction to the discovery of her adultery.

In addition, the taking in of visual and other cinematic cues—the bottle of bourbon, the love song on the radio, the loading of the weapon—coupled with the juxtaposition of the scenes leading up to the murder with the scenes in the courtroom, call upon the viewer to make associations, determine cause and effect, and formulate judgments that may or not conflict based on each sequence (purposely signaled in a cut to and pan over the jury listening to Andy's testimony). As interpreters, we begin making decisions about how to read and understand such a text almost immediately. We figure out what kind of story it is, we make a preliminary interpretation, we adjust our judgments, we make and remake decisions.

Storyworld is the concept developed to capture the robust and multidimensional mental models we create when confronted with narrative. Following from the theory of possible worlds articulated above, storyworld is a possible world that is generated *by us* through the interplay of literary *and* cognitive phenomena. Storyworld is composed of sequences of events and actions in relation to participants who themselves are linked with events and actions as well as states, qualities, even thematic roles (like we saw in worlds devoted to knowledge [K-world], or good and evil [W-world], or duty [O-world]). Herman describes the process:

> Interpreters of narrative do not merely reconstruct a sequence of events … but imaginatively (emotionally, viscerally) inhabit a world in which, besides happening and existing, things matter, agitate, exalt, repulse, provide grounds for laughter and grief, and so on—both for narrative participants and for interpreters of the story. More than reconstructed timelines and inventories of [characters], storyworlds are mentally and emotionally projected environments in which interpreters are called upon to live out complex blends of cognitive and imaginative response, encompassing sympathy, the drawing of causal inferences, identification, evaluation, suspense, and so on.
>
> (Herman, *Story Logic* 16)

When we encounter a narrative, a complex assortment of responses is set into motion; our minds generate and project a storyworld that becomes, for a time, the center of our mental universe. We begin to discern properties, genre, and rules. We order events in time and position them in space, we determine perspective, we pay attention to context and change our minds if a new context calls for it, we recall things from the past or learn new information and adjust our judgments accordingly. All of these—ordering, spatialization, perspective taking, context monitoring, frame modification—allow us to live in and participate in the storyworld.

So, actions can be put together to make sequences, and sequences of sequences make up narrative. But "actions" don't have to be only actions taken, or events. They can also be states of being. Consider the genre of the *bildungsroman*, stories of the development and growth of the individual. We encountered one of these in Chapter 1, when we looked at Tsitsi Dangarembga's novel *Nervous Conditions*. According to Herman, all genres have preferences, and different genres show different preferences. Some kinds of stories actually prefer to have the narrative consist of sequences of states of being for their "action," in addition to events. This is a bit similar to Seymour Chatman's idea of the plot of revelation we saw in Chapter 1; the difference here is that Herman is interested in how we recognize the "preferences" of a genre or type of story, and so then cognitively understand that sequences of states of being are in fact the "action." Narratives rely in many ways on both action and changes in being: "intentionally bringing about or preventing a change in the world . . . . Change occurs when some state of affairs either ceases to be or comes to be" (Herman, *Story Logic* 55). We need to look at the state the world might have been in initially, the state the world has taken on once the action has been taken, and what the world might have been like had the action not been taken. The state can be left alone, the state can continue to change, the state can be destroyed or cease to exist. Determining who took the action, how, when, and why the action was taken—all of these need to be added to the equation, too. In a *bildungsroman*, the protagonist performs actions: goes to school, takes a job, moves away, encounters difficulty, learns lessons. Events occur: people are born and die, secrets are revealed, etc. Yet fundamental to the "action" of the narrative is not simply what the protagonist does; it is also the changing states of the protagonist, the sustaining of some states and the ending of others. A lot of the story depends on the protagonist "being," developing, becoming, and the "action" of "being" takes on a wide range of forms, with a wide range of results: possible states, unactualized states, unrealized states.

Engagements: Exemplary text

Take Edna Ferber's coming of age novel *Fanny Herself*, the story of a precocious Jewish girl growing up in a small Wisconsin town at the turn of the century. (We'll consider this novel again from a different perspective in Chapter 4.) Early in the novel, Fanny decides to undertake her first fast for Yom Kippur, the Day of Atonement. The first action in the sequence is to decide not to eat, a non-action which is actually a deeply significant action. The next action is to uphold the decision not to eat when tempted with pastries by a malevolent schoolmate; again, the action is a non-action (not eating) while also being an action (deciding not to eat) while also being another iteration of a deeply significant action (fasting). At the same time, Fanny's state is altered, as is the state of her relationship with her schoolmate and the state of her mother's perception of her daughter as she takes on this challenge and succeeds. We also see nonactualized, unrealized, possible actions: Fanny might have taken the pastry, broken her fast, and had her state altered in a different way, perhaps finding her mother disappointed in her, which would thereby change their relationship. This deeply formative experience in Fanny's development ends one state and begins another; it is one node in the trajectory of Fanny's growth, one that encapsulates the importance of change, state, and event in the narrative of development. More broadly, these are preferences for the genre of *bildungsroman*; preferences around action here are different from, say, preferences around action in, for instance, a detective story.

As we said earlier, the more a narrative gives us to work with, the richer the storyworld. The more we are called upon to process a sequence of actions or states of being according to expectations generated by our scripts; the more that sequence activates scripts we have based on our experience in the world; and the more cues we receive from that sequence that tell us to process it as a narrative (which we understand how to do based on the scripts we possess as experienced readers)—the richer the storyworld (again, see Box 2.5). Sequences that look like narrative activate scripts that tell us what to do; they show us how to fit participants in that narrative into recognizable slots, and how to monitor and re-evaluate those decisions based on changes.

At the same time, recognizing a sequence is not enough to make a storyworld. A storyworld is made, projected like a image on a screen, through a series of activities generated by the reader's using of processing strategies, of "narrative competence" (Herman, *Story Logic* 104). A storyworld is a combination of schemas and scripts, like other schemas created by our minds and other scripts we follow (like my wedding example), and it both shapes how we interpret and adds more information to our existing repertoire. In other words, the more stories we encounter, the better we get at figuring out how narrative works. A somewhat lengthy quote detailing this process might be worth sharing:

> Story logic involves a two-stage parsing procedure. First, in mentally modeling what is being narrated, readers, viewers, or listeners use textual cues to distinguish participants from circumstances, that is, nonparticipants. Then they use those same cues to match participants (and also nonparticipants) with an inventory of roles deriving from the types of processes involved and from how those processes are instantiated in particular events. The matches that result afford a sense of how participants relate to one another and to circumstances in the storyworld.

Moreover, these role assignments have to be monitored and updated during narrative comprehension since a given participant's role can change; such role changes may also alter the network of relations between various participants and between participants and circumstances. Thus . . . in order to create higher-order narrative units based on interpretations of characters' emergent beliefs, desires, and intentions— recipients must frame and reframe inferences about participant roles over time. Interpreters must also work to infer what roles participants impute to themselves and to others through analogous, but storyworld-internal, processes of inference.

(Herman, *Story Logic* 116)

We might look at "Bliss," a very short story by Katherine Mansfield, for illustrative purposes, especially when it comes to character. Mansfield, a New Zealand writer who emigrated to England and died at a young age of tuberculosis after a rather turbulent personal life, takes such finely drawn character studies and psychological portraits as subjects in many of her remarkable short stories; "Bliss" is no exception.

Engagements: Exemplary text

When we first meet the main character, Bertha, we see her as a lively young wife and mother, delighted with the ways her marriage, baby, and social life are turning out. Over the course of the day, as she prepares for a party, we regard her thought process and see how, for the first time in her marriage, her desire turns towards her husband. We begin to question the sense she had held all along that she and Harry are "great friends," and wonder if we are actually witnessing a woman on the cusp of a new kind of erotic revelation, a new form of maturity. As the party begins and we meet Bertha's guests, we make a distinction between Bertha's role as hostess and her role as desiring wife; we follow her lead in this as this is the first time she herself has recognized that distinction, acknowledging she wishes everyone would go home so that she might be alone with Harry. At the same time, we consider each guest and wonder what role each might play in the conclusion of the story, particularly Bertha's friend Pearl, to whom the text devotes attention through specific images and reflections on the part of Bertha; she imagines she and Pearl are also "great friends." As the party draws to a close, Bertha witnesses her husband and Pearl together, and the final moments of the story are her undergoing a radical reassessment of her husband, her friendship with Pearl, all of the feelings she had had over the course of her day, and how she might even begin to imagine the rest of her life. In large part this transformation occurs because of the shift in Pearl's status from one kind of participant in the sequence to another. Furthermore, in the case of this story, our processes of inference and mind-changing very much parallel Bertha's, as we share the same cues. Where this gets interesting, however, is if the reader is able to process the cues differently from Bertha, and perhaps sees what's coming all along. In that event, the reader may experience something different with regard to Bertha: sympathy, perhaps.

The example of "Bliss," used to illustrate Herman's theories about participants in the storyworld, helps us think about character. Herman's concept of "participants" allows for us to think of "role bearers whose combinations and interactions produce larger narrative structures" (Herman, *Story Logic* 123). We can begin to think of characters in terms of our human experience, because we watch them behave in certain ways and it activates our scripts. We can consider material processes, such as when a character creates something like a work of art; mental processes, such as when a character has a thought, feeling, or perception; relational processes, such as when a character is defined as having an attribute or identified as existing in relation to a category available to her in the story; behavioral and verbal processes, as in the doing or saying of something; and existential processes, as in when a participant is noted as being in a particular way. So, if I see Bertha planning for her party—a material process—I know to interpret her as a social person, so that when I see her mental processes shift from wanting to be with her friends to wishing they would go home so she might be alone with her husband, I know something kind of dramatic has happened to the character.

   A character's primary role may shift over the story, forcing the reader to adjust. The roles and states of characters are not fixed, which might be another way to think about the notion of static and dynamic characters given to us by E. M. Forster. The personality of a character might change, but so might the part they are expected to play in the action, which then in turn might reveal even more about the character. A brief example might be found in the character of Linus, played by Matt Damon, in the Steven Soderbergh film *Ocean's 11*. At the start of the film, Linus is a young, inexperienced pickpocket recruited to help Danny Ocean (George Clooney) and his sidekick Rusty (Brad Pitt) rob a Las Vegas casino. In Herman's terms, Linus would be an *experiencer*, rather than an *actor*; he observes, he learns, he remains on the outside while the action unfolds. Once he realizes that Danny is not just trying to rob the casino but also attempting to regain his ex-wife (Julia Roberts), who is now the girlfriend of the owner of the casino Danny and his gang are trying to rob, Linus becomes an *actor*: he fills Rusty in and is made an integral part of the plot because the gang is no longer sure they can trust Danny once his ulterior motive is revealed. Likewise, Danny's role changes: he goes from being the main agent behind the robbery to lovelorn husband and sidelined as the guy in charge. Yet both roles are actually important; the emphasis shifts, but Danny inhabiting both roles is essential for the plot to unfold as it does.

   Characters and their roles and actions are not the only elements needed to make a storyworld, however; we also need to be able to conjure up time and space, because all stories take place in time and space (Herman, "Narrative" 158). Herman is particularly interested in what he calls "fuzzy temporality."

This accounts for vagueness around how many times an event may or may not have taken place, or a form of inexactness around the order in which events occurred, or a lack of clarity around over how long of a duration an event happened in time. If our conceptions of narrative depend upon events sequenced in a particular order over a certain amount of time, then we are going to receive different cues in our construction of a storyworld should we suspect an author is using fuzzy temporality. This often leads to us attempting to come up with multiple interpretations of what actually happened, and that ambiguity can have important thematic considerations as well.

Engagements: Exemplary text

A look at Pia Juul's *The Murder of Halland* might serve to illustrate not only Herman's theorization of polychrony and fuzzy temporality, but also the important ways that such cues disrupt generic expectations and prompt the reader to rethink the limits of narrative particularly in the face of trauma, guilt, and fear. Juul, a Danish novelist, offers an elliptical, elusive crime novel that subverts every expectation we might have for the genre. We never find out how Halland was murdered, who did it, whatever role his partner Bess, the narrator, might have played, why Halland was a victim—really, we find out very little. Instead, Bess is revealed as a character through episodes detailing her grief and bewilderment in a sort of collage of loss. The clearly defined sequential order that characterizes murder mysteries is here transgressed, and with it the clear presentation of temporality.

The story is narrated by Bess, a homodiegetic or "I-narrator." Noting her perspective is important here because it is from her subjective orientation that we get the representation of time. She seems to have slipped out of time once Halland is murdered and the subsequent events unfold (or don't, as the case may be). The novel begins with a seemingly clear temporal marker: "The night before" (loc. 64). What follows in the first chapter is a recounting of time over the course of the night before Halland is murdered. Halland says he needs to leave at seven the next morning; Bess, an author, says she wants to write and "won't be long"; then she loses track of time (loc. 64). Bess falls asleep on the sofa, then wakes up the next morning to find Halland gone and a police officer on her doorstep announcing "It is seven forty-seven. I am arresting you for … bear with me …" (loc. 76). The strangely specific noting of time is in contrast with the eliding of the reason for the arrest. We know the time and precious little else. By the start of chapter two, our sense of time is destabilized; Bess calls her mother to try to find her daughter, from whom she is estranged, and her mother scolds her for calling "in middle of the night" (loc. 116). It seems clear that no time has elapsed since the discovery of Halland's body and the phone call, so why this time marker that troubles our notions of order and duration? In another scene, the police leave Bess's home and she thinks about looking for photographs—although it is not clear she does—and "lost myself

in … memory" (loc. 197). The paragraph is not long, and consist
reminiscing about Halland, but the duration of time it is supposed to
is several hours. We see aspects of Bess's mental activity in the repor
of her memory, but not much otherwise, and time passes without us real
knowing what occurs except the activity of her mind.

A substantial portion of the novel is composed of these scenes of reported
mental activity, Bess narrating what she is thinking about, and it has the
effect of rendering temporality "fuzzy." The combination of reverie and
absence of clear events—kernels to anchor and move the story along towards
resolution—renders the novel dreamlike. Chapter thirteen begins "Ten days
had passed," but there is no indication that this is so in the reading experience
(loc. 593). Things happen: a pregnant niece of Halland's appears, Detective
Funder shows up every once in a while and asks questions. But none of
these events leads anywhere, and Bess slips back into her inner world. An
instance where she has to be somewhere—the funeral—at a specific time also
slips away: "I told the pastor I would arrive an hour before the funeral, but
I didn't manage" (loc. 680). Chapter five consists entirely of such remem-
brances and reverie, and then re-enters seemingly real time, clearly marked
time, in chapter six. The novel uses such a pattern throughout. The beginning
of chapter six is filled with time markers: "If I lay awake for more than two
minutes"; "I had managed an hour or so of sleep on the sofa"; "All the books
I had bought … and which I had never read. Time was too short"; "It was
five o'clock in the morning" (loc. 309, 321). The effect is to make certain
parts of the novel feel of long duration, slow moving, and other parts feel like
Bess is hyperaware, counting the minutes of each day.

As the novel progresses Bess begins to suspect that Halland had a secret
life: "Secret pregnant nieces. Secret rooms … I know what goes on in
Halland's mind. I fell in love with him, of course I know. I can read his
slightest passing thought; I can sense him without touching" (loc. 837). Here
is another instance of fuzzy temporality: the use of tense. Bess, in reading a
secret journal of Halland's found at his niece's home, begins thinking of him
in the present tense: "I can read his slightest passing thought." Bess is further
disoriented by the discovery of Halland's secrets, and they compound her
grief and confusion, marked by fuzzy temporality. One of the final events
that signifies Halland's continual presence, and her need to break free, is a
mysterious message she receives from Halland's mobile phone. The message is never explained, and the final act of the novel is Bess throwing the
phone into the fjord on a beautiful spring day. Halland's murder seems to
take place in early spring—"Despite the sunshine, a chill lingered in the air"
(loc. 360)—and the novel concludes in late spring, providing a clue to the
duration of the entire diegesis. The penultimate paragraph brings together
several layers of past and marks time not with temporal signs or verbal
markers and cues but with memory and experience: "Soon you would be
able to buy strawberries over there. We had bought some last summer. Or
Halland had. They smelled delicious and tasted of the childhood you didn't

ed for" (loc. 1666). Halland features in memory at the
sense memory of childhood, and the temporal arc of
t from time markers but from sense, from taste, from
rience. One wonders if being freed from the weight of
ed from the weight of time, from the hands of the clock
endless day.

.... to constructing a storyworld in our minds too; we have
to be able to visualize physical space, the space in which the story is taking
place. Herman offers six concepts to help define how we might understand
space in narrative (Herman, *Story Logic* 270–271):

- *Deictic shift:* the persons on the receiving end of a story "relocate" themselves from the present wherein they are experiencing the communication
  to the "space-time coordinates of the storyworld." An example would
  be the beginning of Joseph Conrad's *Heart of Darkness*, where Marlow
  invites the men on the ship to listen to his story, thereby transporting them
  from the Thames to Africa; the opening crawl of *Star Wars* works in a
  similar way, literally referencing the "space-time coordinates of the storyworld" with the famous "A long time ago, in a galaxy far, far away...."
- *Figure v. ground:* an object which is the focal point of attention is positioned *vis-à-vis* reference to something else. An example would be the
  depositing of Franny's overnight bag in the car as she arrives to spend what
  is supposed to be a romantic weekend with her boyfriend in J. D. Salinger's
  Franny and Zooey—as they leave for the weekend, the relationship begins
  to deteriorate almost immediately; another example can be found in the
  scenes of the classic 1930s screwball comedy *Bringing Up Baby*, where the
  dog belonging to the aunt of Katharine Hepburn's Susan steals a dinosaur
  bone and buries it—the object is the focal point around which the ensuing
  chaos, spreading over the entire space of the estate, revolves.
- *Regions, landmarks, and paths:* an example would be the movement of
  Clarissa Dalloway through the streets of London in the early pages of
  Virginia Woolf's *Mrs. Dalloway*; or the movement of Leopold Bloom
  through the streets of Dublin in James Joyce's *Ulysses*; or the road trips
  in Jack Kerouac's *On the Road*; or the trek into the wilderness under-
  taken by Chris McCandless in Jon Krakauer's *Into the Wild*.
- *Topological v. projective locations:* the difference between geographical
  places and spaces and the ways in which location is relative to a viewer. An
  example would be the ways Sasha Jensen moves through the streets of Paris
  from bar to bar in Jean Rhys' novel *Good Morning, Midnight*, while also
  thinking about where she might go or should not go; or the well-known
  use of maps as orienting points for the viewer in the *Indiana Jones* movies,
  which appear on the screen every time Indiana Jones embarks on a quest.
- *Motion verbs existing on a continuum with come and go:* an example
  would be from Winifred Holtby's novel *South Riding*, in a scene where

a man and woman who are antagonistic to each other have a long discussion, after she has assisted him with an emergency calving on his farm, about whether she should drive him home or whether he should walk, how far it is, whether she should then come to his house and clean up or go on her way, etc.; or, in a scene also dedicated to evoking the tension between men and women as well as ethnic tension, the moment in E. M. Forster's *A Passage to India* when Dr. Aziz realizes Miss Adela Quested has gone missing at the Marabar Caves—they go together to the caves, and as Dr. Aziz tries to figure out what has happened and convince others he is not at fault, there is much coming and going.

- *What v. where:* the ways in which objects exist in space. An example would be the configuration of offices at home and at work in John Williams' novel *Stoner*—as Stoner's professional and personal lives take increasingly dark and confining turns, the space of the offices and the books and papers within them are altered; or the emphasis on the beautiful glass figures in the shabby apartment which take on such symbolic resonance in Tennessee Williams' play *The Glass Menagerie*.

Imagery provided in the text can generate a perception in the reader of her own embodiment, her own physicality of the experience of her body and its movements in space. This in turn facilitates the enactment of the storyworld wherein the reader "feels" and perceives spatial experiences via narrative. In his conceptualization of space, most famously articulated in *The Production of Space*, the French philosopher Henri Lefebvre shows that space is also a social construct, determined by social acts and social identities. Space is shaped by the human interactions that take place within it, and descriptions of space and the ways characters interact with the borders of social spaces, the tropes associated with particular settings, the relationships among small and large, neighborhood and nation, self and landscape are all important components of storytelling. We will return to space, and objects in space, in Chapter 3, when we look at Chris Ware's graphic novel *Jimmy Corrigan; or, The Smartest Kid on Earth*.

Mind reading

Within the world of story we are able to interpret (often with some accuracy) the mental processes and emotional states of characters, based on the cues provided to us by the narrative itself. As scholars bridging cognitive science and literary studies such as Lisa Zunshine have shown, cognitive science allows us to develop rich understandings of how character functions in narrative. Zunshine, in her pioneering work applying *Theory of Mind* (ToM) to literary study, writes,

The very process of making sense of what we read appears to be grounded in our ability to invest the flimsy verbal constructions that we generously call "characters" with a potential for a variety of thoughts, feelings, and desires and then to look for the "cues" that would allow us to guess at their feelings and thus predict their actions.

(10)

Cognitive theory allows us to consider those cues as narratively significant. The cues that tell us how to interpret characters, their actions and thoughts and intentions, are fundamental to how narrative works; without those cues, and without our ability to "mind-read," or attribute actions, expressions, and behaviors to mental activity and emotional states based on those cues, narrative would be incomprehensible.

Part of how narrative functions—a really important part—is getting us to care about imaginary people. As Blakey Vermeule writes in a study asking, quite simply but necessarily, "why do we care about literary characters?," "Fictional characters come trailing many cognitive puzzles .... The tools that artists use to prod us to care about the people they create run along the grain of our minds" (xii–xiii). Vermeule shows that the work of "caring" about literary characters is severalfold. We have to be willing to be "hailed" by a character, whom we perceive as another mind (21). We have to pick up on the cues writers of stories give us that allow us to make inferences about characters (Vermeule 20). And we have to be able to do both of these things while running in what Vermeule calls, drawing from cognitive psychology, our "decoupled mode" (17). What this means is we are able to process information even if it is coming not from the "real world" but from hypotheticals, counterfactuals, or, simply, our imagination. All of these features of our cognitive capability allow us not only to deal with fictional characters—they also allow us to empathize with other people. In my mind, this is a key claim for the ethical work of narrative, an idea to which I will return in Chapter 4.

Comprehending our processes of "mind-reading" even allows for a rendering of elements like descriptive detail into narratively significant components. Description might be focalized through the perspective of a character; we begin to see those moments as part of the mental processes belonging to the characters with whom we are engaged (Zunshine 26). Zunshine suggests that even landscape detail and nature imagery depend upon a perceiving consciousness, and therefore a set of mental activities that are there for us to interpret. This calls to mind the formulation of William Wordsworth in "Lines Composed a Few Miles Above Tintern Abbey," wherein the eye "half create[s]" as it "perceives" (ll. 106–107). The appearance of nature serves the specific purpose of drawing our attention to imaginative processes, to the work of memory, to the activity of the perceiving consciousness.

If we look at narrative from a Theory of Mind perspective it is composed of levels of thinking, wanting, knowing, believing, and intending, layered with descriptions of body language and setting, as well as physical actions, that provide further clues to the mental activity occurring. These combine with "noise," the "competing" discourses that make interpretation such a complex activity, even in life. For instance, during a holiday, I might be working with my sister in the kitchen to prepare dinner for the family. Our mother might come in and begin criticizing what we are doing with the turkey. Is she actually criticizing what we are doing with the turkey? Or is she trying to express her desire to feel like she is participating in the work of preparing holiday dinner for her family? Many years of life-experience in this context with these relationships is required to effectively interpret what might be happening here, accepting the possibility that there might be several layers of intentionality—wanting dinner to go well, wanting to participate in cooking, believing that thirty-something daughters have less experience with roasting turkey successfully. Additionally, mistaking criticism for something negative, rather than seeing the negative as "noise," means that "noise" gets in the way of what might be a more constructive interpretation.

We try to "mind read" characters, but characters also try to "mind read" each other; sometimes they fail, and that is how conflicts—and plot—emerge. There is a social element to the representation of minds. Characters try to "mind read" in order to understand other characters, but they also work together to try to understand the world and achieve goals. We might see this in the interactions of characters over the course of a sequence of dialogue, let's say, as they work together mentally to create or resolve a situation; the scholar of narrative Alan Palmer has been instrumental in demonstrating how these processes of "social mind" and what he calls "intermentality" work.

Social minds

As noted above, cognitive science provides a spectrum of tools and concepts we can use to more deeply understand how narrative works. Alan Palmer's development of the field around intermentality and social minds—which builds on both storyworld and possible worlds theory—provides further insight into how character functions, how characters interact, and how readers interact with minds to make narrative.

Palmer is interested in what we mean by "the mind" beyond simply the representation of inner speech, and he tries to analyze how different kinds of mental activity are represented in storytelling. He's come up with three ways that narrators tell us what characters are thinking: thought report (He wondered whether his wife would be home in time for the party.); direct thought (He wondered, "Did Alice remember we had plans for tonight?"); and free indirect thought, which captures not only the content of the thought but the subjectivity of the thinker (He paused for a moment in the kitchen. When on earth would Alice be home?). But there are other ways to represent thought, too. These include:

- presentation of a variety of mental events;
- presentation of latent states of mind;
- presentation of mental action;
- presentation of character and personality;
- presentation of background information;
- presentation of intermental thinking;
- expression of consensus;
- interpretation, analysis, judgment.

Key to all of these is the social function of mental activity, made possible by linking the character to his/her/its environment through the narrator (Palmer, *Fictional* 81–85).

Engagements: Exemplary text

A good example of how all of these different kinds of mental activity show up in storytelling is James Joyce's *Portrait of the Artist as a Young Man*. This novel tells the story of the development of the mind and imagination of Stephen Dedalus, an Irish Catholic boy who, as he says, wants to "fly by the nets" of "nationality" and "religion" and become an artist (220). Joyce's novel has long been read as classic example of free indirect thought. Much of the novel is the narrator describing Stephen's thoughts in a style and voice that subtly changes over the course of the text as Stephen matures; we might recall from Chapter 1 that this is called *focalization*. For instance, here is Stephen thinking about his mother taking him away to school for the first time:

> Nice mother! The first day … when she had said goodbye she had put up her veil double to her nose to kiss him: and her nose and eyes were red. But he had pretended not to see that she was going to cry. She was a nice mother but she was not so nice when she cried.
>
> (5)

There is a marked contrast between the representation of early Stephen and more adult Stephen, both in style and content of his thoughts. Here is Stephen as a university student, anticipating his need to break with family and friends in order to become an artist, and trying to find inspiration for poetry around him despite the poverty of his surroundings:

> The full morning light had come. No sound was to be heard: but he knew that all around him life was about to awaken in common noises, hoarse voices, sleepy prayers. Shrinking from that life he turned towards the wall, making a cowl of the blanket and staring at the great overblown scarlet flowers of the tattered wallpaper. He tried to warm his perishing joy in their scarlet glow.
>
> (240)

What *Portrait of the Artist as a Young Man* is doing that is so distinctive has to do with the concepts of focalization, voice, and perspective, some of our key ideas from Chapter 1. The narrator not only has access to Stephen's thoughts, but also tries to communicate them in a style that captures the voice of Stephen's inner consciousness. There is a kind of semi-permeable membrane between the narrator and Stephen, as the narrator channels the character not only by telling what that character knows and sees, but also speaking in a way it imagines that character might speak.

Joyce works to show the relationship between mind and voice because the development of the mind and the imagination of the artist is his subject. The novel itself, in a way, is about the mind, so Joyce tries to make that mind "transparent," to pick up Dorrit Cohn's phrase again. But if we consider Stephen Dedalus in light not only of his own private mind but of *social mind*, we can actually learn quite a bit about who he is as a character, and we can foreground the tension he feels between his inner life and his developing and changing social roles. We can trace his growing desire to break free. Friendship is actually quite important to the novel, especially the process of realizing that your friends might be holding you back. A lot of the second half of the novel happens not in reported thought but in quoted dialogue, so that we can see Stephen in the highly social context of being with his friends.

We also get a much different perspective on him because we see him not through the workings of his own mind but through the perception of him by others, and how he responds to (especially unwanted) social situations. In Chapter 2, Stephen is seen talking to friends before the Whitsuntide play at school. Over several pages we see an assortment of instances of thought report: "He had often thought it strange that Vincent Heron had a bird's face as well as a bird's name" (80); "Any allusion made to his father by a fellow or by a master put his calm to rout in a moment" (80); "A shaft of momentary anger flew through Stephen's mind at these indelicate allusions in the hearing of a stranger . . . . All day he had thought of nothing but their leavetaking on the steps of the tram at Harold's Cross" (81); "Stephen's movement of anger had already passed. He was neither flattered nor confused but simply wished the banter to end" (82). Each instance of thought report captures Stephen in a social moment, reminding us of his relationships with others and how he behaves and performs in his environment. Our access to these moments of narrated thought report highlights our growing understanding of Stephen's isolation, as the mental activity is both prompted by social interaction and hidden from the others around him.

Yet foregrounding thought report alone does not accomplish the larger project of "widening and deepening" the concept of the mind "beyond the phenomenon of inner speech" (Palmer, *Fictional* 87). Looking at how characters think helps us understand them better both as beings with inner lives and as social beings thinking about relationships with other people. Palmer's concepts of "whole mind" and "social mind" provide insight into

ife and consciousness. The *whole mind* perspective accounts for
ntal processes, especially those responsible for language, non-
nsciousness, non-consciousness, dispositions, emotions, action,
achieving goals, and our ability to ascribe motives and intentions to ourselves.
The *social mind* perspective accounts for socially directed processes that
include public thought, or how the workings of a character's mind are
rendered visible to others; our ability to ascribe motives and intentions
to others; purposive thought, or thinking that facilitates communication
with others and problem-solving; dialogic thought, or thought that reflects
the multiple viewpoints of the beings in the world inhabited by the character
(Palmer, *Social* 42). My examples from *Portrait of the Artist as a Young
Man* show both whole mind activity and social mind activity. Whole mind
activity would be the examples from both young and old Stephen thinking,
including thinking about "warming his perishing joy." Social mind activity
would be the instances of Stephen thinking about his mother's emotional
response to his leaving home, as well as his judging his friends while simultaneously trying to pretend that nothing is wrong. Palmer notes that in
order to fully grasp characters in narratives, and how character works, we
have to account for the ways characters exist within social networks, as
social beings. We also have to account for how sharing knowledge, both
in life and in storytelling, is integral to social relationships; the social mind
provides insight into how knowledge is given, and how it is given to shape
the progression of a narrative (Palmer, *Social* 63–64). Palmer categorizes
many types of social activity and relationship, dividing such activity into
encounters between people (as in moments of dialogue), the creation of
small units (as in getting married), the creation of medium-sized units (as in
workplaces or neighborhoods), and the creation of large units (as in cities);
his categories capture the ways individuals exist as thinking beings within
large and small networks (*Social* 47–48). Thought must be understood as
being part of a network that includes action, communication, and problem-
solving, all of which can be seen in a social context.

Common sense (and all of our most useful reading strategies come, for
the most part, from common sense) tells us that we require a way of thinking
about "social minds" in stories because we ourselves exist as social beings,
in intermental connection with others. Because of this important aspect of
who we are, as we have already seen in the work of Zunshine, we perform
the task of reconstructing the mental processes of others when we encounter
stories. We try to make sense of one instance of mental activity within the
larger context of a story as it unfolds (Palmer, *Fictional* 184). Not only do
we process the individual mental functioning of characters, we also process
how those instances work in relation to the rest of the story. The fictional
mind creates a world "inhabited by intelligent beings who produce a variety
of mental representations such as beliefs, wishes, projects, intents, obligations, dreams, and fantasies" (Palmer, *Fictional* 188). These representations

are embedded within other representations, and the job of the fictional mind is to exercise mental activity to access and make something of the story-world—much as we do with the minds of the people around us.

Important themes in this chapter have included identity, community, and the role narrative plays in our understanding of social roles and relationships. These will continue to be important as we turn to Chapter 3, and place these themes in the context of media and technology, story and screen.

Works cited

Chambers, Ross. *Story and Situation: Narrative Seduction and the Power of Fiction.* Minneapolis: U of Minnesota Press, 1984. Print.

Chatman, Seymour. *Story and Discourse: Narrative Structure in Fiction and Film.* Ithaca, NY: Cornell UP, 1978. Print.

Cohn, Dorrit. *Transparent Minds: Narrative Modes for Presenting Consciousness in Fiction.* Princeton, NJ: Princeton UP, 1978. Print.

Donahue, James J. Personal communication. 6 April 2015. Email.

Herman, David. "Narrative Theory after the Second Cognitive Revolution." *Introduction to Cognitive Cultural Studies.* Ed. Lisa Zunshine. Baltimore, MD: Johns Hopkins UP, 2010. 155–175. Print.

——. *Story Logic: Problems and Possibilities of Narrative.* Lincoln: U of Nebraska P, 2002. Print.

Homans, Margaret. "Feminist Fictions and Feminist Theories of Narrative." *Narrative* 2 (1994): 3–16. Print.

Lanser, Susan. *The Narrative Act: Point of View in Prose Fiction.* Princeton, NJ: Princeton UP, 1982. Print.

——. "Toward a Feminist Narratology." *Style* 20 (1986): 341–363. Print.

Lefebvre, Henri. *The Production of Space.* Trans. Donald Nicholson-Smith. New York: Wiley-Blackwell, 1992. Print.

Palmer, Alan. *Fictional Minds.* Lincoln: U of Nebraska P, 2004. Print.

——. *Social Minds in the Novel.* Columbus: Ohio State UP, 2010. Print.

Prince, Gerald. "On a Postcolonial Narratology." In *Companion to Narrative.* Ed. James Phelan and Peter Rabinowitz. New York: Blackwell, 2008. 372–381. Print.

Richardson, Brian. "U.S. Ethnic and Postcolonial Fiction: Toward a Poetics of Collective Narratives." *Analyzing World Fiction: New Horizons in Narrative Theory.* Ed. Frederick Luis Aldama. Austin: U of Texas P, 2011. 3–16. Print.

Ryan, Marie-Laure. *Possible Worlds, Artificial Intelligence, and Narrative Theory.* Bloomington: Indiana UP, 1991. Print.

Vermeule, Blakey. *Why Do We Care about Literary Characters?* Baltimore, MD: Johns Hopkins UP, 2010. Print.

Warhol, Robyn. *Gendered Interventions: Narrative Discourse in the Victorian Novel.* New Brunswick, NJ: Rutgers UP, 1989. Print.

Wordsworth, William. "Lines Composed a Few Miles Above Tintern Abbey." *Norton Anthology of English Literature.* Vol. 2. 9th ed. Ed. Stephen Greenblatt. New York: W.W. Norton, 2012. 288–292. Print.

Zunshine, Lisa. *Why We Read Fiction: Theory of Mind and the Novel.* Columbus: Ohio State UP, 2006. Print.

Exemplary texts

Anchorman. Dir. Adam McKay. Perf. Will Ferrell and Christina Applegate. Dreamworks, 2004. Film.

Austen, Jane. *Pride and Prejudice*. New York: Penguin, 2002. Print.

Bringing Up Baby. Dir. Howard Hawks. Perf. Cary Grant and Katharine Hepburn. RKO, 1938. Film.

Brontë, Emily. *Wuthering Heights*. New York: Penguin, 2002. Print.

Conrad, Joseph. *Heart of Darkness*. New York: W.W. Norton, 2005. Print.

Eliot, George. *Middlemarch*. New York: Penguin, 2003. Print.

Everett, Percival. *Percival Everett by Virgil Russell*. Minneapolis: Graywolf Press, 2013. Print.

Ferber, Edna. *Fanny Herself*. Urbana-Champagne: U of Illinois P, 2001. Kindle file.

Forster, E. M. *A Passage to India*. New York: Penguin, 2005. Print.

Holtby, Winifred. *South Riding*. London: Virago, 2011. Kindle file.

Joyce, James. *Portrait of the Artist as a Young Man*. New York: Penguin, 2003. Print.

——. *Ulysses*. New York: Vintage, 1986. Print.

Juul, Pia. *The Murder of Halland*. Trans. Martin Aitken. London: Peirene Press, 2012. Kindle file.

Kerouac, Jack. *On the Road*. New York: Penguin, 2002. Print.

Krakauer, Jon. *Into the Wild*. New York: Anchor, 1997. Print.

Lessing, Doris. *Stories*. New York: Knopf, 1978. Print.

Mansfield, Katherine. *The Short Stories of Katherine Mansfield*. New York: Ecco Press, 1983. Print.

Miller, Laura. "Your Brain Loves Jane Austen." *Salon*. 19 September 2012. Web. 4 May 2015.

Ocean's 11. Dir. Steven Soderbergh. Perf. George Clooney, Brad Pitt, Matt Damon. Warner Bros., 2001. Film.

Rushdie, Salman. *East, West*. New York: Vintage, 1994. Print.

Rhys, Jean. *Good Morning, Midnight*. New York: Vintage, 1999. Print.

Salinger, J. D. *Franny and Zooey*. New York: Little, Brown, 1991. Print.

Thompson, Helen and Shankar Vedantam. "A Lively Mind: Your Brain on Jane Austen." *NPR*. 9 October 2012. Web. 4 May 2015.

The Shawshank Redemption. Dir. Frank Darabont. Perf. Tim Robbins and Morgan Freeman. Castle Rock, 1994. Film.

Torres, Alissa and Sungyoon Choi. *American Widow*. New York: Villard, 2008. Print.

Williams, John. *Stoner*. New York: NYRB Classics, 2006. Print.

Williams, Tennessee. *The Glass Menagerie*. New York: New Directions, 2011. Print.

Woolf, Virginia. *Mrs. Dalloway*. New York: Harcourt Brace Jovanovich, 1990. Print.

Recommended further reading

Aldama, Frederick Luis. *Postethnic Narrative Criticism*. Austin: U of Texas P, 2003.

Fludernik, Monika. *Towards a "Natural" Narratology*. New York: Routledge, 1996.

Herman, David. *Basic Elements of Narrative*. New York: Wiley-Blackwell, 2009.

Herman, David, James Phelan, Peter J. Rabinowitz, Brian Richardson, and Robyn Warhol. *Narrative Theory: Core Concepts and Critical Debates*. Columbus: Ohio State UP, 2012.

Richardson, Brian. *Unnatural Voices: Extreme Narration in Modern and Postmodern Fiction*. Columbus: Ohio State UP, 2006.

Engagements: Interview with Sarah Copland

Sarah Copland is Assistant Professor of English at MacEwan University in Edmonton, Alberta. She received her Ph.D. from the University of Toronto in 2009. She has published work on modernist narrative, rhetorical and cognitive approaches to narrative theory, and narrative theory and short story theory in *Narrative, Modernism/Modernity, Blending and the Study of Narrative* (de Gruyter, 2012), and *Narrative Theory and Ideology* (forthcoming). She is also co-editing, with Greta Olson, a forthcoming special issue of the *European Journal of English Studies* on the politics of form. She is working on two larger projects, one on the rhetoric and pedagogy of modernist prefaces and the other on the relationship between narrative theory and short story theory. Prior to joining MacEwan University, she held the position of Visiting Assistant Professor of Humanities in the Integrated Program in Humane Studies at Kenyon College (Ohio) and completed a two-year appointment as a postdoctoral fellow in the Department of English and as a visiting scholar with Project Narrative, both at the Ohio State University.

How would you describe your approach to narrative studies and/or narrative theory?

I take a rhetorical or communication-based approach to narrative theory, conceiving a narrative text (in whatever medium) as the product of authorial design and as an invitation to readers to participate in a particular interpretive, affective, and ethical experience. As leading rhetorical theorist James Phelan observes, individual flesh-and-blood readers, with their own experiences and beliefs, have varying abilities and willingness to join the authorial audience and thereby participate in the authorially designed experience. For me, one of the delights of reading is pushing the limits of my ability and willingness to participate in a textually guided experience. I find this approach productive for my scholarship and for the way I approach teaching narrative (prose, graphic, and filmic) in the classroom.

Describe your most recent project. What prompted your interest? What were you hoping to achieve? What questions or ideas in the field do you see it responding to?

Two of my essays bring narrative theory into conversation with other theories: short story theory and postcolonial theory. The first, an essay entitled "To Be Continued: The Story of Short Story Theory and Other Narrative Theory" (*Narrative*, 2014), responds to the first sustained conversation involving these two theoretical approaches, a conversation published as a special issue of the journal *Narrative* in 2012. The short story theorists published in that issue were, on the whole, less than sanguine about the potential of narrative theory to illuminate short story theory, and vice versa. My response, based on a reading of the Alice Munro short story they used as their shared case study, "Passion," radically reinterpreted the text using various concepts from narrative theory, in turn suggesting a more productive and promising beginning for work that seeks to bring short story theory and narrative theory into conversation.

My other essay, "A Contextual Rhetorical Analysis of Audiences in E. M. Forster's Preface to Mulk Raj Anand's *Untouchable*" (for a forth-coming collection, tentatively entitled *Narrative Theory and Ideology*, edited by Divya Dwivedi, Henrik Skov Nielsen, and Richard Walsh), questions the assumptions that both structuralist narratology's paratext theory and postcolonial theory share about the allographic (non-authorial) preface as inherently appropriative and colonizing. I offer a contextual rhetorical analy-sis of flesh-and-blood and authorial audiences for Forster's preface to Anand's *Untouchable* to demonstrate that the preface-text dynamics of this particular pairing belie existing paradigms and offer grounds for an approach to form and ideology that draws on both narrative theory and postcolonial theory.

What scholars and texts have influenced your approach?

My work is indebted to and influenced by the scholarship and guidance of my postdoctoral co-advisors James Phelan (rhetorical) and David Herman (cognitive) and my doctoral advisor Melba Cuddy-Keane (cognitive neuro-scientific). While my late postdoctoral and early-career work has drawn on and contributed to the rhetorical approach, my doctoral and early postdoc-toral work drew on and contributed to the cognitive approach, particularly Mark Turner and Gilles Fauconnier's conceptual blending theory. During this period, I immersed myself in Herman's and Cuddy-Keane's work, and both scholars remain, along with Phelan, models of the kind of narrative scholarship I most admire and hope to emulate: using theory and text to illuminate each other, resulting in profound, widely applicable theoretical payoffs and innovative readings of narrative texts in various media.

My work has also been influenced by the scholarship and guidance of Henrik Skov Nielsen (fictionality studies and unnatural narratology) and Greta Olson (the politics of form). My two-year postdoctoral fellowship and visiting scholar appointment at Project Narrative at the Ohio State University, where Nielsen was also a visiting scholar, led to several productive visits to his Centre for Fictionality Studies at Aarhus University, Denmark, where I benefitted greatly from his expertise and exposure to the work of his colleagues. Regular attend-ance at the conferences of the International Society for the Study of Narrative (ISSN) has enabled me to stay up-to-date with the latest work in narrative theory and has enabled me to meet scholars who would go on to be collabora-tors, such as Greta Olson, with whom I am now editing a special issue of the *European Journal of English Studies*, dedicated to the politics of form.

What do you see as big questions confronting the field?
Where's the cutting edge? What are the trends?

Following the publication of Richard Walsh's *The Rhetoric of Fictionality* (OSU, 2007) and Henrik Skov Nielsen's founding of the Centre for

Fictionality Studies at Aarhus University, Denmark, work in fictionality studies has redefined fictionality as a rhetorical or communicative strategy as opposed to a generic designation. The consequences of this move will be far-reaching for narrative theory, which has long observed a distinction between narrative fiction and narrative non-fiction. A recent essay by Nielsen, Phelan, and Walsh (*Narrative*, 2015) outlines the impact of this move and suggests future directions, many of which are already being pursued by scholars working on narrative across media at the Centre for Fictionality Studies.

In addition to fictionality, work on the politics of form seems to be gaining ground. As Greta Olson so cogently noted in a contemporary narratology talk at the 2015 Narrative conference, narrative forms do political work (including reifying and challenging social conditions), but concepts from narrative theory may themselves be inherently political (historically situated as opposed to universal) and thus require contextualization. My own work broaches this latter question *vis-à-vis* conceptions of the allographic preface in structuralist narratology's paratext theory and in postcolonial theory, but the aforementioned forthcoming collection *Narrative Theory and Ideology* and a special issue of the *European Journal of English Studies* (forthcoming as of this writing) take up the issue of the politics of form as it pertains to many different subfields of narratological inquiry.

In recent years, we have also seen growing interest in approaches to teaching narrative and narrative theory, perhaps nowhere more evident than in the *Teaching Narrative Theory* collection edited by David Herman, Brian McHale, and James Phelan (MLA, 2010). I have taken over organization of the Narrative conference's annual pedagogy lunch, which Irene Kacandes founded and organized for more than a decade. Organizing the pedagogy lunch and working at a teaching-focused institution have offered me exposure to work at the intersection of narrative theory and scholarship of teaching and learning, work that will no doubt continue to develop.

Although I do not work in these fields directly, they continue to produce excellent work that constantly re-shapes both the corpus we work with as narrative scholars and the concepts and tools we use to examine that corpus: cognitive and cognitive neuroscientific approaches, unnatural (antimimetic) narratology, feminist and queer narratologies, affect and emotion theory, trauma theory, econarratology, narrative and medicine, and inter- and trans-mediality.

What are you working on next?

I continue to toggle back and forth between two book-length projects, both of which have already yielded published essays. The first is my long-term work, drawing on my expertise in modernist studies and narrative theory, on the ways in which modernist writers used their prefaces as pedagogical aids for readers to negotiate experimental narrative techniques. This project is tentatively entitled *Front Matters: The Rhetoric and Pedagogy of Modernist Prefaces*. The second project, which emerged more recently in the form of the aforementioned 2014 article in *Narrative* and has been developed through my ongoing teaching of the short story and short story theory, seeks a more productive and mutually illuminating relationship between narrative theory and short story theory and will be organized around key concepts with case studies from a range of historical periods.

Engagements: Interview with Jennifer Ho

Jennifer Ho is an Associate Professor in the Department of English & Comparative Literature at UNC Chapel Hill, where she teaches courses in Asian American literature, multiethnic American literature, and Contemporary American literature. Her first book, *Consumption and Identity in Asian American Coming-of-Age Novels* (Routledge, 2005) examines the intersection of coming-of-age, ethnic identity formation, and foodways in late 20th century Asian American coming-of-age narratives and American popular culture. Her second book, *Racial Ambiguity in Asian American Culture* (Rutgers UP, 2015) considers various forms of racially ambiguous subjects (such as transnational/transracial Asian adoptees, multiracial Asian American authors/texts, and Tiger Woods).

*How would you describe your approach to narrative
studies and/or narrative theory?*

I am most attracted to a rhetorical approach, but I also think that my own take is a hybridity of the fields I am most comfortable with (Asian American/critical race theory) so I would say my approach is to make race the center and then think about how narrative theory can help me/others understand the role of race/ethnicity in narrative.

*Describe your most recent project. What prompted your interest?
What were you hoping to achieve? What questions or ideas
in the field do you see it responding to?*

I am co-editing (along with Jim Donahue and Shaun Morgan) an edited collection of essays, "Narrative, Race, and Ethnicity in the Americas" (currently under review), and I've also contributed an essay to this collection, "Racial Constructs and Narratological Constructs or Whose Narrative Is This Anyway?" (which uses David Mitchell's *Cloud Atlas* as a central narrative to interrogate our ideas about authorship, narrators, race and nationality). This all began as a conversation on Facebook where I said I wished there was an edited collection of essays on race and narratology that focused on American literature. Jim and Shaun agreed and

I forget who joked that we should do it. The next thing I know I'm email-ing James Phelan to gauge whether there'd be interest in the Literature, Interpretation, Narrative series that he co-edits, and then from there Jim, Shaun, and I crafted a call for papers, gathered abstracts, and put together this edited collection.

I think our impetus for doing this was that we wanted to make race a central and inextricable factor in considering narratological questions/issues—to do what Susan Lanser has done for understanding the primacy of gender in narrative theory. We were interested in seeing what people in the field interested in ethnic literature and what folks interested in narratology would do with putting these concerns into conversation—so we chose essays (from among the riches that we got) that really delved into both areas—that looked at the role of the narrator or considered the storyworld or thought about sequences and temporality not just applied to works that are written by/about African American, Latino, American Indian, and Asian American people, but that consider how these things are negotiated when race is intro-duced as a salient narratological issue.

What scholars and texts have influenced your approach?

I think a scholar whom a lot of people point to, especially working in gender/sexuality studies, is Susan Lanser—her essay, "Toward a Feminist Narratology." Reading her work was really revelatory and was a great cor-ollary for thinking through the centrality of race in narrative/narratology. I've also been influenced by James Phelan's work (his rhetorical approach) and Robyn Warhol's work (in feminist/sexual studies). And Sue Kim's work in post-colonial and critical race theory/Asian American narratology has been very influential for me.

What do you see as big questions confronting the field?
Where's the cutting edge? What are the trends?

Honestly, I am not sure I feel confident enough to answer this as a rela-tive newcomer to the study of narratology. Certainly I'd like to think that engaging in questions of race, ethnicity, multiraciality are new and innova-tive issues that the field of narrative studies is just recently taking up. There really hasn't been a single authored monograph, that I know of, looking spe-cifically at this topic (in the way that we have work from Robyn Warhol for example and Susan Lanser)—I imagine Sue Kim is going to write that book soon—and Frederick Aldama has been a pioneer in this field, particularly through his cognitive approaches to thinking about race and his attention to issues of Latina/o narratives. I think post-colonial has been a recent trend, but again, as someone who feels still in a beginning stage myself, I don't know that I really know.

What are you working on next?

My next project is going to be what I'm calling a critical autobiography of breast cancer narratives. I'm going to start with my own story of being diagnosed with breast cancer and move out to look at the various narratives and discourses around breast cancer specifically, cancer more broadly, and disease/illness generally. I want to also consider my position as an Asian American woman in her forties who was diagnosed when she turned forty and the messages of positivity and pink washing that were overwhelming to deal with in the face of my diagnosis.

3 Stories beyond the page, stories on the screen

You're reading *Romeo and Juliet* for an English class; maybe you're reading it by yourself in the evenings for homework, or maybe you're reading it out loud in class, and possibly even collaborating in groups to act parts out. Then the instructor decides to show a film version, maybe the 1968 Franco Zeffirelli version—a lush costume production generally considered to be a "faithful" adaptation—or the 1996 Baz Luhrmann version—generally considered to be taking some liberties in order to appeal to a contemporary audience steeped in postmodern popular culture. Or maybe you're procrastinating on your reading of *Romeo and Juliet* by playing a video game; for a while you're Neku in *The World Ends with You* or fighting the Dredge in *The Banner Saga*, making choices you hope will lead to good results for your characters and analyzing how those choices affect the story as you go. Perhaps, procrastinating some more, you log in to Facebook or Tumblr, and read through some posts, collecting and commenting on stories from your assorted social networks.

All of these are ways that stories show up in our everyday lives, and all of them depend on engaging with narrative through a variety of media. In some cases, we're engaging with narrative through several different media at once. This *multimodal* engagement can be listening to the soundtrack of a movie or game as you watch or play; it can be thinking about how the words and images go together in a comic book; it can be interacting with friends in the digital world by clicking a thumbs-up, a heart, or a retweet button; it can be using a game console or swiping an iPad to keep the story moving and make choices that lead to different possible resolutions. In this chapter, we will take a closer look at the ways we engage with a wide variety of narratives in a variety of media, and we'll pay special attention to the ways digital culture and digital media have transformed how we make, experience, and share stories. To start, I've clustered some ideas around key features of multimodal, visual, and digital narrative: image, interactivity, adaptation, and community.

Image, interactivity, adaptation, community

Thinking about *image* as a kind of story has always been a component of studying narrative. A painting that depicts a story, or at least a narrative moment, like Breughel's *Landscape with the Fall of Icarus*, is not necessarily seen to have a series of events set into motion by characters who can think or make choices, told in a particular order through a particular perspective. Yet we can look at this painting and see that something has happened and we are being told about it. The event *has* occurred in space and time; the order of events before and after might reside outside the frame, the effect of the event might not be immediately clear. One might even argue that conflict and change—two key elements of narrative—are present: the conflict between the landscape itself, the movement of ordinary life, and the dramatic event of the fall; and the imagined alteration in those who witnessed Icarus's plummet from the sky. When we talk about film, we can certainly think of the importance of image for storytelling. Comic books and graphic narratives also make clear the narrative potential of image, and the ways word and image complement. Both film and comics are clear cases of multimodal storytelling: narrative information being conveyed and storyworlds being constructed via the interplay of more than one medium (word and image in comics, image and sound in film, etc.).

Interactivity is changing how we think about narrative. All narratives are in some ways always, by their nature, interactive; we create storyworlds as we engage with the components of narrative, and we fill in gaps as we read. On the other hand, plot depends on a series of events occurring in a particular sequence, characters' actions unfold in particular ways based on specific motives, and there is not much room for a reader to make choices to influence the action. The gimmicky book series from my childhood *Choose Your Own Adventure* offered the opportunity to make decisions about what could happen next—you'd go down into the cave or climb up the mountain, for instance—but the consequences of whatever choice is still fixed. There are only so many branches off the path you might take, and the path is still pointing in the same direction. Yet true interactive fiction, games, and virtual reality offer new ways of thinking about how storytelling might be interactive beyond two people interacting in the telling. Story might become a space for a participant to enter into the structure of the story, altering the nature of character and the ways choices affect plot, or point of view and levels of narrative. Might interactive stories change how we think about narrative and its most basic elements? Will *our* point of view become as important as the narrator's? How will the choices of characters and *our* choices work together to move the story along?

Adaptation has been part of thinking about narrative for as long as humans have been telling stories. Shakespeare adapted well-known stories to make plays such as *Hamlet* and *Romeo and Juliet*. An even more interesting case would be *King Lear*, based on a true story that ended much less unhappily in real life, and then turned into another version altogether by Nahum Tate after the playwright's death that had Cordelia and Lear being reconciled and Cordelia getting married; well into the nineteenth century this was the only version of *Lear* playgoers knew, until the original ending was restored by Edmund Kean. *The Odyssey* has inspired versions as varied as James Joyce's novel *Ulysses* and Joel and Ethan Coen's film *O Brother Where Art Thou?* Much discussion about adaptation, especially book-to-screen, for a long time rested on the concept of "fidelity": whether or not the adaptation was "faithful" to its "source," and this judgment was made based on whether or not the film did a good enough job of showing what was on the page, casting actors that looked like how the characters appeared in our minds, following the plot accurately, and capturing the tone and themes. Two examples of adaptations that make much better films than they did books in part because they elected to be "unfaithful" in creatively viable and artistically compelling ways would be *Jaws* (novel by Peter Benchley and film by Steven Spielberg) and *The Ice Storm* (novel by Rick Moody and film by Ang Lee). In both cases, the filmmakers teased out themes and developed characters that made for a richer experience of the fictional world. From the early days of cinema to our own era, one way to get audiences into a movie theater, and one way to earn actors and directors awards, has been to make a "prestige" picture that takes as its source a work marked as "high culture," like *Wuthering Heights* or *Pride and Prejudice*. Likewise, a sure way to make money is to make a comic book film, like the many iterations of *Batman* movies. At the same time, a hindrance to recognizing the potential of film to generate art from "source material" is quite simply snobbery: the privileging of the literary text over the pop culture product of movie-making, or the critical denigrating of cultural forms like comic books and their blockbuster movie versions.

More recently, however, adaptation itself has been seen as a meaningful artistic process that creates real artistic products. Furthermore, the concept of adaptation has expanded beyond "translation," turning a work of art from one medium into another (book to screen, again, most obviously), and has come to encompass not only translation but a kind of dialogue, where the "original" text and the "new" text speak back and forth to each other. The multiverse of Marvel Comics, for instance, demands this dialogue as the world and the canon continually expand through *transmedial adaptation*: adaptations that exist in and across many media continuously at the same time, like comic books, films, and games. Another example would be Michael Cunningham's *The Hours*, which could be read as an adaptation of Virginia Woolf's *Mrs. Dalloway*, but could also be read as an attempt to interpret Woolf's novel through adaptation and encourages a re-reading of the "source" text through a new lens. Likewise, the film adaptation of *The Hours*, starring Nicole Kidman, Julianne Moore, and Meryl Streep, presents an opportunity to move back and forth among different interpretations and media to come to new readings. The possibility of interactivity and stories that let us immerse ourselves has also changed how we think about adaptation. A game version of *The Simpsons* is not merely an adaptation of the long-running cartoon series; it is an interactive experience wherein a player/viewer can enter into a narrative world using his or her actual body (consoles, swiping) because the continuities between show and game create a lot of opportunities for immersion. If you already know Springfield really well, then getting into the game is that much easier. We might even, as Linda Hutcheon and Henry Jenkins have done, extend adaptation to amusement park experiences, where a child (or a patient adult) can go on a Winnie-the-Pooh ride, for instance, as another way of engaging with beloved stories. As we shall see, the digital context has transformed how we think about adaptation, which has in turn prompted a reconsideration of the relationship between adaptation and narrative.

Individual readers often talk about curling up with a good book (or a fully charged Kindle); we bury our noses in our novels when we are on a long flight and do not wish to engage with our neighbor. Virginia Woolf in *A Room of One's Own* advocated for women writers to have rooms of their own in order to fully engage in the stories they were meant to tell, new kinds of stories for new ways of thinking about women's lives. Yet despite our fairly modern idea of reading and writing as solitary acts, narrative has for centuries been considered as for and of *community*. Narrative has shaped communities, stories are shared, and—as we shall see in Chapter 4— thinking of narrative as an act of communication among humans has deep ethical implications, particularly in thinking about empathy, identity, and how we are different from each other. The digital context has provided new ways of defining the relationship between narrative and community: we share stories, we create networks and communities through stories, we collectively turn our lives into stories. All lives are worth telling, as seen in our use of Twitter and blogs, the use of storycircles as part of community organizing and advocacy, the curating of individual stories through projects like StoryCorps, and the featuring of multimedia stories (including film, photos, and sound) on sites like the Center for Digital Storytelling or through the work of NPR's Visuals Team. Apps like Storify and Evrybit make it easy for people to create and share multimedia stories, generating a new model for interactive narrative—although how new, really, is the creation of community through shared stories, and the attempts to turn our lives into stories as a form of meaning-making? Perhaps this new context has simply directed our attention to these processes in new ways, and provided a greater variety of tools upon which to draw.

So looking at how stories work in games and on the internet, in films and in comic books, lets us ask new and interesting questions about engaging with narrative. Do we have to rethink certain concepts like character and plot when we try to apply them to games? Does *The Walking Dead* change from medium to medium, from graphic novel to TV show to video game? We see stories everywhere, and technological innovation has made it possible to tell stories in ways both really new and totally familiar.

Let's begin with frameworks and concepts that have emerged from what Michael Toolan calls "old-tech" narrative (130). We can start with the relationships among word, image, and sound or music. Marie-Laure Ryan has helpfully outlined a conceptual framework for these relationships (and here I quote):

Language:

Can easily do: Represent temporality, change, causality, thought, and dialogue. Make determinate propositions by referring to specific objects and properties. Represent the difference between actuality and virtuality or counterfactuality. Evaluate what it narrates and pass judgments on characters.

Can do only with difficulty: Represent spatial relations and induce the reader to create a precise cognitive map of the storyworld.

Cannot do: Show what characters or setting look like; display beauty . . . . Represent continuous processes.

Images:

Can easily do: Immerse spectators in space. Map storyworld. Represent visual appearance of characters and setting. Suggest immediate past and future through "pregnant moment" technique. Represent emotions of characters through facial expressions. Represent beauty.

Cannot do: Make explicit propositions . . . . Represent flow of time, thought, interiority, dialogue. Make causal relations explicit. Represent possibility, conditionality, or counterfactuality. Represent absent objects. Make evaluations and judgments.

Makes up for its limitations through these strategies: Use intertextual or intermedial reference through title to suggest narrative connection. Represent objects within the storyworld that bear verbal inscriptions. Use multiple frames or divide picture into distinct scenes to suggest passing of time, change, and causal relations between scenes. Use graphic conventions (thought bubbles) to suggest thoughts and other modes of nonfactuality.

Music:

Can easily do: Capture flow of time in pure form. Suggest narrative pattern of exposition-complication-resolution through relations between chords. Create suspense and desire for what comes next. Arouse emotions.

Cannot do: Represent thought, dialogue, causality, virtuality. Single out distinct objects, characters, or events in a storyworld. Tell a specific story, since its stimuli have no fixed meaning.

Makes up for its limitations through these strategies: Use titles and subtitles to suggest a "narrative program." Individuate characters through musical motifs or distinct instruments.

(*Avatars* 19–20)

Each medium has "preferences," the favoring of different variations in how to tell stories with differing results in how we use those narratives

(Ryan, "On the Theoretical" 18). So, choosing to use one medium rather than another lets you do different things in telling a story, and combining different media has different effects as well. Likewise, different media will provide different experiences to spectators or participants. Those experiences might involve more effort in terms of navigating the storyworld or performing gap-filling than traditional narratives might. These experiences might involve the effort of actually contributing to the expansion and growing of the storyworld through the creation of new narratives, as in the case of fan fiction. They might involve keeping up with multiple worlds across multiple platforms, as in the case of those who follow the Marvel Comics universe. Whether this work is cognitive or cultural, multimodal storytelling places demands on the reader/spectator/participant (Box 3.1).

Box 3.1 Engaging with multimodal narrative

Part of what stories that work in multiple media need is the competency of the reader/spectator/participant. The more one participates in narrative and the storyworlds generated by a particular narrative, the higher the degree of narrative competence required and gained. As a participant in a narrative, I use the context and the medium to generate the storyworld. Through the engagement with different media, I can expand my ability to participate in and navigate a complex narrative world. Take, for instance, David Lynch and Mark Frost's influential (and occasionally maligned) television series *Twin Peaks*. Here is what I need to know and do to fully manage the experience of that text:

- I need to know how serial television works in terms of genre, plot, time, and narrative levels. Viewers who have learned to appreciate what Jason Mittell calls "complex television," twenty-first century shows such as *The Wire* and *Breaking Bad*, might not be aware of how difficult it was for viewers in 1990 to grasp what Lynch and his co-creator Mark Frost were trying to do. Now I might recognize "centrifugal," or world-driven, television; I might see that *Twin Peaks* was more interested in making a world and then extending that world as far as it would go. Or perhaps I might think of it as "centripetal," character-driven, taking characters and putting them in unusual situations and using idiosyncratic secondary characters to extend that world (Mittell 264, 270). I may or may not feel compelled to pin down genre; I might instead recognize how the show plays with generic conventions. Was this a soap opera? Was it a detective show? What did the multiple plot lines and narrative layers have to do with each other? Would they ever resolve themselves into integration and closure? Would I be comfortable adjusting my expectations to account for the possibility that they wouldn't?

- I need to know something about David Lynch's thematic universe and visual repertoire. A viewing of *Eraserhead* will offer insight into what certain visual choices might mean. A viewing of *Blue Velvet* will offer insight into how Lynch views the relationship between the ordinary world and our subterranean impulses and subconscious desires, and what happens when they rupture the fine membrane that keeps darkness in check.

- I need to recognize when a narrative is positing multiple worlds, each with its own ontology. *Twin Peaks* draws on this kind of competency very explicitly in its juxtaposition of the world of Twin Peaks and the Great Northern Hotel alongside that of the Black Lodge, "another place," that may or may not be the iconic room with red curtains and black and white zig-zag floor. I also might need to be comfortable with the possibility that these worlds exist separately and are equally viable.

- I need to be aware of what Gérard Genette might call paratexts, and what Jason Mittell calls transmedia narrative extensions: other iterations and components of the narrative universe that use other media to do their work. I might even need to participate actively in these transmedia extensions. I might need to read *The Secret Diary of Laura Palmer*, a novel written by Lynch's daughter Jennifer (who is possibly the inspiration for *Eraserhead*), in order to fill in gaps in the story and uncover psychological motivation for what occurs on the show. I would certainly need to read it to understand what's going on in the cinematic "sequel" to the show, *Fire Walk With Me*. I might even need to immerse myself in the world of the Black Lodge by playing the computer game *Black Lodge*; the immersive power of the Atari-like video game is limited, but it does capture the otherworldly and surreal quality of trying to navigate that imaginative space.

So multimodal narrative demands multimodal thinking. It also demands that we rethink certain core concepts of narrative. Jan-Noël Thon, for instance, who has done a great deal of work on computer games, comics, and films, writes that the view that there is always a signal, however weak, that a narrator exists "becomes significantly less plausible since most narrative media are not limited to verbal narration and, hence, do not as easily or self-evidently activate the cognitive scheme underlying" our understanding of how mimetic narrative works ("Toward" 27). Once we broaden our definition of narrative, and our competency in dealing with it, beyond "the verbal representation of storyworlds"

(Continued)

(Continued)

(Thon, "Toward" 28), we cannot take the presence of a narrator for granted. On the other hand, we might be able to say across media that the subjective representation of consciousness is a key factor (Thon, "Subjectivity" 67). I might wonder who is telling the story of Agent Dale Cooper in *Twin Peaks*. We might not be able to discern a "narrator," but we might be able to consider an "author collective" (Thon, "Toward" 29), the group of directors who made the episodes, such as Lesli Linka Glatter, Caleb Deschanel, Tim Hunter, even Lynch himself, each with their own style and thematic concerns; when we bring all of these elements together, a storyworld begins to emerge. We can certainly say, though, that the subjective representation of consciousness is crucial to the narrative working of *Twin Peaks*: from the representation of memories of watching their babysitter dance shared by the Horne brothers, to the psychic turmoil and murderous impulses of Leland Palmer, to the embodied manifestations of consciousness represented by the killer BOB and Agent Cooper's entry into the Black Lodge, the show depends heavily on recognizing the multitude of ways we can depict the working of the mind.

So, looking at how narratives work in different media can give us the equipment we need to ask new kinds of questions. For instance, how does moving a narrative from one medium to another change that narrative? How is storytelling affected when one medium imitates the techniques of another? How do changes in technology fundamental to the use of a medium change narrative? (Ryan, "Introduction" 32–33). Rather than considering narrative solely from the perspective of what happens with words on the page, we can think about narrative through film, graphic novels, games, social media, and real-world interaction.

Narrative and film

The list above outlining the capabilities and limitations of word, image, and sound is a good starting point for thinking about narrative and film. In some respects, we can "read" aspects of film the same way we would any other narrative; on the other hand, film by the very nature of the medium "does" story differently than what we might find in a novel.

There are some fundamental distinctions between film and other media, like novels. Because of the continual roll of images, we often feel like time is happening differently in film than it does when reading a novel. There are also moments in a movie where plot seems to stop happening and the narrative gives itself over to instances of visual spectacle. For instance, is there any plot-relevant purpose to pausing the progression of the narrative for an explosion or a sex scene?

Chatman points specifically to description and point of view as significant differences. In the first case, "narrative pressure" makes it difficult for film to linger on the visual equivalent of descriptive passages ("What Novels Can Do" 122). A filmmaker does not need an extended passage describing a landscape, for instance, if she can use an establishing shot to do the work. In the second case, film is limited in the ways it can show perspective ("What Novels Can Do" 128). The camera is always there to "see" and to show, but the range of movement available to it is more limited than the range of voice and perspective available to an author creating a narrator. Film is also inherently multimodal: it is a hybrid form that uses words, spoken language, sound, and of course image (Box 3.2).

Box 3.2 **Storytelling in film**

Here is a by no means exhaustive list of everything we can find in film that we cannot find in novels and what they do in terms of storytelling:

- *Use of voice-over:* can represent mental activity, interior monologues, subjective representation of consciousness (example: Bradley Cooper as Pat Solitano in the final scene of *Silver Linings Playbook*); can also serve as a "narrator" or a framing device or a cue towards perspective (example: Jena Malone as Chris McCandless' sister in *Into the Wild*).
- *Use of sound:* can disconnect voice from actor; can create dissonance and disorientation or a feeling of closeness; can set mood or tone (example: acousmatic sound, where the source of sound, like a voice on a telephone, is not seen on-screen).
- *Use of music:* can set mood; can comment on action; can prompt an emotional response; can create a distinction between the diegetic and non-diegetic (example: a John Williams score in a Steven Spielberg movie; the use of James Taylor's "Carolina In My Mind" in *Funny People*).
- *Use of lighting:* can set mood; can create dramatic effects related to character and theme; can establish time of day and time passing (example: film noir, such as *The Maltese Falcon*).
- *Use of space/proximity:* can establish relationships; can establish setting; can generate a sense of world and scale using close-ups or long shots (example: filming scenes of dialogue or kissing; the use of close-ups).
- *Units—frames, scenes, sequences:* can work as both narrative units and as "pregnant moments"; can establish narrative arc or pause narrative movement; can show the passage of time, the development of character, cause and effect (example: montage, freeze frame).

(Continued)

(Continued)

- *Editing:* can create pacing; can transition from one scene to another with fades, dissolves, or cuts; can create coherence or confusion through long takes or jump cuts; can facilitate or hinder gap-filling (example: the famous no-cut Steadicam tracking shot in the nightclub scene in *Goodfellas*; the intertwining of scenes from the staged reading, the State Department, and the hostage crisis in Iran during the first third of *Argo*).
- *Camera POV (point of view):* can create a sense of perspective using low angles or wide shots; can direct our attention to characters, actions; can foreground certain elements or shift attention (examples: the shifting back and forth between the perspectives of Chief Brody and the shark in *Jaws*; the use of foreground/background and focus or lack thereof in *Eternal Sunshine of the Spotless Mind*).

Clearly, this list draws upon certain narratological functions and concepts. The camera "eye" can give us the perception of focalization in a way that we recognize as the subjective representation of consciousness, either through a narrator or a character (within limits). The establishing of scenes and editing can move the story along in sequence, with a particular fixed order, in the way we expect stories to move from exposition onward.

Engagements: Exemplary text

I would like to now consider Terrence Malick's *The Tree of Life* to show how to read movies. To say "Terrence Malick's film *The Tree of Life* tells the story of a young boy growing up in Texas and the ways the death of his brother as a young man reverberates throughout his life as he reaches middle age" would be a summary of the "plot," but it would not be entirely accurate. First of all, the film doesn't really "tell a story." It presents certain recognizably narrative elements that a viewer can piece together into a story, and part of the film is dominated by the narrative mode, with a discernible arc, events, and characters. But it depends just as heavily on purely visual components whose purpose is not immediately clear. (In this regard it reveals a debt to Stanley Kubrick's *2001: A Space Odyssey*, and in fact the same techniques were used to create special effects representing outer space, manipulating chemical compounds rather than relying on CGI; this manipulation of chemical compounds to make art out of light is called *lumia*.) Second, my capsule makes it sound like a clear narrative arc is present, that narrative time moves through the film and moves the film forward, and that we can map the arc and time passing onto the life of the protagonist. Finally, it suggests that there is a protagonist, a singular guiding consciousness throughout.

Plot, time, duration, order, perspective: none of these appears the way one might expect in a narrative film. The film is framed by the present day; the middle takes place over an extended flashback to Waco, Texas in 1956 but is also punctuated by images of the creation of the universe and of outer space. In the present, the main character, Jack O'Brien, played by Sean Penn, is a middle-aged architect working in a city: the visual mode is dominated by shots of Jack walking through the streets, riding elevators in a high-rise, looking out the window of conference rooms or his apartment, walking through the atrium of his building with the camera gazing up at glass ceilings. This is a built world, inorganic, cold with the blue and gray tones of steel and glass, in contrast to the natural world of Jack's childhood. There are a number of jump cuts, as well as tracking shots which follow Jack's movement and then pause and look upwards: up to the sky, up through the glass ceiling, up through treetops. The effect is to feel constant motion punctuated by moments of contemplation— literally gazing heavenward. The scenes of Jack's present are interrupted by his visions of walking on a beach, first alone and then, at the end, joined by his parents as younger people and his brothers as children—the same as we see them in the middle, narrative, section of the film. That middle section essentially constitutes whatever narrative arc the film might possess. We see Jack and his two brothers born, and we watch them grow up together until Jack's father, played by Brad Pitt, loses his job and the family has to move house.

So far, so good. The extended flashback narrative of the main body of the film is itself framed by spectacular visual sequences seemingly prompted by Jack's mother, played by Jessica Chastain, learning of the death of her son, Jack's middle brother. He is depicted throughout the film as artistic and sensitive, quick to forgive; his death is unexplained. This is a kernel—an essential plot event without which the narrative cannot occur—but it also is the event which throws us out of the narrative entirely.

In Figure 3.1 we see Mrs. O'Brien, walking down the street, her grief-stricken face filling the space of the screen. We next see her in a forest; the camera takes on her perspective as she gazes up at the sky, and her prayer is heard in voice-over. The perspectival technique is the same as in the very beginning of the film, with Jack in the city. Voice-over is used throughout the film, all from different perspectives, sometimes Jack as a boy, sometimes Jack as a man, sometimes his mother. Sometimes voice-over is used to relay mental activity—such as Jack wishing his authoritarian father would die— sometimes it is used to relay the very particular mental activity of prayer. It is never used simply to narrate. Individual perspective slips around in the film, and while specific visual strategies are used to cue us to notice perspective, one single guiding consciousness cannot be identified (unless one wanted to make a claim for it being God).

Mrs. O'Brien's prayer for her son in the forest hurls us out of plot and time. The narrative is paused and a symphony of images and music commence showing the creation of the universe and the beginnings of life on earth. This culminates in the image of a flame in darkness, an image which recurs

Figure 3.1 Still from *The Tree of Life*. (Dir. Terrence Malick, Fox Searchlight, 2011.)

throughout the film as a transition from narrative time to what we might call "geological time" and from past to present—reminding this viewer of Alfred Tennyson's use of Charles Lyell's theories of evolution for his own extended meditation on grief, *In Memoriam*. At the very least, we could say that the distinction between the clearly defined arc of Jack's childhood, and a more symbolic way of thinking about time is made visible. Once the "symphony" is over, we return to story-time and the "plot" with the birth of Jack, and the flashback narrative goes on. Throughout the film, music by such composers as Bach and Brahms is used; it serves as pure form, much the way the lumia-inspired images of space do. Writing on another of Malick's films, *Days of Heaven*, Chatman has said, "[The] visual effects [in the film] are too striking for the narrative line to support. Narrative pressure is so great that the interpretation of even non-narrative films [like *Days of Heaven*] is sometimes affected by it" ("What Novels Can Do" 122). Here, the visual effects are necessary because the narrative arc itself is ruptured. The grief of the mother renders narrative impossible. The death of Jack's brother is unnarratable. It cannot be shown. It cannot even be told, except in voice-over, and in Malick's use the voice-over itself becomes sound and thought and prayer. Narrative stops and form takes over; language can only be used for prayer.

For all of its experimentation with form, Malick's film does ultimately seek to offer resolution and closure; however, it is the resolution and closure of elegy, of coping with grief, not of narrative. We return to Mrs. O'Brien in the woods. Her moment of reflection cuts to another of Jack's visions of the beach, and as he is joined by his young brothers and his parents, Mrs. O'Brien's voice returns in voice-over: "I give you my son." Mapping the form of elegy onto *The Tree of Life* facilitates an alternative way to make meaning of the film, and we also see Malick simultaneously using and pushing the form and limits of narrative.

Graphic narrative

Graphic narrative—comics, graphic novels, comics journalism and reportage, autography—is inherently multimodal, or using multiple forms of media. It depends on the interplay between word and image, and it uses a range of visual conventions to tell its stories (the "POW!" to show a punch in a superhero comic book, for instance, or voice balloons to show talking). Graphic narrative also has the potential to expand what stories can do and expand our idea of the storyworld.

Let's start by defining graphic narrative and some of its core components. Essential to telling a story through graphic narrative is the use of the panel and the page, and the relationship of the part (panel) to the whole (page). The space of the page is divided into a grid, with panels separated from each other by gutters. Sometimes a panel can take up a whole page with no border or space at all; this is called a bleed. Sometimes a panel can exist on a page with no borders, creating an effect wherein a moment "escapes into timeless space" (McCloud 103). The panel establishes space and time. Effective use of foreground and background positions a character in space and contributes to the representation of perspective. The panel positions the perceiving subject through one panel's relationship to another and through the composition of the panel within the border (or lack thereof) and on the page as a whole. Durwin Talon and Guin Thompson refer to panels as "containers of story" (22). The space between panels—the gutter—can also serve as a space where story happens, holding narrative captions, information pertinent to time or place, or the thoughts of the characters. Comics take some of their language from film. A graphic narrative might begin with an "establishing shot," a panel that provides information about setting and opens up the process of making the storyworld; or it might introduce character or an early plot kernel.

Once panels are strung together, we begin to have story, events occurring over time. Panels can depict action, but they also can depict static moments, mood, or multiple events occurring simultaneously. Individual panels on the grid might lay out sequential action, but a bleed might depict many events happening all at the same time. Scott McCloud, one of the foremost writers about comics art and storytelling, has also created categories for how one might use panels in terms of transitions: moment to moment, action to action, subject to subject, scene to scene, aspect to aspect, and non-sequiturs (74). If we recall learning about order, duration, and frequency in Chapter 1, we can see that the panel is an effective device for storytelling. Panels can depict events occurring in order, and then shuffle the order. The horizontal space of the panel can be elongated to show duration, or made into much smaller components of the grid to quicken the pace of the story. Panels can be repeated to show repeated action, or the same event from different perspectives. Spreading action out over several panels can heighten the drama of an event.

The elements within a panel, both word and image, can also contribute to story. In fact, we could say that a core element of graphic narrative is that the discourse depends upon the interplay of word and image. Lines can be used to show mood or character; jagged lines might show anger, swirling lines confusion. Even the lines of the borders of panels can be manipulated to show time passing, speed, emotion. Sound is visualized through sound balloons or visual effects, and dialogue is provided in word balloons. Pictures and words can be linked, or they can be juxtaposed in such a way as to show contrast or contradiction. The conventionally and deceptively simple "comics" style can be used but it might also be joined with a more deliberately "realistic" visual style to draw the reader's attention to the defamiliarizing capacity of the medium and the relationship of the storyworld to the "actual" world. The verbal element can also help to structure the interior space of a panel. Text boxes might frame the panel, providing narrative, and then the rest of the panel is filled in with image. A panel might be pure image, with no dialogue or narration at all, creating a "pregnant moment," a pause, a moment of realization or reflection. Finally, all of these elements, all of the parts, come together in a reader's perception of the whole, what McCloud calls "closure" (63). He says, "If visual iconography is the vocabulary of comics, closure is its grammar" (67). Closure could be considered in light of our understanding of the storyworld: the components of the graphic narrative allow for the making of the storyworld as we read both word and image, and as we comprehend how the visual vocabulary is arranged in a narrative grammar.

A quick example from the satirical strip *PhD Comics* (Figure 3.2) shows a classic, conventional strip with clearly defined gutters and borders, and panels that progress from set-up to punchline. The facial expression in the first two panels depict increasing aggravation. Then, the absence of the human figure in the last two panels is meant to show she has gotten up to put a stop to her friend's internet addiction: absence, rather than presence, conveys the progression of the micronarrative, and the empty panel shows she has left the frame for another off-screen space. The voice bubbles, complete with sound effect ("... sob"), show the resolution.

Does the multimodal nature of graphic narrative, the fact that it operates along at least two channels, word and image, change our thinking about story? Robyn Warhol has suggested that comics ask us to think about "us[ing] 'the space between' words and pictures to extend possibilities for the representation of consciousness" (3, 5). Kai Mikkonen claims that comics have a unique power to represent "minds in action" (302). The layer created by words and the layer created by image might function as two different layers. Each might be devoted to the subjective representation of consciousness, but the space between might lend itself to the creation of yet another way of reading the story.

The "word layer" can have several different parts embedded within it, too. Comics artist-writers can use captions in the gutter or within inset text boxes to convey the work of a narrator. Dialogue can be shared in voice

Figure 3.2 "Addicted to the Web." (Published 8 May 2000. © Jorge Cham. PhDComics. com.)

balloons, or interior mental workings in thought balloons. There are multiple ways to report thought. Layers can consist of the reporting of a narrator, commenting upon action; and the arrangements of panels themselves can break through the boundaries of the different layers, crossing from one part of the narrative, or space, or time to another. So different verbal layers can contradict one another, or word and image can contradict one another. Gaps in knowledge can be revealed. Likewise, the "image layer" can create assorted ways of reading. In the same way that a novel might show different ways of using language, like letters, legal briefs, dialogue or face-to-face storytelling, graphic narratives can use different kinds of images as well. Photographs, maps, drawings in different styles, the replication of print or typewriting by hand, computer-generated images, visual "quotes" or allusions to other works of art all go beyond simply "word and image" to activate a multimodal engagement with the storyworld.

Comics can also use the visual medium to capture character in a variety of ways: facial expression, body language, close-ups (either on the entire face or on just a part of the face, like the eyes). It can depict through image how a character changes over time, and characters' relationships to each other. Both of these enable the artist-writer to forgo words in favor of image: showing a child growing to adulthood through changing clothes in a set of serial images, or showing emotional relationships through facial expressions or proximity within a panel. At the same time, comics art is not photography (though it might use photographic elements); it renders the human form and face into a cartoon. Comics might use a certain level of realism, but the medium calls for simplification or defamiliarization so that the narrative can achieve its ends (McCloud 36, 41). Certain features can be exaggerated for effect and to highlight particular traits. In some cases this is extreme, as in Art Spiegelman's *Maus*; in this memoir of the Holocaust,

Jews are depicted as mice and Nazis as cats. Characters can also step outside the diegetic space—perhaps outside the borders of a panel—and directly address readers, adding to both engagement and defamiliarization. Viewing the face of a character might create in us a sense of empathy, but it also creates some critical distance (Hatfield 115). Drawing a person makes them seem simultaneously real and not; the cartoon human is a version, an imagined and defamiliarized version that calls attention to how we construct both real and fictional selves.

Additionally, the bringing together of the verbal and the visual has implications for perspective. Perspective can be discussed in terms of both seeing and knowing, as well as through a character experiencing the narrative or a narrative consciousness separate from the story. Furthermore, to use Seymour Chatman's terms from Chapter 1, that narrator can be overt—making its presence known either through being part of the story or exceptionally interventionist with comments and judgments and voice—or covert—hidden and not character-bound. The character experiencing the narrative can also take a different perspectival position from the narrator, based on knowledge or judgment. A narrator can convey what it knows based on what it sees; it can lead us to make judgments about reliability. What it sees or knows may "color" how it presents the narrative. Perspective may be inflected by perception, as well as by "ideological and moral orientation" (Horstkotte and Pedri 334; Jahn 244). These affect our own understanding of the narrative, not only of consciousness but of events and characters, as we build the storyworld. In prose fiction, perspective can manifest itself through voice and style; in graphic narrative, it can appear through different uses of "visual vocabulary," via repetition and shading, and through the "braiding" and intertwining of repeated visual elements like panels to show relationships of parts to the whole (Horstkotte and Pedri 335). The story might be told by a narrator, but aspects of the story may be focalized through one or more characters, "seeing" and relaying elements differently or with a particular perspective. A reader-viewer cannot always pin down for sure who is doing the "seeing," but such ambiguity does lead the reader-viewer to cognizant of multiple layers of narrative within the storyworld.

Let's take a look at a few examples.

Engagements: Exemplary text

When traditional narrative forms, like novels, have used space, they have done so in terms of setting; perhaps they have shown how characters are situated in a room or how they live in proximity to one another. It might be significant, for instance, to consider the distance Elizabeth Bennet has to travel to be with her ill sister in *Pride and Prejudice*. Graphic narrative uses space differently. The medium relies on depicting characters in space, and placing characters in space or manipulating the space of panel or page allows an artist-writer to complicate our perception of who is seeing what when.

One of the more innovative practitioners of graphic narrative in recent years is Chris Ware. His project *Building Stories* turns a book into a work of art, presenting the narrative in a boxed set of 14 different kinds of print materials (books, broadsheets, etc.). *Jimmy Corrigan; or, The Smartest Kid on Earth* draws attention to itself as a book object in similarly self-conscious ways; the endpapers of the hardcover book, for instance, offer instructions for how to read comics, and several pages (206 and 207 for instance), are designed as cut-outs, where readers could conceivably cut out the diagrammed shapes, fold them up, and make paper versions of the homes featured in the novel. Thus Ware points to the spatial relationship of book to world, of the potentially multidimensional nature of engagement with the storyworld.

Ware's book tells the story of a man named Jimmy Corrigan, a true sad sack of a person, alone entirely in the world; upon meeting his estranged father for the first time after many years, he learns that he had a grandfather, also named Jimmy Corrigan, whose father abandoned him at the World's Columbian Exposition of 1893 in Chicago. A parallel storyline, positioned in time midway through the far past of Jimmy's grandfather and the narrative present of Jimmy's adulthood, depicts Jimmy as a lonely child being raised by a divorced mother. Many of the pages of the novel feature a tight grid, with heavily drawn borderlines and almost no gutter. The panels are predominantly small squares, creating the impression that Jimmy's world and outlook are small and constrained. Even as a grown man, he is still a small child, emotionally stunted and trapped in his life. The panels featuring 1893 Jimmy use a script text to convey his internal thoughts and his narrating of childhood; after his father leaves him at the Exposition, we never see him again.

The pages I would like to focus on here are those a little more than half-way through the book (most of the pages are not numbered), where 1893 Jimmy is left by his father.

The small panels open up into large panels as Jimmy and his father climb to the top of the main exposition hall. The grand white building fills the space of the panel; surrounding the large panel are tiny panels where Jimmy is shown in a boy's home post-abandonment, imagining his father hurling him off the top of the building. The last tiny panels before we turn the page show Jimmy standing on the roof, watching the people below (featured in a tiny panel, representing how tiny they would have looked to Jimmy); the script says, "So I just stood there, watching the sky, and the people below, waiting for him to return." The tiny panels cut back and forth between Jimmy and the people, showing his perspective. The next page is a full-page panel, one of only a few (and all of those panels depict buildings of great scale), of the exposition hall, now colored a rosy shade to show the sun setting and that time has elapsed (Figure 3.3); at the top, almost impossible to see, is the tiny figure of Jimmy, alone. Directly opposite, in the upper right-hand corner, is script saying: "Of course, he never did." Ware exploits the

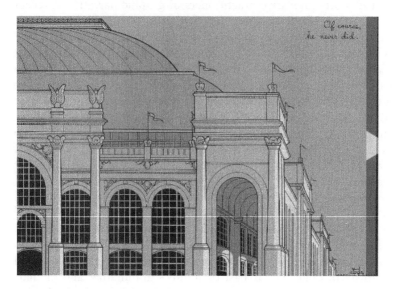

Figure 3.3 Illustration from *Jimmy Corrigan: The Smartest Kid on Earth*. (Chris Ware, © 2000, 2003, by Chris Ware. Used by permission of Pantheon Books, an imprint of the Knopf Doubleday Publishing Group, a division of Penguin Random House LLC. All rights reserved.)

scale of the building and the space of the panel to heighten the poignancy of Jimmy's situation, and to have us receding from him as he leaves the story. Being able to capture the monumental nature of the building juxtaposed with the vulnerability of the boy is essential to the emotional impact of the scene and his position in the multiple plotlines, all of which tell stories of loss and abandonment. Thus space here is vital not only to constructing the storyworld but to the elucidating of thematic elements as well.

Engagements: Exemplary text

In her consideration of what constitutes a medium, Marie-Laure Ryan suggests that it would be something of a stretch to claim smell or taste as experiences that can be engaged as part of the construction of the storyworld. We do not generally think of perfume or food as media, and she deliberately excludes them from her discussion of "media" (*Avatars* 18). What if we did, however, think of food as a medium for telling a story? What if we thought of recipes as a plot, with a beginning, a middle, and an end, consisting of a communication from a narrator with a specific goal in mind?

Food and foodways have always been a rich source of narrative. Memoirs focused around food, like the essays of M. F. K. Fisher or Ruth Reichl's *Tender at the Bone*, are a genre unto themselves. The growth of digital culture has led to numerous food blogs, many of which narrate the making of dishes alongside the recipes that provide the instruction (including the expository moment of trying to figure out what to do with whatever is in the cupboard that day, or the plot-like quest to find the perfect barbecue sauce). Cookbooks have always included shards and traces of story. As Anne Bower writes, the textual components of cookbooks, "the discourse of the discrete textual elements and their juxtapositions contribute to the creation of" story (2). Narrative is an essential component of food writing, and I would like to suggest that food narratives themselves are multimodal, particularly when they include recipes. Food narratives seek to engage the reader in the storyworld via two channels: one sensory, through taste, and one verbal, through recipes. I might even suggest that recipes themselves are narrative. They rely on sequences of events, duration, people doing things and making choices, and interactivity. They have a beginning, a middle, and an end, which as we saw in Chapter 1 and learned from Aristotle, is absolutely essential.

Here we might consider how graphic narrative can serve as a medium for life writing as well as for fiction, and we might also see how a graphic memoir about food can be multimodal in several respects: with the inclusion of recipes. Lucy Knisley's graphic memoir, or "autography," *Relish: My Life in the Kitchen*, tells the story of assorted episodes in her life from the point of view of food, cooking, and sharing meals: growing up in Rhinebeck, NY with a bohemian caterer/farmers' market mother; spending time with her gourmand father after her parents' divorce; traveling to Japan; moving to Chicago for art school; memorable meals and food cravings. Chapter 8, "The Apple Doesn't Fall Far From the Cheese," seems to exemplify Virginia Woolf's claim from *A Room of One's Own* that "if we are women, we think back through our mothers" (75). We can see Knisley exploiting techniques that are both essential to narrative and specific to her medium. The chapter begins with her imagining her parents' life in the Village prior to her birth; when her mother gets pregnant, Knisley draws her mother's belly with herself as a baby within in a kind of cut-away (reminiscent of illustrations from eighteenth-century medical textooks). A horizontal panel filling the bottom of the page shows herself at different stages, each version representing the passage of time and development influenced by her mother.

Chapter 6, "The Craver," is another episode where the connection to the mother is made explicit. In this chapter, Knisley explores how she and her mother share similar cravings for certain foods: steak, tomatillos, mushrooms. The chapter ends with "The Way Mom Makes Mushrooms," a recipe for sautéed mushrooms (Figure 3.4). The recipe includes the expected instructions: equipment one might need, tips for drying the mushrooms prior to cooking, how much olive oil and how high the heat should be. But Knisley also combines this with narrative elements, generating story through the telling of the recipe. Knisley, or a drawing of her face, appears throughout the four-page illustration to comment and directly address the

Figure 3.4 "The Way Mom Makes Mushrooms," from *Relish*. (Illustration from
Relish: My Life in the Kitchen © 2013 by Lucy Knisley. Reprinted
by permission of First Second, an imprint of Roaring Brook Press,
a division of Holtzbrinck Publishing Holdings Limited Partnership.
All rights reserved.)

reader. She depicts herself at her mother's side while cooking the mushrooms, reminding us that the recipe is indeed part of the storyworld which
is constituted in large part by the telling of the mother–daughter relationship.
She even includes a microtelling of her mother meeting Julia Child. Knisley
exploits the narrative capability of the recipe by telling the story of making
the mushrooms—including a "resolution" where the reader is presented
with a plate of mushrooms and exhorted to eat with her hands. But she
also includes a number of strategies to make the giving of the recipe seem
like the telling of a story: bringing in characters from the "story" part of
the narrative and depicting them at work and in relationship; embedding
microstories within the recipe itself; and showing herself as narrator
commenting upon the process. Such an example might be useful for thinking
about the ways recipes and food writing use aspects of narrativity to tell
stories and engage sensory experience, and how the form of the graphic
narrative provides tools to do this.

Engagements: Exemplary text

Can things tell stories? Things are often part of the furniture of the storyworld; they can also be helpful cues for theme, symbolism, and character.
For example, in *The Great Gatsby*, a number of objects generate significance

(something exploited to good effect in Baz Luhrmann's film adaptation): Gatsby's shirts, the green light at the end of the pier, the car that is the instrument of Myrtle's destruction. There is an entire virtual "shelf" on the social networking site for bookworms, GoodReads, devoted to "Unusual Perspectives," with nominations suggested in the comments feed for stories told from the points of view of cats, dogs, and so on. Yet all along, as we've talked about character, we seem to have been presuming that we meant humans. Can we have a story told from the point of view of a thing, like a shopping cart, which is the premise of Bo Fowler's novel *Skepticism, Inc.*? If we use graphic narrative, does that alter the capacity of objects to "tell" stories? The answer is an easy yes: the assigning of captions to panels consisting entirely of the representation of objects in narratives like Alison Bechdel's *Fun Home* or Marjane Satrapi's *Persepolis* show us that even as those captions offer the perspective of the narrator, important things to be told gather around objects.

Things are signs of the material world. They also provide necessary furniture for conjuring a storyworld. Like food, narrative constellates around things; stories can be made with things at the center, but our question here is whether they can be seen to play an active role. Thing theory, as formulated by the philosopher Bill Brown, might suggest that things—objects—can themselves act and have agency in a narrative. They can have perspective, and by positioning them as entities with a particular perspective we might have a different experience of the world of the story. They can be agents of plot, and by positioning them as beings that can take action we might have a different experience of how events unfold and what they mean. Attending to things in narrative requires us to think of stories in the context of everyday life, as well as the relationships they establish between subjects and objects.

Leann Shapton's *Important Artifacts and Personal Property from the Collection of Lenore Doolan and Harold Morris* tells the story of a couple and their break-up through a fictional auction catalog. A series of 325 captioned photographs details the objects accumulated over the course of the relationship, creating an intimate world of artifact and memory—literally, souvenirs. Are they objects or things? Artifacts? Are we readers, consumers, voyeurs? Is this private or public, narrative or event? The use of objects, artifacts, things, which call upon readers to fill in the gaps of Lenore and Harold's intimacy, serve as storymakers in and of themselves. Objects become things tossed away that, in a sense, find a second life as storymakers.

The cover of the book indicates the auction was to take place on, of course, February 14th, Valentine's Day. Epigraphs from the writers Graham Greene and Novalis indicate the dual nature of things and objects with which Shapton grounds her project: "If ashtrays could speak"; "We seek the absolute everywhere, and only ever find things." The timeline of both the relationship and the relationship of the relationship to the event of the auction is mysterious: the auction is taking place in 2009, it begins with a postcard from 2008, which references an encounter in 2007, after the breakup in 2006; the relationship begins in 2002, when Lenore is 26 and Harold is 39. Is the auction the ending? Is it the final ending? Shapton seems to have begun with the ending, but to what extent did her characters participate? Did they agree to have their things put up for auction? Is this truly the end of Lenore and Harold?

Because we know the objects, the things, are the detritus, or the relics, or the artifacts, of an ended relationship, because we know the ending, we are nudged to read with anticipation in a kind of flashforward, as well as retrospectively. One particular area of interest, as well, is Lenore's lists: food she's eaten (she's a food and wine writer at the *New York Times*) mixed in with questions and anxieties about the relationship, quick mentions of arguments ("sort-of fight over water bottle"; "poss preg") that extend backwards in our mind's eye as we attempt to visualize what might have happened before the textual moment. Shapton also manipulates narrative causality: the photograph positioned after Harold writes to Lenore telling her he doesn't want to be there when she takes her pregnancy test is of a white-noise machine irreparably damaged "as if struck by a hammer." No other comment is provided.

For all of the information we are provided, it is in some ways not the right kinds. Furthermore, our objects seem to have failed: meant to create a connection, to express preference, to serve as gifts, they have failed, and they are rendered merely things by their failure. For all of the intimacy engendered by the objects, perhaps in the end they are merely things: they are the furniture of an intimate world, they concretize an intimate landscape, they render a "we," but as we peruse the catalog further, we see evidence again and again of a failure for each human actor to enter the world of the other and for the objects to sustain their significance. Our humans have created a world for their "we," without ever having fully entered the worlds of each other. Past lovers and hints of new attachments appear and reappear, leaving their own clues, like sunglasses, behind.

Without the relationship and our own work to make a storyworld out of the objects presented, this is not a "collection," even though that's what it calls itself: it may be wrought and ordered with a kind of affective impulse, with a chronology of the couplehood, with giving and taking and relational logic, but where's the meaning without the "we"? It's just junk. What is its value? Objects are as particular as this love, as particular as each beloved is to her other. How did these objects become things; without the relationship, they are meaningless, but they originally garnered meaning by existing in a web of significance created by the relationship itself. The state that gave them their meaning and functionality is also the thing that strips away that functionality. If no one "buys" the important artifacts and personal property from the collection of Lenore Doolan and Harold Morris, these things will be obsolete, relics, rubbish. They will enact the rejection and discarding of a failed love affair. Thus the presentation in the catalog is part of the structural understanding of the objects, the things. They are collectively and individually perceived—collectively by the purported audience for the auction, individually by the readers of the catalog. The intimacy of the couplehood becomes a public spectacle (potentially), while the private experience of looking through the catalog, performing a certain kind of interpretation on the relics therein, performs the work of narrative itself—what are these objects, and what would they mean to me should I make them part of my world? In Shapton's hands, the collection becomes a story, the curator becomes an arranger and a narrator, objects are transformed from things and given the agency of storymaking.

Narrative and the digital

The kind of navigation between word and image we see in film and graphic narrative is one way a reader or viewer interacts with a story. Managing word and image when we read is something we learn how to do as children, and our ability to do this, to participate in different kinds of interactivity, is something that allows us to make, share, and experience stories in the digital world. Let's consider an example that draws on this complex set of activities. One of the more notable children's books in recent years is Jon Klassen's *This Is Not My Hat*. Like a lot of children's literature, it is inherently multimodal, depending on the interplay of word and image. The story begins when a small fish steals a small hat from a very large fish, and proceeds by the little fish narrating his understanding of the consequences in a way that is contradicted by the images themselves. So, the small fish imagines he will get away with stealing the hat because the big fish "probably won't wake up for a long time"; this piece of text is matched with an image of the big fish, in fact, waking up. After a series of these counterfactual word/image pairs, the small fish turns to directly addressing the reader: "I will tell you where I am going. I am going where the plants grow big and tall and close together." The story continues along two separate narrative levels emerging from the kernel of the theft of the hat, one that has the small fish telling his conviction that no one will find him, and one that has the images showing what is happening outside the realm of the small fish's knowledge: the big fish getting closer, a lobster pointing the big fish in the direction of where the little fish went. The two levels meet on a spread of two pages; on the right-hand side, moving in the direction of our reading and the linear narrative, is the tiny fish getting to where the plants are big and tall and close together, and on the left-hand side is the big fish catching up. The story exploits our ability to hold two levels of narrative in our heads at the same time, and it plays with the pleasure of seeing them meet up in the climax because, of course, it's bad news for the tiny fish once the big fish catches him. This is revealed, sadly, in the final images: the big fish swims off, and at first we see only his tail, his head outside the frame of the page. The final spread is of the big fish wearing a tiny hat. These images, without words, call upon us to fill in what happened to the little fish; his fate is not shown, much like the murders that happen off-stage in Greek tragedy or Shakespeare, and it is reported to us via wordless image.

The slightly chilling effect of the unseen demise of the little fish is heightened by a digital video book trailer produced by Candlewick Press, Klassen's publisher. The 35-second video is available on YouTube, and has generated about a dozen comments from readers who love the book and the accompanying trailer. In the video, *Psycho*-esque strings play over a rapidly rolling image meant to capture the movement of the tiny fish escaping with his booty. The tiny fish swims into the frame and stays there while words play over his head: "I've got a plan to get away with it. So everything's going to be okay. Everything's going to be fine." He swims into the plants that grow big and tall and close together, and the trailer ends. The transmedial artifact, existing in conjunction with the book itself, takes advantage of the element of sound to capture or anticipate the experience of reading about the tiny fish's attempt to escape. It uses motion along with word and image to generate suspense and to facilitate readers' sense of what the reading experience might be like. And, it inhabits a digital environment that encourages sharing and commenting as forms of engagement and community-building.

This small, slightly silly example, highlights just a few of the ways that digital allows us to think about narrative, interactivity, adaptation, and community. Digital media facilitate the creation and dissemination of transmedial narratives, stories that draw on the same world and exist in multiple forms in multiple media at the same time. Furthermore, digital media and stories that use them call upon us to rethink how we engage with narrative given the growing possibility for greater interactivity. Reading is, of course, a form of interacting with narrative; in fact, as Chapter 2 has shown, this interaction is a complex cognitive process that calls upon us to recognize cues, fill in gaps, and construct worlds. Reading can be, inherently, an immersive experience, as anyone who has ever looked up from the pages of a book and realized an entire day has gone by can tell you. The point of focusing on digital is not to suggest that the ways it allows us to do narrative through adaptation, interactivity, and community are radically new, or will take the place of other experiences. It is to suggest that as we are exposed to new and different forms of storytelling and storymaking, as our experience of narrative widens, our competencies around our dealing with narrative will change. We can always be adding new forms of narrative to our repertoire, and we can always be finding new ways to read them—even as those qualities that make narratives familiarly and recognizably narrative ground us. We will always want stories that have interesting plots, engaging characters, immersive settings, intelligible actions and thoughts. These are the things that make up narrative, no matter the form. How those things get made and used might change depending on medium, and that will change our experience.

Here are just some of the ways digital media and narrative work together:

- creating and sharing multimedia stories on social media or through digital storytelling/digital journalism tools;
- following a serial podcast or web series;
- circulating stories among a network through Facebook, Twitter, blogs;
- expanding a narrative universe through fan sites and wikis;
- participating in an immersive narrative experience through video games;
- reading interactive fiction on an iPad or a piece of virtual-reality journalism using Oculus Rift (such as "Harvest of Change," produced by the *Des Moines Register*).

All of these instances share several characteristics: the necessity of computers and digital technology to the making and consuming experience, interactivity, immersion, sharing and networking, and use and integration of multiple media. Page and Thomas define the qualities of "online discourse." It is "hybrid in nature," hybrid meaning the blending of the "literary" work of storytelling with the kind of "face-to-face" narratives we find in situated life contexts, as well as

> blending the written word with near-instantaneous communication . . . . In particular, the narratives that emerge in Web 2.0 environments where personal expression is inextricably woven with dialogue (for example, through the use of conversational metacommentary) require paradigms [or models] that account for both their interpersonal and expressive qualities.
>
> (4–5)

We might think of digital media as modular, communal, fragmented, and process-oriented. The stories that emerge from these media might be open-ended, unlike the closed experience of a novel. They might have infinite permutations, with no real gesture towards closure. Thus Page and Thomas provide three central areas of interest for studying digital narratives, and these are all potentially interesting issues for us to keep in mind as we go forward:

- how these texts generate progression, coherence, and closure while also exhibiting qualities of deferral and open-endedness;
- how "producing narrative in digital media is an embodied experience," one that calls upon models of authenticity and foregrounds issues of identity;
- how digital texts facilitate, possibly even demand, interactivity and collaboration (11).

At the same time, practitioners should be mindful of what digital narratives are not. They are not all about infinite choice or randomness. As we have seen, narrative depends on a highly structured process of selection and ordering on the part of the maker or author, and recombination into particular schemas and scripts on the part of the user or reader. They are also not all about, or entirely all about, immersion. As Aristotle taught us, a satisfying narrative depends to a certain extent on our feeling a distance from a character's experience while also participating in it—*not* on our *being* that character. Even when we take on an avatar or virtual persona, as we shall see, we are still our own persons, living in the real world (one hopes).

Interactivity

Narrative is not necessarily supposed to be wholly interactive. Narrative consists of specific events, occurring in a specific order, determined by a controlling consciousness: the author in the making, and the narrator in the telling. There is not a whole lot of room for choice here. Nevertheless, when we turn our attention to other ways texts generate narrativity, such as setting, character, mental life, the establishment and maintenance of certain social rules and natural laws, we can see the potential for reconciling interactivity and narrative, particularly if we focus on what our minds do when we "read." Interactivity comes in multiple forms: cognitive, functional, metacultural (engaging with the "metaverse" of, let's say, *Star Wars*, or participating in social stories). For Ryan, interactivity is an essential component of digital media, in its "responsiveness to a changing environment . . . . The interactive character of digital texts manifests itself as a feedback loop . . . situat[ing] us inside a system that continually produces a dynamic object" (Ryan, "Digital Media" 329). We can think of interactivity as being able to participate in a system due to the system's having an architecture that permits us to enter the structure of the system. We adapt cognitively to the experience of interactivity, creating new schemas in order to take appropriate actions to fulfill tasks, and using scripts to quickly recognize situations and fill in gaps. With true interactivity, the architecture that permits this is not simply our own cognitive architecture; it is a system external to us. As with other kinds of narratives we might find ourselves immersed; unlike with other kinds of narratives, however, we are given the opportunity to participate. In this formulation, it is not choice that is important; *Choose Your Own Adventure* books, and even hypertext fiction, are not truly interactive, even though a user can make choices, because all one is doing is navigating through a limited number of prescribed options. True interactivity would mean that interacting with the system changes the system in a reciprocal manner. Our participation changes the very architecture of the system, and thus the story.

Ryan has defined several kinds of interactivity across two axes: internal/external involvement and exploratory/ontological involvement.

- *Internal/external.* Users inhabit the virtual world, in the form of an avatar or by evincing a first-person perspective; or users are outside the virtual world manipulating it from beyond.

- *Exploratory/ontological.* Users move around the virtual world without having any impact on plot, without changing the history or destiny of the virtual world; or users make decisions and take actions which determine the development of possible worlds and thereby story (*Avatars* 108–11).

What do these categories look like in practice? Most of my examples are taken from games; a true interactive fiction, which is hard to come by, would be internal/ontological. The example of interactive fiction I discuss below, *Device 6*, is internal/exploratory.

- *Internal/exploratory.* The classic Nintendo game *Super Mario Bros.*: the player takes on the role of Mario or Luigi—the avatar—and moves through the world collecting coins, jumping on mushrooms, achieving levels, saving princesses, etc.; there is a feeling of triumph in making one's way through the game, but the world itself is unchanged by the actions or choices of the player.
- *External/exploratory. Civilization*: the player chooses a civilization from history to build, and tries to create empires. More roles and abilities are made available as technology progresses, and the characteristics of the civilizations are drawn from historical record. Players have some choice, and the appearance of shaping the "destiny of the world," but this is somewhat limited given the framework of the game. Much hypertext fiction, like Michael Joyce's now-classic *afternoon*, falls along these axes.
- *External/ontological. The Sims* games: the player creates the world of the Sims, directing emotions, needs, moods and aspirations; placing the characters in situations, etc. Originally I might have placed *The Sims* under "external/exploratory," because the characters as created did not necessarily take actions, have thoughts, construct goals, etc., which are necessary to plot—in other words, a player could create "people" and move them around in the world, but not to any end we would associate with making a narrative. More recent versions have introduced this capability, however, making the possibility of story more plausible.

One way a digital or interactive story can show itself to be an especially engaging narrative is to be an "emergent story," where there is a convergence between "textual architecture" and "user involvement" such that the storyteller or designer creates patterns and platforms that make a meaningful story and allow for generation of worlds, while also creating the illusion that the choices of the user matter, "giving users both the confidence that their efforts will be rewarded by a coherent narrative and the feeling of acting of their own free will" (Ryan, *Avatars* 100). In other words, the story "emerges" from the choices made and actions taken by the user, and the story is able to do that because the system creating the story changes with the experiences and actions of the user. Narrative must become a part of the system that renders a more complex whole, "conceived as the interaction between a user and a simulated environment" or between a user and digital agent; it also becomes "reciprocal and recursive" (Walsh 76). Good design will facilitate user exploration and participation while also exploiting the mutually enhancing relationships among word and image to generate good stories. Emergent narrative happens when a system allows for reciprocal interaction; we feel ourselves part of the system, acting within an architecture which permits meaningful choice that serves the creation of a storyworld. We do the work of choosing, and what we choose allows us to do the cognitive work—the pleasurable work—of making a storyworld.

Engagements: Exemplary text

Rosamund Davies' interactive fiction *Index of Love* (indexoflove.net) uses text, image, and video, as well as cues to guide users' choices, to create a complex set of pathways which, if one moves through it long enough and deep enough into the network structure, one is able to build a storyworld. This strikes me as an example of "emergent narrative," because we interact with the technology to create a good story, and our using of the technology to make the story in turn changes the architecture that makes the story possible: it is responsive. Using Ryan's typology, we might consider Davies' fiction as an example residing somewhere between external/ontological and external/exploratory interactivity (southwest on Ryan's interactivity "compass" [*Avatars* 121]). A user manipulates the site from outside of it—not taking on an avatar—but the manipulation generates a series of possible worlds within the wider textual world of the site.

The structure operates along several different axes; each axis functions as an entrypoint into the network. The further you go into the network, the more pathways open up. The architecture is recursive rather than linear. Making one's way through the story is rather like making one's way through a maze (Ryan, *Avatars* 104). The more pathways one takes, the more story is generated.

On the homepage for *Index of Love* (Figure 3.5), within a frame in the middle of the teal screen, along the y-axis, is a list of words: trace, token, vestige, fragment, keepsake, baggage, memento, souvenir, stain, residue, detritus, talisman. Different gestures or actions generate different results: hovering the mouse over words as opposed to clicking has different consequences and leads users down different pathways. Holding the mouse over each word calls up a photograph or a phrase. "Souvenir" generates "I remember." "Stain" calls up a photograph of a bed. The same elements occur every time, but the placement on the grid within the frame changes. Clicking on words brings up fragments of text or video. The frame also adjusts, and along the x-axis appear "where," "what," and "when." Clicking again takes

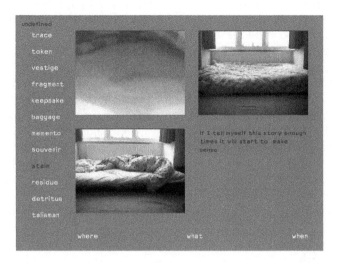

Figure 3.5 Screenshot of *indexoflove*. (© Rosamund Davies 2010.)

one of these words away and adds "why," so users have to go through several levels to get at any hint of motivation, cause and effect, etc. To begin, we are on the level of event or thing, setting, and time. In this way, Davies uses narrative logic and narratological elements to build her architecture and guide users' experiences.

Clicking on "where" provides setting: the bedroom where the sofa appears or a train station, and so on. All of the images appear as individual squares on the grid. Clicking on "what" creates another list along the y-axis, a list of things: "2 plastic bags," "a part of me," "sugar and spice," "my one and only." Clicking on "when" replaces whatever previous list had appeared along the y-axis, with a list of time-related items: "summertime," "tomorrow," "morning," "forever and ever," "once upon a time." It might be worth noting that while these items are all part of the semantic field of time/temporality, they are all different ways of thinking about time. Temporality, narrative time, is here marked as subjective; it is clearly of the realm of discourse. Above all, the network is organized in such a way as to have users continually choosing between the logic of narrative or the logic of memory or impression. I can choose what, where, when, why—or I can choose the image or phrase that serves as the fragment of whatever story is being told.

Here is one small example of moving through the network. Within each choice described here there were a number of choices that could have been made that were not.

1   Begin by clicking on "memento" on the homepage y-axis.
2   An image of a teddy bear holding a stuffed heart placed on a bed appears.
3   Hover over "where": an image of the bed itself appears.

4   Click on "where": an image of the same bed, unmade, appears. In this case, are we experiencing the passage of time? Cause and effect? Was someone in the bed and left?

5   As the image of the unmade bed appears, the word "residue" along the y-axis is highlighted, a shift from my original choice of "memento."

6   On the x-axis the choices are "what," "when," "why." I elect to defer discovery of motivation or explanation and so choose not "why" but "what." Hovering over "what" reveals: "You are the part of me that I/ wanted to be the part of me/that I never was that I no/longer believe in the part of me/that I tried to destroy."

7   Clicking on "what" brings me to the screen with the list of objects along the y-axis. I choose "the pulse of a vein." This brings me back to the homescreen and the word "trace" is now highlighted.

8   I decide to hover over "why" on the x-axis. A video appears of a man getting into an elevator and the door closing. I click "why," and the same video continues on a loop with the line "the time it takes for an intake of breath."

Were I to follow these paths for several more steps, and were I to proceed with the gap-filling natural to me as a consumer of narrative, I would be able to build a storyworld. Part of what Davies' interactive fiction depends on is our own expectations about love stories, narratives of breakups and loss, and so on. I might be interacting with the text via my computer and the architecture of Davies' website, but I am also interacting with the narrative via my own understanding and expectations of storytelling.

The problem with games

The debate around whether or not digital games are narratives highlights the challenge interactivity poses to storymaking and storytelling. One of the challenges in thinking about games as narrative is the difference between playability and tellability. The point of a narrative is to tell a good story, with everything happening in a particular fixed order; the point of a game is to be fun and challenging to play, and one plays until one wins. As Ken Perlin writes,

> Linear narrative forms and games are intended to serve very different purposes. The traditional goal of a linear narrative is to take you on a vicarious emotional journey, whereas the traditional goal of a game is to provide you with a succession of active challenges to master.
>
> (15)

Another challenge is the difference between player and character. In a narrative, as we have seen, character—figures who exist with subjectivity and legible mental states, who perform actions with goals and motivations and partake of events—is crucial. Games do sometimes have characters, as in the case of *Lara Croft*, but it is debatable whether such a "character" is really a *character*. Games that are based on graphic narratives or television shows might also have "characters," but in this context such characters would be versions of the familiar entities that are in place to facilitate the player's interaction with a recognizable storyworld; they would be objects to be manipulated by a player. Above all, it is the actions of the player which are important; it is the player who functions as the guiding consciousness. Finally, if a defining criterion for narrative is the presence, or at least a trace, of a narrator, this would seem to be a deal-breaker.

On the other hand, games can draw on certain narrative competencies. Narrative can become a way to live in a game world, and games that draw on existing familiar narratives can be a way to extend the storyworld. We might be able to claim, along the lines of Marie-Laure Ryan's work, that games might not always be narratives, but they can possess some qualities that look like narrative; they can have story-like stuff in them. Furthermore, narrative might play a role in how games achieve their own ludic, or playful or game-like, and aesthetic goals. The study of story might seek to account for everything from the way narrative frames gameplay, to the role script-writing plays in design, to the structuring effect of genre on the make-believe world. If we follow Ryan's lines towards a "functional ludi-narrativism [or idea that games and narratives can go together] that studies how the fictional world, realm of make-believe, relates to the playfield, space of agency" (*Avatars* 203), then we may be able to account for the multilayered nature of video games and answer some of our persistent questions about the relationship between narrative and interactivity.

As we have already seen, a number of discussions about interactivity and narrative focus on the extent to which readers have choices, the ways the architecture of the system facilitates those choices, and whether those choices are meaningful to understanding the story. Anastasia Salter has written about the capability of the Apple iPad to engender new forms of interactive storytelling that actually depend on the physicality of the user: the gesture (the "swipe") as a way into reading, as a mode of interaction with text. The interface itself becomes a platform whose "directness allows for conscious manipulation, and a hands-on approach to storytelling elements that can offer responsiveness well beyond the current model of triggering animation or sound" (Salter). In the case of narratives made for a device like an iPad, the potential for a blurring of the boundary between interactive fiction and game-playing is greatly increased.

Engagements: Exemplary text

The Simogo interactive fiction (IF)/game *Device 6* for iPad combines characteristics of a thriller novel with an exploratory quest game (Figure 3.6). The narrative proceeds like a thriller novel; it also proceeds like a puzzle game, with users completing tasks in order to unlock subsequent chapters. It is not interactive in the sense of an endless recursive feedback loop wherein users alter the architecture of the game and the narrative, which makes it, as I said before, residing along the internal/exploratory axes. However, it is interactive in the sense that Salter describes, where the IF depends on the physical gestures of the user; not only does it require users to swipe their way through the story or retrace steps, it also requires users to turn the iPad around as the protagonist moves through space (rotating the device to turn a corner, for instance). The requirement to solve puzzles—to uncover and input codes to unlock doors, thereby unlocking chapters—calls upon the kind of responsiveness Salter sees in IF. The game also exploits readers' desire to find out what happens next by putting obstacles in their path: if you don't know the code to unlock the door to the mysterious room, you don't get to move to the next chapter. It merges the desire to overcome challenges in play with the desire to know what happens at the end, suggesting these two very human impulses have something in common. *Device 6* combines an internal/exploratory interactivity with a highly self-conscious relationship to narrative and its own story. In fact, embedded within the game are references to the narrative functions themselves.

The story involves a protagonist, Anna (Player 248), who wakes up groggy in a castle. Over the course of six chapters, she realizes she is on an island in the middle of the ocean; there are two identical castles on the

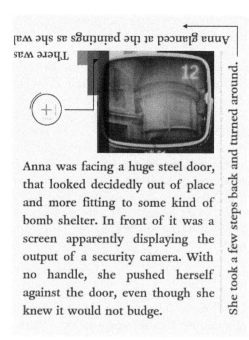

Anna was facing a huge steel door, that looked decidedly out of place and more fitting to some kind of bomb shelter. In front of it was a screen apparently displaying the output of a security camera. With no handle, she pushed herself against the door, even though she knew it would not budge.

Figure 3.6 Screenshot of *Device 6*. (© Simogo 2013.)

island, a theater, a cemetery, a lighthouse. She moves through the space of the text, finding clues that reveal that some kind of experiment has been taking place on the island and chasing a nefarious-seeming man in a bowler hat. A vast surveillance system monitors individuals as they move through the island solving clues in order to find, finally, the room that houses a giant computer called Device 6. Device 6 is at the bottom of all of the tricks and illusions; and, once the quester gets to it, all truth is revealed. The quester is called a Doubter until she gets to Device 6, at which point she realizes that the qualia of participating in the world of the island have been pro-grammed by Device 6 itself. She can either accept this, thereby ceasing to be a Doubter; or she can reject it and shut Device 6 down. Upon replaying the game, a user realizes that the cemetery Anna encounters is the Doubter Cemetery, and Doubters, upon attempting to shut Device 6 down, do not end well. Thus, in a sort of endless loop of narrative play, Anna is Player 248, but the user is also Anna in that the user is the one observing Anna through the story and participating in her movement through the story and the solving of the mystery. The user is also Player 249, and playing Device 6 is presented as a simulation, a beta version of a game called Device 6. The simulation is cast explicitly in narrative terms, with each "device" provided with "developer's notes" that detail flaws in generating qualia for the user, that document whether "input" of information (story details) results in the right "output" (user response). The narrative also plays with the classical notion that we must doubt fiction because it is very close to lies, and the truth of narrative lies within ourselves and our relationship to narrative devices, and here "devices" is entirely literalized.

Each site in the game is marked with a place name; directions are pro-vided with arrows or cardinal direction markers like north and west. Anna is embodied through the sound of footsteps heard through the iPad speaker, and her mental activity is captured in gray italicized font distinct from the black roman font of the telling on the white screen. Swiping not only moves Anna through the story but also reveals layers: "beneath" the layer of text, visible through "cut-aways" in the whitespace of the "page" are black and white images with which the user can interact. They heighten the surreal mood of the piece—a recurring motif is a "creepy doll" that Anna keeps encountering—and they also sometimes feature buttons the user can press to hear sounds, learn clues, and enter codes. An additional layer would be the developer's notes mentioned above, which clue the user into the possibil-ity that the narrative is itself a metanarrative, and these are the traces of an external manipulative narrative source (a "narrator"? an "author"?).

The conclusion of the story/game has Anna entering the room where she discovers Device 6. Her realization that she is herself a character in the story/game and the human subject of a beta test is described:

> It [the text on a wall monitor that is playing the story as Anna is "living" it and the user is playing it] continued to scroll constantly and

it seemed as if it were being written as Anna read it. She put her finger on the screen and swiped it to check the preceding text.

(Device 6)

The layers of narrative merge, as do the personae participating: we realize that Anna is our avatar, yet we also maintain a distance from the story-world as she maintains a separate identity as a character. The final moment showcases the way the story/game has manipulated time and perspective throughout the user experience. The story unfolds in real time: as we read and move Anna through the story, her actions are happening as we swipe. She can go backwards in space, back down hallways or back into rooms, but she cannot go backwards in time. Furthermore, we take on Anna's aspectual perspective: we see what she sees. The storyworld of *Device 6* depends on our physical interaction with Anna and the narrative space through movement and sound; it depends on our ability to navigate multiple layers of narrative breaking in on each other; it depends on our sharing of Anna's perspective, what she sees and what she knows.

The storyworld is disrupted at the end by our realization that we cannot escape the narrative, and that the narrative might be manipulating us in ways we cannot see, which might only be visible upon replaying. In the epilogue, Anna is close to escaping the island by boat. As the user swipes through the last set of screens, a series of images appear of the man in a bowler hat approaching from the end of the pier. The series of images appears in landscape over horizontal lines of text—close-ups indicating his approach nearer the camera and presumably Anna—and the text seems to be proceeding from Anna's perspective as though she does not see the approach of the man in the bowler hat. But we do. Each still image has him moving progressively closer to Anna/us, until the final image has him pointing a gun at us (*à la The Great Train Robbery*). A final swipe activates the sound of a gunshot and a splatter of bright red "blood" across the screen. The last words are "she felt the warmth of the sun." Has Anna been shot? Has she been shot after having that last thought? Is *that* her last thought? Does she escape and the user is the one who is shot, having somehow failed the test and remained a Doubter? Can a character have a thought simultaneous with being shot? *Device 6* bears replaying to answer these and other questions, and it exploits narrativity and interactivity in very compelling ways.

Adaptation

While discussion of adaptation has long been a part of narrative, after a quick overview of some important ideas about adaptation, I will focus my attention specifically on how adaptation occurs particularly in the digital context.

Adaptation can occur along three not necessarily mutually exclusive planes, and we need to think of it as both a process and as a product. Geoffrey Wagner defined these planes and processes in his early and important work on adaptation, and Linda Hutcheon expanded them. An adaptation might be *transposition*, moving from one genre or medium to another. It might be *commentary*, performing the adaptation in order to comment on the source text, or doing "a creative and an interpretive act of appropriation or salvaging" (Hutcheon 8). Finally, it might be an *analogue*, something that exists along-side the original but that can be enjoyed independently or in a relationship of "intertextuality" (Hutcheon 8; quoted material is from Hutcheon; non-quoted material is Wagner paraphrased from McFarlane 10–11).

Engagements: Exemplary text

The Bennett Miller film *Moneyball*, starring Brad Pitt as Oakland A's manager Billy Beane, is a good example of an adaptation that performs all three actions: transposition, commentary, and analogue. The film is an adaptation of Michael Lewis' extended nonfiction investigation into sabermetrics, or the ways man-agement in baseball uses statistics to build a team, rather than old-fashioned horse sense or the experience of scouts. The film is a transposition, in that it takes a book and turns it into a movie. It also makes a number of choices based on that initial move, like placing the charismatic and intelligent Beane at the heart of the movie rather than presenting a collection of episodes and players as Lewis does, as well as giving the Beane character a lot more of a backstory in order to render him sympathetic and explain his motives, something Lewis leaves out. The film is also a commentary, in that it uses the themes and motifs of inspirational sports movies in order to reflect on whether the ideas in Lewis' book are good for the sport of baseball or not, and what the changes in the sport mean for our culture at large. For instance, Pitt's Beane believes that sabermetrics is important for taking some of the romance out of baseball; a more objective approach means players will be chosen by rational measures rather than "for the love of the game." However, the climactic moment of the film is a game-winning home run hit by one of the underdog players who had been sitting out most of the season. Of course, the A's are losing, and if they lose this game they lose their chance at the playoffs and at the record for winningest team. In a burst of glory and stirring music right out the inspirational sports movie playbook, the underdog hits the ball out of the park. As Pitt's Beane says, "How can you not be romantic about baseball?" For all of the objectivity of sabermetrics and for all of the ways it is part of our increasingly data-driven society, there is still a certain cultural romance with the sport of baseball that our films reflect, and *Moneyball*, counter to its source text, participates in that. Finally, *Moneyball* is an analogue: like so many other baseball movies, it is about much more than baseball, and like so many other adaptations, it ignores a lot of its source material in order to tell a good story that stands on its own.

At least two challenges arise when talking about adaptation. First, we are often maneuvering between word and image, in the case of book to film adaptation, or the transformation of a novel into a graphic narrative. Even the move from graphic narrative to film can be tricky, as we transmediate from still to movie image. As Jack Boozer puts it:

> The versatility of the visual and sound palette available to screenwriters and filmmakers . . . can provide a wealth of alternative ways to convey the intricacies of the source text, and therefore disobliges a simplistic comparative cataloging across the two media.
>
> (9)

Second, we often privilege the (often literary) source text. A symptom of this privileging is what is called "fidelity discourse," wherein an evaluation of an adaptation rests solely on whether the cinematic "derivation" did justice to the original literary work. In order to consider adaptation as a more robust process, we need to pay attention to precisely the kinds of multimodal capabilities upon which film and digital can draw.

A great deal of work on adaptation until recently has focused on book to film, beginning with George Bluestone's *Novels into Film*, published in 1957, and this has informed thinking on adaptation. Linda Hutcheon's theory of adaptation has broadened the framework to account for digital products, as well as products that depend on the use of the body and physical action, like games and amusement park rides. She argues for reading adaptations "laterally," "challenging the authority of any notion of priority": what if we read the adaptation and the "original" "out of order" (xiii)? This subversion of authority around a "source" or "privileged" text will very much come into play when we turn to Robert Berry's comic book adaptation of James Joyce's *Ulysses*, *Ulysses "Seen."*

Hutcheon also calls upon us to think about these relationships not as "adaptations" but as "remediations": a kind of re-seeing through shift in media. We should embrace the "oscillation" among texts, as well as the multiple levels of engagement—telling, showing, and interacting—made possible (xv). Furthermore, she notes the implications remediation has for how a story is told: "Pacing can be transformed, time compressed or expanded. Shifts in the focalization or point of view of the adapted story may lead to major differences" (11). One instance might be the film adaptation of Jon Krakauer's work of long-form reportage, *Into the Wild*. The book tells the story of Chris McCandless, a young man who ventured into the Alaskan wilderness and died. The film, starring Emile Hirsch and Jena Malone (as McCandless's sister), compresses the story (removing many passages consisting of Krakauer recalling his own foolhardy wilderness adventures) in order to focus on McCandless, but it also makes the somewhat startling move of having large portions of the film narrated by Malone in voice-over. This alters the story by shifting the focus away from the "man alone in the wilderness" and foregrounding the family he left behind. (It also significantly de-masculinizes the telling by making a young woman's voice, rather than the macho Krakauer's authorial voice, more dominant.) Adaptation can actually alter the way a story is told, which then can in turn change things like theme and tone.

These transmedial alterations and the potential they have for new thinking about narrative are my reason for attending to adaptation and digital culture. I see the dramatic changes in technology over the last decade playing a significant role in how users—readers, viewers, audience members —make and engage with stories. Due to increased access to tools of storymaking and a wider network with which to share those tools and their results, and due to our heightened sensitivity to the nature of interactivity in storymaking and narrative consumption—and adaptation is, in many ways, a form of interactivity—it seems that the rise in new thinking about adaptation is tied very much to digital culture. Furthermore, these examples are easily available to any reader who wishes to engage—and engaging with them, as a means of generating an evergreen and continual process, is part of the point of adaptation itself. Our digital adaptations are continually adapting, and with them our reading.

Engagements: Exemplary text

In thinking through the nature of Robert Berry's digital comics adaptation of James Joyce's *Ulysses*, *Ulysses "Seen,"* I might suggest it operates along all three planes described above: it is a *transposition*, in that it takes Joyce's novel and translates it into the comics medium; it is a *commentary*, in that it functions on the level of interpretation particularly in illuminating specific narrative strategies when read alongside Joyce's novel; and it is *analogue*, in that one can enjoy the comic on its own without putting it in relation to the novel.

Berry's artistic moves in the adaptation of the "Calypso" episode (the fourth in the novel, and the second released by Berry's studio Throwaway Horse), especially in his engagement with the conventions of romance comics, coupled with his representation of multiple perspectives and voices, all dramatically highlight Joyce's concerns with intimacy, empathy, and the question of how we know and love. To illustrate, I've chosen a panel from "Calypso": it depicts Bloom returning to his house at 7 Eccles Street after buying a kidney for breakfast (Figure 3.7). It is still early in the novel, and early in Bloom's day, before he commences his wandering around Dublin in order to avoid being at home while his wife partakes in an adulterous tryst in their marital bed.

Berry created a visual vocabulary for dealing with what Hugh Kenner calls "Joyce's voices." In the more realistic-seeming early Bloom chapters of *Ulysses*, there are usually only two "voices" or perspectives, at work: Bloom's interior monologue and the narrator. Sometimes we shift from one to the other in mid-paragraph—even mid-sentence—and so two different visual/textual styles are required. The yellow text box is the narrator, while the thought balloon is Bloom. (Here we do have one speech balloon; this is Molly, calling from off-screen. There is also the "jingle" sound effect, representing the quoits of the Blooms' bed, a sound that will linger in

Figure 3.7 Screenshot of *Ulysses "Seen."* (© Robert Berry 2011.)

Bloom's mind throughout the day as he tries not to imagine his wife in bed with another man.)

This trio of panels generates movement and drama resonant of romance comics: the betrayed husband/hero enters his home to see it has already been violated by the presence of another man. But the splitting of the scene with the clearly defined borderless gutters mirrors the splitting of Bloom's self. The action is drawn out, almost in slow motion, over time and space, while the character himself in that time and space is fragmented. This is echoed by other visual elements on the page. The clear delineation between text box/narrator and thought balloon/Bloom represents the protagonist's separateness from his own experience in moments of sexual anxiety and trauma. Bloom has lost control of the story. His participation, his processing—his making a story of his own life—is reduced to fragmentary thoughts that he cannot quite complete. Furthermore, we do not see Bloom's face. Berry uses the drawing of the face throughout the episode very strategically in ways that speak back to Joyce's own questions about intimacy and knowledge. Bloom's face is obscured, off-screen, or turned away in all three panels. Our access to him is limited, and so is our knowledge of his emotional life.

In addition to the flexibility afforded the adaptation by the comics mode and the digital medium, Berry also takes advantage of the collaborative possibility of the digital space by offering a readers' guide upon which users can comment through a blog-like interface. This taps into an already-existing community of Joyce readers, and creates the potential for a new form of community dedicated to re-envisioning the novel.

Community

Several of the examples we have considered here so far have already provided an opportunity to consider how digital culture, digital media, and transmedial storytelling have transformed our sense of the relationship between narrative and community. As Page and Thomas write, "The ability to harness the textual resources and networking capacities of the World Wide Web has been exploited by a proliferation of storytelling communities" (2). We saw the ways readers engage with one another through the social media site GoodReads, sharing recommendations, reviews (some quite extensive), and reading habits. YouTube, one of the first sites to allow users to share and comment upon content (specifically video), has become a place to engage with narrative, not only through user-made media like short films and adaptations in the form of mashups, but also in the form of book trailers and other transmedial extensions, as we saw with *This Is Not My Hat*. Finally, we considered how user interaction and the building of community is integral to the design and purpose of *Ulysses "Seen,"* where readers collaborate with one another to create a community dedicated to crowdsourcing interpretations and annotations of Joyce's notoriously multilayered novel. The ability to create many stacks of meaning and engagement in the digital context is well-suited to reading Joyce's work in collaborative ways. Similar endeavors have emerged around similarly complex texts like David Foster Wallace's novel *Infinite Jest* and Junot Diaz's *The Brief Wondrous Life of Oscar Wao*, both of which have wikis devoted to navigating their labyrinthine and allusive worlds.

In some senses, all of these instances replicate the experience of a book discussion group, like something one might participate in with one's friends or at the local library. Book groups dedicated to deciphering James Joyce's last novel *Finnegans Wake* have been meeting for decades. (In some cases, like the group in Boston, individual groups have been meeting continuously for years.) But narrating itself has also become a public or interactive activity, a social and communal practice. In her work on blogging, Ruth Page says we need to think about how the ways readers can interact with narratives online should change how we study stories: we have to think about giving up "control of the text" ("Blogging" 223). The study of digital narratives thus depends on a culturally informed, real-world way of thinking about reading, writing, and interacting with texts. It also, to echo one of Page and Thomas' earlier points, calls upon us to find a way to "read" authenticity and identity. We can look at how digital storytelling, and digital culture more broadly, provides a "way of constructing a more or less coherent personal identity cut to the exact measure of the personal cultural obsessions we assemble in our digital archives" (Collins 654). Digital tools facilitate the process of making our stories our own, as well as of sharing that meaning-making.

Engagements: Exemplary text

The Center for Digital Storytelling (storycenter.org) is an important place for storymaking and community-building around narrative. The center runs workshops for people interested in learning how to do digital storytelling, and in addition to featuring individual stories on their website, they curate a list of stories by theme: health, cancer, adoption, refugees, education, place, activism, youth, identify, family, fathers, mothers. The list captures digital storytelling's concern with identity, community, and the ways storymaking can have meaningful social impact. One short piece, a little over a minute long, is called "Pete's Grill," by Kyle Little. Like many examples of digital storytelling, it is told from a first-person perspective. It combines the voice-over of a young man with a series of shifting images. The images are photographs, and they appear to be cut into pieces and reassembled in a collage style over a black background, but the pieces are not always all accounted for; there are gaps in the reassemblage. The first screen has pieces of photographs, slices taken from different images (building fronts, cars, people walking down a street in a working-class neighborhood) that fill in to compromise the entire screen. After that, black gaps are left. For instance, when the narrator speaks of the long counter of the diner "embracing" him, a vertical slice of a photograph of a counter appears perpendicular to a long horizontal slice (Figure 3.8). A sliver of the image of a bowl is visible in the horizontal slice, and another shot of a bowl surrounded by ketchup squeeze bottles and small metal milk pitchers for coffee appears to fill in the gestalt-like arrangement. The rest of the screen is black.

These disjointed images seem to do the work of memory or impression, while the narrator fills in details about his life in order to convey the significance of Pete's as imagined place. The final image is a fully assembled, full screen image of Pete's Grill, presented after the final line is spoken: "Just another customer, another worrier, another empty stomach, looking for breakfast." This image holds the screen in a "pregnant moment" for three seconds. The images do the work of filling in setting and elements like class, while the voice-over narration provides access to character and the mental work devoted to imagining place on the part of the narrator. It is debatable whether an artifact like "Pete's Grill" lends itself to the creation of a storyworld on the part of the viewer/listener. A viewer/listener of a particularly receptive nature, one possessed of a mindset geared towards empathy, may very well be able to conjure a storyworld from "Pete's Grill": we learn about the narrator's parents' divorce and get hints of his difficulty being a working-class young man at university. We are provided with details of sensory experience, glimpses of faces. "Pete's Grill" is not necessarily a complete narrative, but does show important elements of story.

Figure 3.8 Screenshot of "Pete's Grill." (Kyle Little, available at the Center for Digital Storytelling channel on YouTube, 2012.)

"Pete's Grill" is also an instance of the ways storymaking and digital culture combine to create community and collective story-sharing. The microblogging platform Twitter is another instance, and an interesting one. The 140-character limit that is the defining feature of Twitter has led many to suggest that it is not suitable for storytelling, unless one's idea of story is to let the world know what your cat ate for breakfast. (The scholar of digital media Mark Sample has a long-running gag on his own feed parodying Twitter nay-sayers who claim this is all the social media site is good for.) Yet storytellers have found ways to exploit the Twitter feed and its ability to manipulate the pacing of both reading time and discourse time: what if you only tweet one 140-character segment of a story a day, as Jennifer Egan did with her 8,500-word story "Black Box." Twitter also allows users to embed images and video, and creates the potential for readers to interact with story through replying and retweeting.

Engagements: Exemplary text

John Fugelsang used Twitter to tell the story of his parents' courtship and marriage; the piece was then reported by Claire O'Neill on NPR's *Morning Edition* and turned into a digital narrative (with sound and video) by the NPR visuals app team, called "Look At This: A Brother And Sister in Love." In the original piece, Fugelsang exploits the 140-character limit of Twitter to evoke emotional response through minimalism and the interplay of words and image, in this case family photographs. The creation of narrative demands selection and ordering, something Twitter as a platform is a uniquely suited to do. In order to tell the story and engage readers emotionally, Fugelsang had to choose the right details to convey character and significance of event: in this case, his parents falling in love with each other and leaving their respective religious orders to get married, and then living a long and happy life together until his father died in 2010. Additionally, the parceling out of details over the course of a 26-tweet feed allows for the generation of suspense and the manipulation of time through compression. At last, even perspective is activated through the storytelling, as Fugelsang's point of view is made clear; he is, in fact, an outsider to his parents' lives and love, retracing their path to each other and watching them grow old together. To achieve the level of aesthetic satisfaction using Twitter that Fugelsang is able to do here is rare, but it is an instance of digital storytelling that deploys a surprising choice of platform in effective ways.

Digital storytelling has changed the way we make and read stories. Stories remain of the highest importance to how we are human, to how we relate to other human beings, to how we make meaning of the world. The rise of digital culture has had a profound impact on our world and the stories we tell about it, which means it should have a profound impact on the study of what it means to be human. In a compelling call that serves to lead us into our final chapter, Jim Collins writes:

> If "narrative theory" is to become relevant again in the twenty-first century, it has to account for how narrative texts—whether they be novels, films, television programs, or web series—are shaped by how we acquire, curate, and "play" them across ever more diversified formats within the devices which are the repositories of all our cultural stuff. When texts become files, when the page becomes a screen, when the book becomes a portable multimedia library and at the same time a portal to reading communities that make the pleasures of narrative as robustly social as they are intensely solitary, then we have to account for the changing use values of narrativity.
> (641)

Such changes mean a rethinking of world-building through story, a redefinition of community, a new understanding of authority. Narrative studies no longer focuses only on structures or storyworlds; it is the study of collaborative world-building among bodies of texts and communities of readers. In the next and final chapter, we will take a look at the ethical implications of narrative, and why for this, and other reasons, narrative theory remains an essential pursuit and a necessary tool in our time.

Works cited

Bluestone, George. *Novels into Film*. Berkeley: U of California P, 1957. Print.

Boozer, Jack, ed. *Authorship in Film Adaptation: Literature to Screenplay to Film*. Austin: U of Texas P, 2002. Print.

Bower, Anne. "Bound Together: Recipes, Lives, Stories, and Readings." *Recipes for Reading: Community Cookbooks, Stories, Histories*. Amherst: U of Massachusetts P, 1997. 1–14. Print.

Brown, Bill. "Thing Theory." *Critical Inquiry* 28 (2001): 1–22. Print.

Chatman, Seymour. "What Novels Can Do That Films Can't (and Vice Versa)." *On Narrative*. Ed. W. J. T. Mitchell. Chicago: U of Chicago P, 1980. 117–136. Print.

Cohn, Dorrit. *The Distinction of Fiction*. Baltimore, MD: Johns Hopkins UP, 1999. Print.

Collins, Jim. "The Use Values of Narrativity in Digital Cultures." *New Literary History* 44 (2013): 639–660. Print.

Fludernik, Monika. "New Wine in Old Bottles? Voice, Focalization, and New Writing." *New Literary History* 32 (2001): 619–638. Print.

Genette, Gérard. *Paratexts: Thresholds of Interpretation*. Trans. Jane Lewin. New York: Cambridge UP, 1997. Print.

Hatfield, Charles. *Alternative Comics: An Emerging Literature*. Jackson: UP of Mississippi, 2005. Print.

Horstkotte, Silke and Nancy Pedri. "Focalization in Graphic Narrative." *Narrative* 19 (2011): 330–357. Print.

Hutcheon, Linda. *A Theory of Adaptation*. New York: Routledge, 2012. Print.

Jahn, Manfred. "Windows of Focalization: Deconstructing and Reconstructing a Narratological Concept." *Style* 30 (1996): 241–267. Print.

Jenkins, Henry. "Game Design as Narrative Architecture." *First Person: New Media as Story, Performance, and Game*. Ed. Noah Wardrip-Fruin and Pat Harrigan. Cambridge, MA: MIT P, 2004. 118–131. Print.

Kenner, Hugh. *Joyce's Voices*. Berkeley: U of California P, 1978. Print.

McCloud, Scott. *Understanding Comics: The Invisible Art*. Northampton, MA: Tundra, 1993. Print.

McFarlane, Brian. *Novel to Film: An Introduction to the Theory of Adaptation*. New York: Oxford UP, 1996. Print.

Mikkonen, Kai. "Presenting Minds in Graphic Narratives." *Partial Answers* 6 (2008): 301–321. Print.

Mittell, Jason. "Strategies of Storytelling on Transmedia Television." *Storyworlds Across Media*. Ed. Marie-Laure Ryan and Jan-Noël Thon. Lincoln: U of Nebraska P, 2014. 253–277. Print.

Page, Ruth. "Blogging on the Body: Gender and Narrative." *New Narratives: Stories and Storytelling in the Digital Age*. Ed. Ruth Page and Bronwen Thomas. Lincoln: U of Nebraska P, 2011. 220–238. Print.

Page, Ruth and Bronwen Thomas. "Introduction." *New Narratives: Stories and Storytelling in the Digital Age*. Ed. Ruth Page and Bronwen Thomas. Lincoln: U of Nebraska P, 2011. 1–16. Print.

Perlin, Ken. "Can There Be a Form between a Game and a Story?" *First Person: New Media as Story, Performance, and Game*. Ed. Noah Wardrip-Fruin and Pat Harrigan. Cambridge: MIT P, 2004. 12–18. Print.

Ryan, Marie-Laure. *Avatars of Story: Narrative Modes in Old and New Media*. Minneapolis: U of Minnesota P, 2006. Print.

——. "Digital Media." *Narrative Across Media: The Languages of Storytelling*. Ed. Marie-Laure Ryan. Lincoln: U of Nebraska P, 2004. 329–337. Print.

——. Introduction. *Narrative Across Media: The Languages of Storytelling*. Ed. Marie-Laure Ryan. Lincoln: U of Nebraska P, 2004. 1–33. Print.

——. "On the Theoretical Foundations of Transmedial Narratology." *Narratology Beyond Literary Criticism: Mediality, Disciplinarity*. Ed. Jan Christoph Meister. Berlin: De Gruyter, 2005. 1–23. Print.

Salter, Anastasia. "Convergent Devices, Dissonant Genres: Tracking the 'Future' of Electronic Literature on the iPad." *electronic book review* (January 2015). Web. 11 April 2015.

Talon, Durwin and Guin Thompson. "Using Panels to Shape Visual Storytelling: Organizing Flow in the Graphic Narrative." *The International Journal of the Book* 7 (2010): 21–36. Print.

Thon, Jan-Noël. "Subjectivity Across Media: On Transmedial Strategies of Subjective Representation in Contemporary Feature Films, Graphic Novels, and Computer Games." *Storyworlds Across Media*. Ed. Marie-Laure Ryan and Jan-Noël Thon. Lincoln: U of Nebraska P, 2014. 67–102. Print.

——. "Toward a Transmedial Narratology: On Narrators in Contemporary Graphic Novels, Feature Films, and Computer Games." *Beyond Classical Narration: Transmedial and Unnatural Challenges*. Ed. Jan Alber and Per Krogh Hansen. Berlin: De Gruyter, 2014. 25–56. Print.

Toolan, Michael. "Electronic Multimodal Narratives and Literary Form." *New Perspectives on Narrative and Multimodality*. Ed. Ruth Page. New York: Routledge, 2010. 127–141. Print.

Wagner, Geoffrey. *The Novel and the Cinema*. Plainsboro, NJ: Associated UP, 1975. Print.

Walsh, Richard. "Emergent Narrative in Interactive Media." *Narrative* 19 (2011): 73–85. Print.

Warhol, Robyn. "The Space Between: A Narrative Approach to Alison Bechdel's *Fun Home*." *College Literature* 38 (2011): 1–20. Print.

Exemplary texts

2001: A Space Odyssey. Dir. Stanley Kubrick. Perf. Keir Dullea and Gary Lockwood. MGM, 1968. Film.

Argo. Dir. Ben Affleck. Perf. Ben Affleck, Alan Arkin, Bryan Cranston, John Goodman. Warner Bros., 2012. Film.

Bechdel, Alison. *Fun Home*. New York: Mariner, 2007. Print.

Benchley, Peter. *Jaws*. New York: Ballantine Books, 2013. Print.

Berry, Robert. *Ulysses "Seen."* 2011. Web. 11 April 2015.

Blue Velvet. Dir. David Lynch. Perf. Kyle MacLachlan and Isabella Rossellini. MGM, 1986. Film.

Candlewick Press. *This Is Not My Hat*. YouTube. 12 March 2013. Web. 11 April 2015.

Civilization. Created by Sid Meier. MicroProse. 16 December 1991. Video game.

Cunningham, Michael. *The Hours*. New York: Picador, 2000. Print.

Davies, Rosamund. *Index of Love*. 2010. Web. 11 April 2015.

Device 6. Created by Simon Flesser. Simogo. 17 October 2013. Video game.

Eraserhead. Dir. David Lynch. Perf. Jack Nance and Charlotte Stewart. Libra Films, 1977. Film.

Fitzgerald, F. Scott. *The Great Gatsby*. New York: Scribner, 2004. Print.

Fowler, Bo. *Skepticism, Inc*. New York: Bloomsbury, 2000. Print.

Fugelsang, John (JohnFugelsang). "Via @nprnews: A Brother and Sister Get Married (And Later, Their Son Tweets It)." 12 July 2014, 9:40 p.m. Tweet.

Funny People. Dir. Judd Apatow. Perf. Adam Sandler, Seth Rogen, Leslie Mann. Universal, 2009. Film.

Goodfellas. Dir. Martin Scorsese. Perf. Ray Liotta, Robert DeNiro, Joe Pesci. Warner Bros., 1990. Film.

The Great Gatsby. Dir. Baz Luhrmann. Perf. Leonardo DiCaprio and Carey Mulligan. Warner Bros, 2013. Film.

The Hours. Dir. Stephen Daldry. Perf. Meryl Streep, Nicole Kidman, Julianne Moore. Paramount, 2002. Film.

The Ice Storm. Dir. Ang Lee. Perf. Kevin Kline, Joan Allen, Sigourney Weaver. Fox Searchlight, 1998. Film.

Into the Wild. Dir. Sean Penn. Perf. Emile Hirsch, Jena Malone, William Hurt, Marcia Gay Harden. Paramount, 2007. Film.

Jackson, Sharyn, Donnelle Eller, Amalie Nash, Mitch Gelman. "Harvest of Change." *Des Moines Register*. 2014. Web. 11 April 2015.

Jaws. Dir. Steven Spielberg. Perf. Roy Scheider, Richard Dreyfus, Robert Shaw. Universal, 1975. Film.

Joyce, James. *Ulysses*. New York: Vintage, 1986. Print.

Joyce, Michael. *afternoon*. New York: Norton, 1987. Print/Web.

Klassen, Jon. *This Is Not My Hat*. Somerville, MA: Candlewick Press, 2012. Print.

Knisley, Lucy. *Relish: My Life in the Kitchen*. New York: First Second, 2013. Print.

Krakauer, Jon. *Into the Wild*. New York: Random House, 1997. Print.

Lewis, Michael. *Moneyball: The Art of Winning an Unfair Game*. New York: Norton, 2004. Print.

Little, Kyle. "Pete's Grill." Center for Digital Storytelling. YouTube. 8 November 2012. Web. 11 April. 2015.

Lynch, Jennifer. *The Secret Diary of Laura Palmer*. New York: Pocket Books, 1990. Print.

Moneyball. Dir. Bennett Miller. Perf. Brad Pitt, Jonah Hill, Philip Seymour Hoffman. Sony, 2011. Film.

Moody, Rick. *The Ice Storm*. Boston: Back Bay Books, 2002. Print.

NPR Visuals Team. "Look At This: A Brother And Sister In Love." 13 February 2015. Web. 11 April 2015.

O Brother, Where Art Thou? Dir. Joel and Ethan Coen. Perf. George Clooney, John Turturro, Tim Blake Nelson. Touchstone, 2001. Film.

O'Neill, Claire. "A Brother And Sister Get Married (And Later, Their Son Tweets It)." *NPR*. 14 February 2012. Web. 11 April 2015.

Reichl, Ruth. *Tender at the Bone*. New York: Random House, 1998. Print.

Satrapi, Marjane. *The Complete Persepolis*. New York: Pantheon, 2007. Print.

Shapton, Leann. *Important Artifacts and Personal Property from the Collection of Lenore Doolan and Harold Morris, Including Books, Street Fashion, and Jewelry*. New York: Sarah Crichton Books, 2009. Print.

Silver Linings Playbook. Dir. David O. Russell. Perf. Bradley Cooper and Jennifer Lawrence. Weinstein Company, 2012. Film.

The Sims. Created by Will Wright. The Sims Studio. First release: 4 February 2000. Latest release: 31 March 2015. Video game.

Spiegelman, Art. *The Complete Maus*. New York: Pantheon, 1996. Print.

Super Mario Bros. Created by Shigeru Miyamoto. Nintendo. 13 September 1985. Video game.

Tennyson, Alfred, Lord. *In Memoriam*. New York: W.W. Norton, 2003. Print.

Tongues Untied. Dir. Marlon Riggs. Perf. Marlon Riggs, Brian Freeman, Essex Hemphill. Frameline, 1989. Film.

The Tree of Life. Dir. Terrence Malick. Perf. Brad Pitt, Sean Penn, Jessica Chastain. Fox Searchlight, 2011. Film.

Twin Peaks. Prod. David Lynch and Mark Frost. Perf. Kyle MacLachlan, Michael Ontkean, Lara Flynn Boyle, Sherilyn Fenn, Sheryl Lee. CBS Television, 1990–1991. Television series.

Twin Peaks: Fire Walk With Me. Dir. David Lynch. Perf. Sheryl Lee and Ray Wise. New Line, 1992. Film.

Ware, Chris. *Jimmy Corrigan; Or, The Smartest Kid On Earth*. New York: Pantheon, 2003. Print.

Woolf, Virginia. *Mrs. Dalloway*. New York: Harcourt Brace Jovanovich, 1990. Print.

——. *A Room of One's Own*. New York: Mariner Books, 2005. Print.

Recommended further reading

Aarseth, Espen J. *Cybertext: Perspectives on Ergodic Literature*. Baltimore, MD: Johns Hopkins UP, 1997. Print.

Bordwell, David. *Narration in Fiction Film*. Madison: U of Wisconsin P, 1985. Print.

Landow, George. *Hypertext 2.0: The Convergence of Contemporary Critical Theory and Technology*. Baltimore, MD: Johns Hopkins UP, 1997. Print.

Metz, Christian. *Film Language: A Semiotics of Cinema*. New York: Oxford UP, 1974. Print.

Mittell, Jason. *Complex TV: The Poetics of Contemporary Television Storytelling*. New York: NYU P, 2015. Print.

Moretti, Franco. *Graphs, Maps, Trees: Abstract Models for Literary History*. London: Verso, 2007. Print.

Murray, Janet. *Hamlet on the Holodeck: The Future of Narrative in Cyberspace*. New York: Free Press, 1997. Print.

Engagements: Interview with Anastasia Salter

Anastasia Salter is an assistant professor of Digital Media at the University of Central Florida. She is the author of *What is Your Quest? From Adventure Games to Interactive Books* (University of Iowa Press, 2014) and co-author of *Flash: Building the Interactive Web* (MIT Press, 2014). Her work engages with digital narratives and electronic literature.

How would you describe your approach to narrative studies and/or narrative theory?

My approach to narrative studies is grounded in an examination of media and platform. Platform studies, as coined by Nick Montfort and Ian Bogost, allows for the consideration of a media artifact from the level of audience and reception all the way down to layers of code, architecture, distribution networks, and hardware. As most of what I study are works of digital media, these platforms can be diverse and play a powerful role in what types of digital narratives we experience. Questions of platforms also drive who gets to participate in shaping narrative, and whose voices get heard and amplified. I believe that considering these underlying forces is essential to understanding narrative's role within the networks that shape our communities of discourse.

Describe your most recent project. What prompted your interest?
What were you hoping to achieve? What questions or ideas
in the field do you see it responding to?

My most recent project is a multimodal study of *Alice's Adventures in Wonderland* (forthcoming in *Kairos* 19.2) in which I adopted approaches of critical making and digital media to explore how Alice's journey down the rabbit hole thrives as a popular metaphor for our understanding and experience of media. This project is fundamentally playful scholarship and remediates the text of Alice throughout each piece. Working with narrative in this hands-on way is very different from my previous practice, which primarily consisted of traditional academic monographs and articles. With it, I hope to explore some of the potential for solo digital engagement with text that echoes some of the conventions of scholarly humanist study. Through it, I hope to make visible the process of moving through remediated concepts.

What scholars and texts have influenced your approach?

I am strongly influenced by the field of electronic literature, with recent projects such as Dene Grigar and Stuart Moulthrop's "Pathfinders" collaboration pushing through some of the difficulties in preserving, documenting, and analyzing digital works that might otherwise be rendered inaccessible by changing platforms and technologies. Within the field of electronic literature, conversations continually involve both creators and scholars, thus offering the potential for examinations of the impact of platforms and works from a range of perspectives. I am currently working with a team of curators on the next volume of the Electronic Literature Collection, a project through which we hope to explore many layers of digital narrative authorship and potential.

What do you see as big questions confronting the field?
Where's the cutting edge? What are the trends?

Defining the sphere of narrative studies and wrestling with the apparent interventions brought on by technology and remediation is one of the challenges confronting this field now. While the legacy of connections and interwoven discourse with interactive media is ongoing, from the ludology versus narratology debates in game studies to the intersection with electronic literature and the inclusion of film and media studies in some literature programs, engaging with narratives on different platforms can provide challenges in finding common terms of discourse and avoiding the oversimplification of so-called new media through over-applying the lens of another media's study. With so many works presenting adaptations, remediations, and translations that morph from one context to another, the opportunity to chart and explore these intersections is only growing.

What are you working on next?

My next project is a collaboration with Bridget Blodgett (University of Baltimore). We are examining geek culture and particularly geek-driven popular narratives with attention to the construction of narratives of marginalization and victimhood. The last decade has seen a rise in the number of misogynist movements in popular culture surrounding narrative media spaces like games, comic books, and even science fiction and fantasy. We want to consider how the archetypes within these media build on similar tropes and provide a blueprint that has proven harmful to attempts to bring greater inclusion and representation to their narratives.

Engagements: Interview with Leah Anderst

Leah Anderst is Assistant Professor of English at Queensborough Community College, CUNY. She earned her PhD in Comparative Literature from the CUNY Graduate Center, and her research interests include film studies, narrative theory, autobiography, and writing pedagogy. Her articles have been published in *Narrative, a/b:Auto/Biography Studies, Senses of Cinema,* and *Orbis Litterarum,* and her edited volume of essays, *The Films of Eric Rohmer: French New Wave to Old Master,* was published in 2014.

How would you describe your approach to narrative studies and/or narrative theory?

I have a strong interest in film and other visual media, so much of my approach to narrative studies has been characterized by analyzing visual media using some of the tools, terminologies, and methods that scholars of narrative studies initially devised in relation to prose fiction.

During my graduate coursework and while writing my dissertation, I was fascinated by instances of free indirect narration as a way to represent the thoughts of characters in certain novels by Jane Austen, Gustave Flaubert, and Henry James, for example, and I began to notice in films, cinematic devices that seemed to mirror the effects of free indirect narration in prose. I built my dissertation research around comparing the various forms of free indirect narration across a variety of novels and films, including *Hiroshima mon amour* and *Memories of Underdevelopment.* So in some ways, my approach is marked by translation. I translate narrative theory's tools to the study of visual media.

Describe your most recent project. What prompted your interest? What were you hoping to achieve? What questions or ideas in the field do you see it responding to?

My most recent projects continue this translational approach. In two articles, I have looked at autobiographical narratives in film, in prose, and in graphic narrative. I once again make use of the tools of narrative studies and apply them to autobiography and to documentary film. Initially, this interest was not born from questions I encountered by reading scholarship; this interest grew from teaching.

In the fall of 2010, I designed a freshman writing course with a thematic focus on life narratives. I had had some success teaching autobiography and personal essays here and there in the past, so for this particular course, I decided to dedicate all of the readings and assignments to this one theme. I structured the units and writing tasks around life narratives across various genres and time periods. The students wrote about autobiographical documentaries, about some of the earliest autobiographical texts in the western tradition, and about graphic memoirs. When I teach writing, I complete many of the written assignments along with my students, especially those that take place during class time, and that semester, I found myself writing a good deal about autobiography both in and outside of the class. I found myself drawing connections between what I was doing with my students and what I had done while working on my dissertation, without suspecting that those two areas would overlap.

The first work I produced from this interest is an article called "'I've spent a lot of time looking at these images': The "Viewing I" in Contemporary Autobiographical Film" which was published in *a/b: Auto/biography Studies*. In this essay, I look at three autobiographical documentaries, Agnès Varda's *The Beaches of Agnès* (2008), Ross McElwee's *Time Indefinite* (1993), and Jonathan Caouette's *Tarnation* (2003) to argue for and exemplify an additional "I" of autobiographical narration: what I call the "viewing I."

Autobiographical narration is generally broken down into two I's: the "narrating I" and the "experiencing I" (that last one is sometimes called the "narrated I"). My goal in this piece was to show how these three films incorporate the act of viewing, viewing family photographs and family home movies in particular, into the process of autobiographical narration. These three autobiographical documentarians narrate themselves in part through their engagements with their personal or familial visual archive.

Another recent article was prompted by the reading I had been doing connected to the article on autobiographical film as well as by articles I kept encountering in mainstream publications like *The New York Times* and on social media, articles that described the positive benefits novel reading have on us. Because reading novels exercises our empathy muscle, many of these articles suggested, reading them will make us better managers or better friends. While perhaps a boon for literature departments facing pressure to defend themselves, these kinds of articles always raised my skepticism. From these articles I came to Suzanne Keen's *Empathy and the Novel*, an important study that works in part to dampen the thinking that narrative empathy experienced through reading novels makes us better, more philanthropically minded people. Keen's book is a welcomed antidote to that mantra.

An important detail in her book for me, though, was the idea that narrative empathy is connected to a work's fictionality. So, nonfiction narratives, including autobiographies, are excluded from the discussion of narrative empathy. And this exclusion is not Keen's alone; many others, including those many popular articles, focus solely on fiction. In an article called "Feeling with Real Others: Narrative Empathy in the Autobiographies of Doris Lessing and Alison Bechdel," which will be published in *Narrative*, I sought to examine the ways that Lessing's autobiography, *Under My Skin*, and Bechdel's graphic memoir, *Fun Home*, present explicit pathways for the empathetic engagement of their readers.

What scholars and texts have influenced your approach?

I've been influenced by a number of narrative theorists, most particularly by those focused on voice and consciousness in narrative. The work of writers like Bakhtin, Ann Banfield, Leo Bersani, Dorrit Cohn, and Gérard Genette had important influences on my graduate and dissertation work.

The following writers, some of whose work sits at the intersection of film studies and narrative theory, have also been hugely influential in my work: Edward Branigan, Seymour Chatman, Inez Hedges, Bruce Kawain, Pier Paolo Pasolini, Robert Stam, and George Wilson.

More recently, as I venture into the space where narrative studies, autobiography studies, and narrative empathy intersect, I have benefited from the work of Roland Barthes, Susanna Egan, Rachel Gabara, Suzanne Keen, Philippe Lejeune, Sidonie Smith and Julia Watson, and Robyn Warhol.

What do you see as big questions confronting the field? Where's the cutting edge? What are the trends?

There has lately been a lot of interest in expanding narrative studies well outside of the bounds of prose fiction. On a rather limited scale, I have tried to participate in this expansion by focusing on fiction film, on autobiography, and on documentary film. Others have (and are currently) doing this to a wider extent in fields well outside of literary studies: narrative medicine, psychoanalysis, and cognitive science. I find fascinating these newer areas and the questions they raise for narrative studies, but very often, they are well beyond my current expertise.

Questions surrounding fictionality have lately taken a central position in at least one major conference and journal. Fictionality studies certainly interests me with respect to the demarcation between novels and auto/biographical narratives. In this regard, Dorrit Cohn's *The Distinction of Fiction*, published in 1999 with many of the chapters having been previously published, got at some of these questions. My point, I suppose, is that some of the big questions confronting the field are questions that periodically return, faced as we are with new primary texts that cause us to rethink old questions. The title of Monika Fludernik's article published in *New Literary History* in 2001 has always struck me as apt for many of the concerns within narrative studies, "New Wine in Old Bottles? Voice, Focalization, and New Writing." I tend to think that some of the best work in narrative studies combines the old and the new, the perennial questions of narrative theory and new ways of approaching them or responding to them.

What are you working on next?

One of my current projects looks at an important documentary film from 1989, Marlon Riggs's *Tongues Untied*. Riggs's third film, *Tongues Untied* is an experimental project without a single overarching narrative. In the film, Riggs sheds light on the experiences of gay black men, a group invisible to and silenced by white gay culture as well as by black straight culture, during the time of the film's making. The film includes spoken poetry, acted-out scenes, archival footage from civil rights and gay pride parades, as well as performative sequences shot in theatrical black box type spaces that feature individual performers or groups of performers. Riggs also includes, however, brief autobiographical sequences where he faces the camera and narrates important moments from his life. I'm exploring the ways that Riggs uses these short but telling moments of autobiographical narration within the space of his experimental films in order to forward the film's important overall agenda: to break silence and to allow the filmmaker to write his own individual self, a self that had been more often written by others for him.

4 Narrative, ethics, and empathy

We see stories everywhere. Stories help us know; they are a way of knowing, as well as a way of making art and sharing ourselves. What do we mean by the idea that stories are a "way of knowing"? Hayden White says that narrative helps us "translate knowing into telling," that it helps us "fashion human experience" into "structures of meaning" (quoted in Kreiswirth 378). Think about all of the ways stories are used to "translate knowing into telling," for all different kinds of knowledge:

- *fields of knowledge*: religion, philosophy, history, law, psychoanalysis, anthropology, medicine;
- *human social activity*: storytelling, jurisprudence, therapy, social media, witness/testimony;
- *types of writing*: family genealogies and archives, journalism, ethnographies, court depositions and transcripts, life writing, blogging, medical histories.

In all of these cases, narrative is an invaluable tool for conceptualizing how we make up the fabric of social, cultural, institutional, and personal lives. In sacred texts we find the use of parables, self-contained stories that serve the purpose of teaching. In trials we find suspects confessing, telling the story of how a crime was committed for the judgment of others. In medical cases and legal cases, we find stories that serve as a springboard for interpretation, resulting in making a diagnosis or passing down a ruling. Parents and grandparents pass down family stories. Therapists encourage patients to narrate their childhoods and their dreams. Narrative can provide opportunities to celebrate and commemorate, sharing stories as a way to make connections. Narrative can provide a means of working through violence and trauma, while also revealing to us the ways in which these forces are fundamentally disruptive—our response to them is wholly human, in narrative, but that response can also remind us that as a means of bridging the gap between ourselves and other humans, narrative does have its limitations.

Engagements: Exemplary text

One area where more and more people are finding value in narrative is in the field of medicine. Doctors and patients have always used stories, something pointed out by Rita Charon, probably the most significant thinker on the subject of narrative and medicine. Charon writes, "Sick persons and those who care for them become obligatory story-tellers and story-listeners" (261). Doctors elicit stories of pain, illness, or injury from their patients as a way to figure out what needs to be treated, and writing up cases is an important process that enables doctors to share knowledge, understand their patients, and document their work. Some doctors even ask their patients to collaborate on the writing up of charts, creating a kind of "co-authoring" relationship that many find therapeutic and empowering (Charon 262). Patients depend upon and respond well to doctors who seem to have a strong sense of narrative; they perceive that as they are telling the story of how they noticed their chest pains or how they broke an arm, they are being listened to, empathized with, treated with the ethical recognition needed for good and wise care. More and more patients and their families, too, are using storytelling as a way to pursue their own healing; many memoirs and blogs, for example, are devoted to voicing and sharing narratives of illness and pain.

Sigmund Freud should be considered not only as a major figure in the history of ideas related to psychology but also as a pre-eminent storyteller. He used the stories of his patients, and his own narratives of treating them, to understand human consciousness. Freud pioneered the use of narrative in his treatment of those who sought assistance for psychiatric troubles. He did so first by having them tell stories of their childhoods, their dreams, the onset of symptoms; and then subjecting those stories to interpretation, much as one works to interpret a literary text. Next, he wrote up narratives of his treatment processes in a series of famous case studies. These case studies show a number of fascinating features relevant to narrative, including a highly self-conscious narrator who subjects every instance of his own telling to scrutiny; a manipulation of the chronology of events in order to shape the progress of our learning of his "characters," or patients; and an attempt to design closure, or a satisfactory ending.

Freud's first, and one of his most famous, cases is "Fragment of an Analysis of a Case of Hysteria," usually known by "Dora," the pseudonym he gave to the young woman in the case. In "Dora," Freud attempts to make not only the mind of his patient transparent, but his own mind, too. He provides exposition by detailing Dora's symptoms: excessive coughing, migraines, "low spirits and an alteration in her character" (181). He also gives background on "Dora's" family, her relationship with her father and mother, the suspicion that her father is having an affair with "Frau K.," and the trauma of "Dora" herself being propositioned by "Frau K.'s" husband, "Herr K.," something she seems (according to Freud) to both desire and find disgusting. Freud also comments on his own work of narrating, and his attempts to capture the character of "Dora" for his readers. When he tells of beginning to suspect "Dora" of homosexual feelings for "Frau K." after treatment had been going on for some time, he writes:

> I must now turn to a further complication to which I should certainly give no space if I were a man of letters engaged upon the creation of a mental state like this for a short story, instead of being a medical man engaged upon its dissection. The element to which I must now allude can only serve to obscure and efface the outlines of the fine poetic conflict which we have been able to ascribe to Dora .... In the world of reality, which I am trying to depict here, a complication of motives, an accumulation and conjunction of mental activities ... is the rule.
>
> (203)

Freud seems to be suggesting that real life is more complicated than allowed for in fiction, and character more inscrutable. Yet, his narrating of "Dora's" story, and his own role in it, reveals both a finely tuned understanding of how to depict character *and* an understanding of the complexity of human experience and the mind which would be entirely familiar to readers of fiction. Freud knows what makes a good story.

Freud is *not* telling the story of "Dora" as a way to generate empathy with her, nor does he seem to perceive her telling of her own story as an opportunity for himself to empathize with her. In fact, this is one of the contemporary criticisms of Freud's case studies; he wrote and published them for other "medical men," not as a means of accessing the humanity of his patients. In fact, Freud seems committed to representing "Dora" the way *he* sees her, and moving through the progression of representing her character as a way to show how he was forced to re-evaluate his judgments of her as more information was made visible. "Dora's" telling of her own experiences, her own dreams, are riddled with gaps that are revealed only upon our "narrator's" further probing. For instance, Freud cannot explain why "Dora" doesn't want to celebrate her uncle's birthday, until finally "Dora" reveals that "Herr K.'s" birthday was the same day; further, Freud discovers that "Dora's" own birthday went unacknowledged by "Herr K.," something which hurt her and prompted jealous feelings even as she rejects his advances. He finds her to "deny" (203) his interpretations, to "not follow" him (211), as he pieces her story together and comments upon his shifts in judgments.

Finally, "Dora" thwarts his very attempts at closure: she cuts off her treatment before it has reached, to Freud's mind, a "satisfactory" ending (230–231). In an interesting narrative move, Freud then uses what he sees to be his own failure, and his own attempts to understand that failure, as a resolution and ending. The narrative becomes about the doctor trying to figure out what went wrong, with a final note along the lines of "whatever happened to": "Years have again gone by since her visit" and he learns she has married, "reclaimed once more by the realities of life" (239). Whatever has happened to "Dora" is beyond her narrator's reach, and all he can really tell us, in the end, is what he knows—what happened to *him* in trying to figure out the mysteries of the young woman's mind.

Narrative ethics

Freud's "Dora" case exemplifies the challenges we face in trying to understand others, in empathizing with them and treating them ethically. People are mysterious, and while stories can help us understand others by giving us access to a variety of individual realities and then teaching us how to navigate them, ultimately ... people stay mysterious. Throughout this book I have been suggesting that the study and practice of narrative has ethical implications. We will now look at two different ways of thinking about narrative ethics: rhetorical criticism, with its roots in ideas from Aristotle about both ethics and rhetoric; and postmodern ethics, particularly the work of the philosopher Emmanuel Levinas and the concept of alterity (or otherness, difference). We will also consider empathy and narrative, and how the ways a story is structured can lead to empathy and ethical judgment on the part of a reader or viewer.

Ethics, rhetoric, and narrative

People who look at narrative from a rhetorical perspective are interested in the relationships created by telling: the relationships among the teller, the audience, and the thing that gets told (Phelan, "Rhetoric/Ethics" 203). James Phelan, a significant figure in rhetorical criticism, describes it as thinking of narrative "as a rhetorical action: an author's attempt to harness all the resources of storytelling for the purpose of evoking a set of effects (cognitive, emotional, ethical) in an audience" ("Imagining" 243). Readers like Phelan have their roots in Aristotle's *Ethics* and *Rhetoric*; they see narrative as using specific rhetorical strategies to create a response in the reader, and they often see that response as specifically ethical. The classic text that has shaped this way of reading is Wayne Booth's *The Rhetoric of Fiction* (1961). For Phelan, Booth, and readers like them, literature provides an opportunity for individuals to practice a kind of moral wisdom; an ethical imagination; an imaginative flexibility and deliberative capacity necessary for understanding others, understanding context, and acting rightly. Deciphering the act of narration itself as a rhetorical act, particularly in the relation of teller to told, is part of this critical and imaginative work. (This is a different kind of ethics from what we will see in postmodern ethics.)

As we did in Chapter 1 when we were discussing the importance of Aristotle's *Poetics*, a brief look at his *Ethics* and the *Rhetoric* will help us understand some influential ideas. In addition to Booth and Phelan, we could consider someone such as Martha Nussbaum a contemporary Aristotelian; she has explored the moral reasoning made possible by literature in her books *Love's Knowledge* and *Poetic Justice: The Literary Imagination and Public Life*. In *Poetic Justice*, for example, she devotes a chapter to Charles Dickens' novel *Hard Times*, and considers the explicitly didactic nature of the book and its lessons—teaching us that a strictly utilitarian view of the world is stifling and destructive. However, Nussbaum also examines the rhetorical strategies that Dickens uses to call upon his reader to develop *her own* critique of the philosophy of utilitarianism, particularly satire on the one hand and the deliberate engagement of "fancy" or imagination on the other.

Several key concepts from Aristotle's *Ethics* (formally known as the *Nicomachean Ethics*) underlie thinking about narrative from an ethical perspective: practical wisdom, balance, reason, the capacity of deliberation to bring about right action. For Aristotle, practical wisdom, or the ability to know what is right in a given situation based on temperance, reason, a desire to do good, and an understanding of context, is essential for acting in an "excellent" manner (1741). Practical wisdom, or *phronesis*, is different from the more abstract concept of virtue, and from the idea of goodwill, which aligns more with friendship. Furthermore, practical wisdom is different from knowledge, either in terms of theoretical knowledge (such as one might gain from going to college and studying math or history or literature) or in knowing how to do things (like knit or play the piano). Practical wisdom is knowing how to apply being good, reasonable, and prudent to different situations. It is the kind of wisdom that comes from being in the world and seeking to do good, and then knowing how to take right action when the appropriate situation presents itself (1805). For Aristotle, practical wisdom is necessary for ethics, because it involves application: it matters in the *doing*. So, for instance, if I have a student who has been doing well all semester, but then gets a concussion during a baseball game in the last week of class and can't attend the final, practical wisdom might tell me that the ethical thing to do is make arrangements for the student to complete the work when he or she is well, rather than fail the student for missing the exam. Experience with students and teaching (and concussions) has taught me that this is the right thing to do, along with my reason and my desire to see the student ultimately flourish. I apply my wanting to do good, my experience, and my reason to this situation, and take what I see to be an ethical action.

Turning to Aristotle's *Rhetoric*, we can now think about the ways that authors of narratives work to get readers to do things, namely exercise good judgment, by way of rhetorical choices that (1) make us feel like our narrators are credible and (2) tap into our logic, our emotion, and our ethical sense. Thus authors teach us how to take the right action, or rather, make the right judgments. Stories appeal to our minds, our feelings, and our sense of good character, thereby initiating our ethical reasoning, because as we navigate the rhetorical choices used in narrative, we are called upon to find new ways to apply that reasoning, that reasoned judgment. As we shall see below in our discussion of the work of James Phelan, the progression through a story, the ways we see a story unfold through a series of rhetorical choices, calls upon us to use our reason, respond emotionally, make judgments, and deliberate—all important steps in applying practical wisdom to highly specific contexts. The more we do this, the better we get at it. Stories, in this way, give us a chance to practice practical wisdom.

Aristotle defines rhetoric, or the art of oratory, as a blending of logic, emotion, and ethics, and he sees it operating along several different lines at once, all to the end of getting an audience to take right action or make right judgments (2161). First, rhetoric creates a relationship among speaker, subject, and audience (a triad we have already seen referenced by Phelan). We can also outline different types of rhetoric: we can speak in order to get our hearers to take action; we can speak in order to attack or defend; or we can speak in order to praise or condemn (2159). Seeking to achieve these different ends in our audience will determine the kinds of choices we make as speakers. Furthermore, in addition to determining the subject upon which an audience needs to be persuaded as well as the right kind of language or diction for the subject, a speaker has to make two other important moves: to establish his or her character for the audience, and to get the audience into the most receptive frame of mind (2194). When we discuss the idea of the unreliable narrator later, we will see the relevance that establishing good character, or credibility, holds for narrative and readerly judgment. The ways a speaker can achieve his or her particular effects on the audience, establishing the right frame of mind for persuasion, is through appeals to logic, to emotion, and to character or ethical judgment (2238). For rhetorical critics of narrative, stories can operate through all three modes, and much depends on how the narrator establishes him or herself in relation to the reader.

Drawing on Aristotle, Phelan has defined the principles underlying rhetorical criticism (Table 4.1), the first and most fundamental being that narrative is the recounting of events through a rhetorical act aimed at achieving a particular purpose. The second principle says that narrative depends upon an endlessly looping relationship among text, author, and reader. The third principle claims that there are five different kinds of audience: actual, the ideal reader, the audience to the narrative (or observer position), the audience being addressed by the narrator, and the ideal audience imagined by the narrator as she or he tells the story. Then, fourth, narrative consists of several components. These components are not just text, author, and reader, but are elements that prompt different kinds of responses depending on how they are used. These are mimetic, or the ways the text presents characters and situations like our own (remember that *mimesis* means imitation); thematic, or the ways the text engages our interest in larger questions and issues; and synthetic, or the ways the text interests us in its made-ness, its artifice, its status as a work of art. The fifth principle claims that narrative communication prompts narrative judgments. These judgments occur in three different realms: interpretive, ethical, and aesthetic. Finally, the

Table 4.1 Phelan's principles of rhetorical criticism

Principles	Definitions	Elements
First	Narrative is the recounting of events through a rhetorical act aimed at achieving a particular purpose	• Events • Rhetorical act • Rhetorical agent
Second	Narrative depends on a triangulated and recursive relationship among author, text, and audience	• Author • Text • Audience
Third	Speaking of audience, there are five different kinds	• Actual • Ideal reader • Audience in the position of observer • Audience being addressed by the narrator • Ideal audience imagined by the narrator
Fourth	Narrative consists of formal as well as communicative components	• Mimetic • Thematic • Synthetic
Fifth	Narrative communication and narrative formal elements prompt judgments	• Interpretive • Ethical • Aesthetic
Sixth	Narrative works by progressions on the textual side and on the readerly side	*Textual:* • Instabilities (corresponding to story) • Tensions (corresponding to discourse) *Readerly:* • Our changing responses to what we're reading

sixth principle addresses narrative progression. These progressions occur on the side of plot (introduction, complication, resolution) and the side of the person doing the reading. Progressions of plot include *instabilities*, which involve characters and situations; and *tensions*, which involve relationships among authors, narrators, and audience, particularly around what is known and what is not. Progressions for the reader are our changing and evolving responses to what we read (Phelan, "Rhetoric/Ethics" 208–212).

Engagements: Exemplary text

A reading of Virginia Woolf's short story "The Mark on the Wall" might briefly illustrate some of Phelan's principles. In this story, an unnamed, overt character-narrator sits before the fire in her room and notices a black mark on the wall. The narrative consists of the narrator speculating as to what the mark might be, letting her mind wander over stories and fancies and the past, and ultimately reflecting on the nature of reality and knowledge until another unnamed person enters and says, "God damn this war .... All the same, I don't see why we should have a snail on our wall" (89). The narrative uses a lot from the realms of the thematic and the synthetic, calling upon the reader to make interpretive and aesthetic judgments. The narrator helps us notice these elements by drawing attention to her process of deciphering the mark on the wall, as well as her questioning the very necessity of doing so:

> No, no, nothing is proved, nothing is known. And if I were to get up at this very moment and ascertain that the mark on the wall is really— what shall I say?—the head of a gigantic old nail, driven in two hundred years ago, which has now, owing to the patient attrition of many generations of housemaids, revealed its head above the coat of paint, and is taking its first view of modern life in the sight of a white-walled fire-lit room, what should I gain? Knowledge? Matter for further speculation?
>
> (87)

The events of the narrative are composed entirely of the narrator's thoughts— the thoughts serve as the events—as she ponders the mark. (Doesn't this remind you of our reading of the Harold Pinter story "Girls" in Chapter 1?) Embedded within this narrative are incomplete micro-narratives, tiny little plots layered into the larger plot, such as the one quoted above: the revealing of the mark, possibly a nail, over time. We are called upon to make interpretive judgments, directed to do so by our narrator: what is to be gained by figuring out what the mark might be? If you desire to read to the end to find out what it might be, what does that say about you? Thus the narrative progresses by both instabilities—what does each thought-event lead to? will we discover what the mark is?—and tensions—how do we fill in the gaps created by the thought-events? To what extent does it matter whether we know what the mark is? More than anything, the narrative depends on the progression of the reader's judgment and interpretation: our continual evaluation of our experience and our judgment, prompted by the narrator herself as she asks: if I knew what the mark actually was, "what should I gain?"

Phelan's set of principles, when taken all together, show that an interpreter brings together the relationships amongst the parts of a text, the parts of the communicative act that is narrative, to define the working of the whole and the effect that whole has on the audience. In other words, an interpreter considers the telling of events in progression; how formal components work in relation to one another and which components a given text allows to dominate; and how all of these parts work together in unity to create opportunity for judgment, whether those judgments are interpretive, ethical, or aesthetic. An interpreter can enter into this relationship at any point—through the text, author, or audience—and doing so might determine which parts of the whole receive the most attention; but shifting one's point on the triangle in any direction will give a different perspective, and synthesizing the different perspectives gives a greater sense of the unified whole.

Implied author and unreliable narrator

We might focus, before departing this arena, on two of the major contributions of rhetorical criticism to the study of narrative: the ideas of the *implied author* and the *unreliable narrator*. The implied author is a figure conjured by the reader in the course of reading, a guiding intelligence who is neither the actual flesh-and-blood author nor the narrator, but who is responsible for using the strategies outlined above. An unreliable narrator is a narrating agent who seems to not be in accord with the norms established by the implied author, or seems to be lacking some important knowledge that the rest of the text bears forth and which the reader is able to perceive. Phelan and Dorrit Cohn have extended the idea of unreliable narrator to include not only a discordance in perception and knowledge but one in ethical judgment as well (Abbott 243). In Phelan's principles above, a story told by an unreliable narrator works via progression by tension: gaps in knowledge or values or perceptions or beliefs ("Rhetoric/Ethics" 212). For Wayne Booth, one of the knotty issues in narrative, and one of the reasons stories are a powerful tool for engaging moral and ethical reasoning, is trying to determine what happens when the story is told in such a way as to generate sympathy in the reader for the position of the narrator, even when other aspects of the text, such as the norms and values seemingly established by the implied author or knowledge to which we have access which the narrator does not, are suggesting deficiencies in moral sensibility or ethical judgment (Phelan, "Rhetoric/Ethics" 208). Is it okay to like or feel sympathy for a bad person in a story?

Engagements: Exemplary text

Two very different examples might serve to illustrate Booth's and Phelan's ideas about how the rhetorical act of narrating generates ethical responses and judgments in readers. The first, the narrator of Geoffrey Household's novel *Rogue Male*, is an unnamed overt character-narrator, and I have chosen this case because of this narrator's clearly unreliable stance which raises precisely the knotty issue mentioned above: "Inside views can build sympathy even for the most vicious character" (378); I see this at work in *Rogue Male*. The second, the narrator of Edna Ferber's novel *Fanny Herself*, an overt narrator outside the story prone to comment and with a clear sensibility, was chosen because the use of narrator commentary in a particularly in-your-face manner highlights Booth's interest at the close of *The Rhetoric of Fiction* in narrators that make their judgments clear as a means of facilitating ethical response on the part of the reader.

Rogue Male begins with an unnamed narrator recounting the aftermath of a failed assassination attempt in what seems to be a central European country in a time immediately preceding the Second World War. The narrator is captured, tortured, and escapes to England, where he hides in an underground tunnel somewhere in Dorset in an attempt to elude his captors. There is quite a lot of attention to space, as the narrator positions himself geographically and in relation to his ever-approaching hunters. Time, on the other hand, is presented via what David Herman calls "fuzzy temporality," as we saw in Chapter 2; not only is the date unclear, but the amount of time that passes is never differentiated, and there are few time markers besides the transition of day into night and night into day (which are themselves confused during the sequences where the action of the novel is occurring underground). Interestingly, space serves to mark time through distance: how long it takes to go from hiding place to hiding place, or to escape from the continent back to England. Fear works to generate instances of fuzzy temporality, as time is stretched and shortened: "That part of me which was unconsciously looking after my safety kept count of the minutes ... while my conscious mind lived through hours of muddled and panicky thinking" (85). There is very little dialogue, and thus most of the novel is narrated along the lines of this quote: we are provided with the presentation of the narrator's inner thoughts, plans, fears, strategizing. Even though our narrator is an assassin, and even though he represents his deed and its consequences in a wholly impersonal and detached way, because we spend the entire novel on the run with him, observing him build tunnels under the English countryside, outthinking and outrunning his predators, we develop sympathy for him.

One key way the novel works to do this is the representation of our narrator narrating being in pain. Our narrator says,

> There had been a terrifying instant of pain. I felt as if the back of my thighs and rump had been shorn off, pulled off, scraped off—off, however done. I had parted, obviously and irrevocably, with a lot of my living matter.
>
> (2)

The highly self-conscious and detached nature of the narration (note the appositive, for instance) seems to suggest that the narrator is aware of some kind of audience, and the attempt to describe the violence in measured tones increases the horror. This seems an example of what Phelan might term the mimetic component: the realistic representation of a body in pain creates in us a visceral response. This then prompts a move towards ethical judgment: do we judge the narrator for his work as an assassin, or do we experience some other ethical response watching him respond to pain? Do we enter into a relationship with him due to the unmediated access to his inner life? The progression of story events, of filling in knowledge, and of our own responses work together to lead us to answer this question. He might indeed be a vicious person, but we spend so much time with him in a situation of such intimacy that we cannot help rooting for him to escape and survive—even though we know that if he does he will return to the site of his original mission and finish the job—itself a complex problem, because who wouldn't have wanted a dictator assassinated in 1939?

We have already encountered Edna Ferber's novel *Fanny Herself* in Chapter 2. The novel features a number of strong characters, notably the protagonist—a lively Jewish girl growing up in the Midwest at the start of the twentieth century—and her mother, Molly Brandeis. However, just as notably strong is the narrator, an inescapable figure with a voice and stance as sharply defined as any of Ferber's characters. It/she seems to be omnipresent and coming from a perspective that permits a great deal of knowledge over time. This narrator seems to have an explicitly gendered presence, and be situated in a world separate from the town of Winnebago while also familiar with it and friendly towards it and its inhabitants and values. It/she seems to be similarly well-disposed to the reader as well, offering thoughts, opinions, and judgments not only on the characters but on how their stories should be told and how the reader should respond. So this narrator attempts to determine the progression not only of the story; this narrator also attempts to directly manage the reader's progression of judgment. The narrator seems to be using a set of rhetorical strategies—directly commenting being one of them—but also *directing* both the story and reader. These moves engage the reader's awareness of the synthetic (or artistic) components of the narrative, and prompt interpretive and ethical judgments; in other words, we are always aware we are being told a story, and we are asked outright to make judgments as we go. These judgments are in part driven by moments where the narrator reaches out of the story, extending something like a hand to the reader—welcoming, as it were, the reader to the small town of Winnebago and to the Brandeis family.

Chapter One begins with a direct address to the reader: "You could not have lived a week in Winnebago without being aware of Mrs. Brandeis" (1). Not only is this a direct address to the reader, but it also seems to be welcoming the reader to a new place, in an almost neighborly way. The narrator proposes to introduce the reader to a member of the community, to important places in the town—to show the reader around. At the same time, the narrator is directing the reader to have certain experiences:

> You saw a sturdy, well-set-up, alert woman ... a woman with a long, straight, clever nose that indexed her character, as did everything about her .... But first you remarked her eyes. Will you concede that eyes can be piercing, yet velvety?
>
> (1)

The predominance of the synthetic component here activates in the reader an impulse to assess the art of the presentation, but also to decide whether and how to enter into relationship with the narrator—a narrator who is clearly predisposed to like Mrs. Brandeis, and who will insist that the reader have the same experience. The narrator even seems to be suggesting in an entirely overt way that by describing Mrs. Brandeis in a certain way, certain storytelling effects are achieved. Throughout, the narrator asserts her presence using the first person pronoun: "I am even bold enough to think that she might have made business history, that plucky woman, if she had had an earlier start" (9). Our narrator is not a character in the plot itself, yet she asserts herself and makes her consciousness and perspective known.

It is not only to the characters of the novel that our narrator works to introduce us. The Brandeis family is one of several Jewish families in the town of Winnebago; they are a small but notable community, assimilated for the most part but still very visible in their religious and cultural difference. Our narrator, in fact, reports on this aspect of Fanny's mental activity:

> It was about this time that Fanny Brandeis began to realize, actively, that she was different . . . . She and Bella Weinberg were the only two in her room at school who stayed out on the Day of Atonement, and on New Year, and the lesser Jewish holidays. Also, she went to temple on Friday night and Saturday morning, when the other girls she knew went to church on Sunday.
>
> (17)

Here the narrative is told through Fanny's perspective, but our narrator is also reporting on certain particulars of Jewish life and practice and is doing so in such a way as to not alienate the reader. Perhaps the reader would know *Yom Kippur* instead of Day of Atonement, or would know the names of "lesser holidays"—but perhaps not. Another instance might be the narrator commenting on the rabbi at Fanny's synagogue, here with her own perspective: "He stuck to the Scriptures for his texts, finding Moses a greater leader than Roosevelt, and the miracle of the Burning Bush more wonderful than the marvels of twentieth-century wizardry in electricity . . . . Fanny found him fascinating to look on" (20). Yet another might be the narrator describing services: "The congregation, rustling in silks, was approaching the little temple from all directions. Inside, there was a low-toned buzz of conversation . . . . Fanny drank it in eagerly" (20). In both of these cases, the narrator seeks to describe Fanny's religious and cultural milieu from the perspective of an external observer, and then reconnect with her protagonist by showing that milieu through her eyes. Through the act of narrating, we ourselves are both inside and outside. The narrator has to walk a line between capturing the alterity of Fanny in her context, showing her difference, and making that context hospitable for a reader.

In the case of Ferber's novel, the narrator establishes a value of hospitality which serves to welcome the reader into an unfamiliar community *and* create a particular kind of ethical framework. This attention to negotiating difference and alterity or otherness will lead us nicely into our consideration of the second ethical turn: postmodern ethics.

Postmodern ethics and ethical reading: Encountering the other

Postmodern ethics, as defined by Jacques Derrida and Emmanuel Levinas, rejects what it sees as an uncomfortable predilection for universals that do not take into account the ethical imperative to recognize alterity, or difference. Readers who see other people as mysterious, as essentially unknowable, can also have an ethical experience of the text itself by recognizing and appreciating its mystery: the refusal of the text to be reduced to any one meaning, the resistance of the text towards readers seeking to pin down a work of art to only one level of meaning, those readers who want to get rid of any ambiguity and look for easy closure. In her writing on this kind of Levinasian ethical reading, Liesbeth Korthals Altes says, "As a reader, one must agree to lose oneself in the submission to the call of the text as Other, and to lose the work as a graspable, coherent whole" (144). Such an experience parallels an individual's experience of the other in life, wherein to appropriate the other and reduce difference to sameness is a kind of violence.

The philosopher Stanley Cavell, in his book *Pursuits of Happiness*, says that 1930s screwball romantic comedies are good examples of stories we can look at from this perspective. In *The Awful Truth*, Cary Grant's Jerry believes his wife, Irene Dunne's Lucy, is having an affair; she starts to believe the same thing about him. They agree to divorce, only to realize when each wants to remarry other people that they are each the love of each other's lives. Each of them realizes that the other is the only one who really "gets" them. Films like *The Awful Truth* show couples that go through a series of misunderstandings based on total misjudging of each other; hijinks and disasters ensue, the man and woman dislike each other, until they realize they were wrong all along: the person they've been misjudging is the person they love, and part of loving that person means taking all of his or her craziness in stride, and understanding we will all always be kind of crazy. These movies do have clearly resolved endings—the couples are reunited (Cavell calls them "comedies of remarriage")—but the lesson learned is that relationships *themselves* are *never* easily resolved. To not accept that your partner is a little bit of a nut means to not respect the ways he or she is different from you and always will be. A good example of a more contemporary film that does this is the Judd Apatow/Steve Carell movie *The 40-Year-Old Virgin*; in this one, Carell's Andy is made to feel like a weirdo because he is, in fact, a 40-year-old virgin, and it is the mutual acceptance of his weirdnesses along with the weirdnesses of the woman who falls in love with him, Catherine Keener's Trish, that allows the relationship to flourish.

So, we can see people as mysterious and unknowable, and we can see our relationships as presenting us with no easy answers, but how is it that we see *stories* that way? How is a text itself *mysterious*, when we can often feel pretty sure we know what's going on at least in familiar terms like plot and character. We've been emphasizing the ways that stories present recognizable persons in recognizable situations, so how can those stories be "mysterious"? One of the key figures defining a narrative ethics beyond rhetorical criticism and practical wisdom is Adam Zachary Newton. Newton uses the work of Levinas and Cavell to liberate narrative ethics from what he calls the "self-adequating ethos of the critic, who ... matches form to content, and content to conduct" (9); in other words, Newton says that reading books does not make us better people, and they do not have moral lessons to teach us. Newton suggests instead that we can use our experience of people as mysterious, people as having minds difficult to fathom, in order to see texts the same way. Reading a narrative can then function as a kind of encounter with something *not-you* that you have to figure out, the same way people are *not-you* and you have to figure them out. Newton proposes a three-part structure for a narrative ethics: a narrational ethics (the narrative act), a representational ethics (the exchange of persons for characters), and a hermeneutic ethics (the responsibilities emerging from the act of reading) (18). In my reading of Ian McEwan's *On Chesil Beach*, I consider the novel from a similar perspective: the stance of the telling, the removal of selfhood from one character as she becomes part of a story not her own, and the ethical imperative placed on the reader as she encounters otherness.

Engagements: Exemplary text

In *On Chesil Beach* McEwan prompts reflection on questions of intimacy and knowledge, bringing us to a practice of reading ethically. The use of elements of narrative such as perspective, time, and order, directs our attention to how we tell stories of intimacy, what is sayable and unsayable in the representation of intimacy, and to what kinds of knowledge narrative provides access. These moves teach us a form of ethical reading: how to navigate the representation of desire, intimacy, and alterity in order to recognize the epistemological and ethical commitments and problems engendered by narrative.

The story concerns the honeymoon night of Florence Ponting and Edward Mayhew, a narrative that unfolds over the course of an evening in 1962, beginning with dinner and climaxing, literally and figuratively, with sexual embarrassment (the groom's "arriving too quickly" all over his horrified bride). This is a catastrophe in every sense of the word, and the novel ends with the just-married couple parting forever on Chesil Beach as a result of the humiliation as night overtakes the strand. Just before they separate, Florence suggests that the two stay together and pursue an open marriage, a proposition taken by Edward to be profoundly insulting, and he rejects her.

Interwoven throughout are flashbacks to the couple's meeting and courtship as well as their family lives growing up, meant to account for, possibly even to predetermine, how it is that their wedding night goes so horribly wrong.

McEwan's use of perspective in the service of exploring intersubjectivity, or how minds work in relationship to one another, specifically when it comes to intimacy, asks us to do ethical reading. As we read ethically, holding spaces open for doubt, we model what McEwan's characters might not be able to do: moving below the surface, moving beyond misperception, and rejecting the impulse to reduce someone or something to a single meaning.

The strangeness and mystery of each individual to the other, even in the most intimate of circumstances, is evident in the first lines of the novel: "They were young, educated, and both virgins on this, their wedding night, and they lived in a time when a conversation about sexual difficulties was plainly impossible. But it is never easy" (3). The tone of this narrator is worldly, able to make universal assertions predicated on some kind of unseen experience: "But it is never easy." The narrator also prefigures a sexual catastrophe by bringing up "sexual difficulties" on this, their (characters as yet unnamed) wedding night. Why bring up sexual difficulties at such a moment? Why assume we are going to have to have a conversation about them? Our entry into the novel—our penetration into the inner sanctum of Edward and Florence's intimate space as yet not quite fully formed, the liminal space of the honeymoon night in a hotel—is based on a series of impressions: what the glimpse of the bed ("whose bedcover was pure white and stretched startlingly smooth, as though by no human hand" [3]) might tell us, the two young waiters who may or may not be giggling at the honeymoon couple, the overcooked food consumed in a halfhearted manner by bride and groom with other things on their mind.

Even in the early days of the relationship, told in flashbacks, Florence and Edward form impressions of each other based in strangeness and not entirely accurate. Moreover, they never quite get to the point where those impressions are revised, where the true self of each is recognized. McEwan's Edward, in forming his impressions of Florence, recognizes the oddity of the experience, not only the peculiarity of falling in love but the particular strangeness brought on by a lack of experience erotic and otherwise. Towards the end of the novel, as detumescence and denouement (falling action) come together to account for what has occurred and to determine what is to come, Edward recalls his visits to the Ponting home, a very different world from the lower-middle-class home he comes from, made chaotic and unstable by his brain-damaged mother. Through Florence, Edward is introduced to classical music, duck *confit*, books by the highbrow British philosopher and novelist Iris Murdoch: "How could he pretend to himself that within his narrow existence these were not extraordinary experiences?" (146–47). The narrator, in his worldliness, realizes that duck *confit* is not especially remarkable; but he also recognizes that the swirl of impressions, heightened by the erotic excitement of first love, is ushering Edward into a new way of looking at the world. In this regard, our narrator is more equipped to understand how another subject might be thinking and responding than the characters being narrated. Furthermore, by manipulating time in order to show these impressions on the part of Edward *after* his humiliation, we are able to see how open he was and how incorrect in his judgment of who or what Florence was: a subject, not merely a collection of moments and sensations for him to experience.

The impressions that Florence and Edward generate over the course of their relationship, and that shape their understanding of each other and their couplehood, turn out to be wholly wrong. They demonstrate an inability to narrate each other to each other. And, they—Edward in particular—subsume all of their limited understanding of each other into a totality that is the marriage and what it means, namely, consummation. Moreover, Edward, in his desire to possess Florence, to *penetrate*, only reveals to her her own strangeness to herself. This defamiliarization does not reveal to Florence the infinite possibilities made available by love and its radical openness to the new; instead, Florence wants to shut down, to be closed rather than open, psychically and corporeally. The narrator describes her thinking:

> Falling in love was revealing to her just how *odd* she was, how habitually sealed off in her everyday thoughts. Whenever Edward asked, How do you feel? or, What are you thinking? she always made an awkward answer . . . . All these years she had lived in isolation within herself and, *strangely*, from herself, never wanting or daring to look back.
>
> (75–76; italics mine)

"Falling in love" has revealed herself to herself, even as she becomes aware of the reality that the person she loves best might not know her at all. We see here the strangeness of Florence, of the erotic encounter, of one's own subjectivity. Their inability to know each other, and the ways that failure predetermines the collapse of their relationship, is sadly only knowledge for the narrator, and for us.

On Chesil Beach maps onto classic plot structure, along with interruptions from flashbacks and narrator commentary, of rising action, climax, and falling action or *denouement*, a structure which mimics the arc of desire: tumescence, orgasm, detumescence. Furthermore, it does so from a specifically male perspective. It is highly masculinized, and it creates the space wherein the deeply unethical nature of Edward's interaction with Florence is made visible. McEwan's use of impressions leads us to see, in a cumulative fashion over the course of the novel, how misreading is counter to ethical reading. McEwan's narrative work is grounded not only in the mind but in the body. The body determines the working of the mind, and because Florence and Edward are experiencing such separate things over the course of their wedding night, for McEwan this leads to a failure of mutual empathy. The two do not understand each other. As Edward strokes Florence, she begins to get excited in spite of herself, and then immediately attributes the unfamiliar sensation to some kind of disorder; Edward mistakes it for "eagerness" (105). Even as their bodies begin to do sort of the same thing, their minds are separate, making connection impossible—an impossibility that becomes clear a few moments later. When the narrator reports her confessing to being scared, she imagines "trust[ing] him utterly," only to promptly revise: "But this was fantasy" (104). Words related to mental activity, cognition, knowing, perceiving, understanding—and misinterpreting—abound. Florence thinks, "What possible terms could she have used when she could not have named the matter to herself?" (11); "She was alone with a problem she did not know how to begin to address" (13); each of them pursue silent hypothetical lines of thought as they remain inscrutable to each other: "might have suggested," "would have been better," "he thought he understood," "she made herself remember" (all occurring between pages 23 and 35). An evening that is supposed to be about union, the coming together of bodies and minds, instead begins with separation and sees increasing mental distance even as bodies draw nearer.

Unity with an ultimately unknowable other recedes infinitely, just as Florence recedes down the beach from Edward after the crisis; to grasp after it is to do a form of violence. For Levinas this becomes how we think about other people, and the process of reaching and recognition forms the foundation of his ethics. While a connection is lost between Edward and Florence as a result of the catastrophe of their wedding night, a connection is gained between Edward and the reader, as we get to see what he has lost in her. We get to have a kind of narrative knowledge that Florence will never have: she not only departs from Edward on that beach, she departs from the novel entirely except as a fantasy. Florence remains a fantasy, "that girl with her violin" (202), amplified by Edward's imagining of the daughter they might have had, wearing a headband like her mother, a "loved familiar" (203). The novel ends with Edward's partial self-recognition of his own emotional and ethical shortcomings, his failure to appreciate the subject, and the gift, that was Florence. At the same time, one is left to wonder if Edward has truly done the work of recognizing Florence: in his final thoughts, she is unchanged, static, recreated in the person of a daughter, sentimentalized through the lens of nostalgia. Where is the real Florence? Is she to be found in the gaps between Edward's impressions, even at the last?

The tragedy of Florence and Edward then becomes their inability to recognize other possibilities, other ways of knowing, either in their situation or in themselves and each other. Misreading has profound ethical implications for McEwan, and Edward's humiliation is a very visible sign of that. The mind of the other is impenetrable. Indeed, in the world conjured by *On Chesil Beach*, the very act of penetration is a violation. A more ethical kind of penetration is imagined instead by connections between minds that depend on the fruitful creation and navigation of impressions.

Gap-filling and ethical thinking

We can suggest that meeting people in books helps us understand people in real life. However, while it is handy to make comparisons between how we process storyworlds and how we process the real world, it is also true that "storyworlds differ ontologically [in their being] from the real world because they are incomplete" (Palmer, *Fictional* 34). People in books are, of course, not real, and the nature of the reality of a storyworld has to be different because stories cannot be about, cannot contain, *everything*; they select stuff to tell us, and leave other stuff out, sometimes because the author judges that stuff to be irrelevant, and sometimes because there are things stories just can't do. The film director Quentin Tarantino, for instance, always creates elaborate backstories for his characters as he is working on a script, but that information rarely makes it into the film itself. He creates an entire world for those characters, and shares it with the actors to help them help him make the world, but we don't get to see a lot of that world in the finished screen productions of *Inglourious Basterds* or *Django Unchained*. What about what stories just can't do because the reality of a story is different from the "real world"? If I am baking a cake at my house and you come over, you can smell the cake. If I write a story about baking a cake and give it to you to read, I can do the best I can to describe the smell, but I can't make you smell anything. Your sense experience of a storyworld versus your sense experience of the real world, and therefore your experience of reality, has to be different.

At the same time, we are able to manage gaps in narrative because we so often encounter gaps in real life. This is, as Ellen Spolsky writes, "the daily business of all human minds" (2). As we saw in Chapter 2, the making of storyworlds is a way to get to completeness and cohesion. However, it has always been the case that reading narrative is considered to be a series of gap-filling maneuvers, and that the developments in cognitive theory described earlier have done more to show both how this works and how ultimately it is incomplete: narrative will often resist our attempts to fill in gaps, and we often derive pleasure from that resistance.

Beginning with Wolfgang Iser's important study *The Implied Reader*, gaps have been given a central place in thinking about narrative. Iser defines gaps as "points at which the reader can enter into the text, forming his [or her] own connections and conceptions and so creating the configurative meaning of what he [or she] is reading" (40). The assumption is that the gaps can be filled, and that this is part of how we make a world when we read. We can have gaps in time (such as flashback and flashforward) and we can also have gaps in knowledge (a character or narrator doesn't seem to know something they should, or we don't seem to know something we think we ought to). Meir Sternberg, in his influential work on the role of exposition in narrative, suggests that exposition plays the vital role it does because of the gaps it generates and the work we proceed to do, as readers, to fill the gaps. Information might be delayed or suppressed or otherwise with either temporarily or permanently, generating ambiguity the reader wants to resolve. The kinds of information catalogued by Sternberg include:

- actions that have led to other actions and the motives thereof, such as what happens in any detective story;
- character traits, such as in the case of Misha Vainberg, the protagonist of Gary Shteyngart's novel *Absurdistan* (is he a coward? is he redeemable? is he truthful about himself?) or in the case of Humbert Humbert in Vladimir Nabokov's novel *Lolita* (what is he doing with this young girl and why and do we believe what he tells us?);
- the details of personal relationships and how the dynamics got to be so, such as George and Martha in *Who's Afraid of Virginia Woolf?* (play by Edward Albee; film by Mike Nichols) or Nick and Amy in *Gone Girl* (novel by Gillian Flynn; film by David Fincher);
- details that indicate space and geography and therefore help the reader place characters, such as the description of houses and neighborhood in the beginning of Jane Austen's *Sense and Sensibility*, where the positioning of houses near one another, and the description of size, numbers of rooms, etc., all play a role in the family's coming to grips with their diminished expectations (director Ang Lee and screenwriter Emma Thompson use this to good effect in the film adaptation as well);
- the expectations and preferences that help the reader generate the story-world, what Sternberg calls "the probability-register of the fictive world" (242), such as in Michael Cunningham's novel *The Hours*, wherein one of the main characters is Virginia Woolf in the process of writing *Mrs. Dalloway* (is this fiction? is it biography? is it a kind of magical realism? at what point do we have enough information to decide?).

Necessary to the work of gap-filling is the formulation of hypotheses about what might be right or true, as well as a recognition that some "fillings" are more probable than others. Our work here as readers is aided by understanding the motivation behind exposition, why writers or filmmakers use it. When we see "exposition-type things" happening, we realize we are in a story and that the story is trying to give us information we need to enter into the world of the story, to start making sense of the characters, to visualize the setting, and so on. The creation and filling of gaps sets the story in motion. Exposition might work to establish patterns. It certainly situates the reader within a particular perspective, which for Sternberg is one of the main necessities of exposition (254); one of the first questions we

whose perspective is this being told? Exposition does communicating a point of view to the reader, and the s from the selection of that point of view.
tive to be a form of communication, then a natural complicate that communication by leaving things out? order? Ellen Spolsky and H. Porter Abbott have argued ctivity, the fun, of not filling in gaps, of trying to figure

out stories that do not make the process easy. Maybe we *don't* always want completeness. Maybe we like to be kept guessing. Spolsky draws on the theory of "modularity of mind," which argues that we process sensory information via independent and interdependent channels, and that our understanding of the world comes from our ability to fill in the gaps created by those inputs in order to make a complete picture. Her example describes what happens when you smell something burning, remember you have a cake in the oven, visualize in your mind a burnt cake, and jump up to run to the kitchen (6–7). The action comes from all of these separate pieces of information being processed via separate "modules," and then integrated through successively more complex mechanisms into one response. Spolsky suggests something similar occurs when we read or view complex narratives, "when the gaps are not filled habitually or conventionally but creatively .... These texts ... are profitably understood as responses to gaps in understanding that are not amenable to repair in conventional ways" (7). Gap-filling is seen to be a creative process, and literary texts call upon their readers to embrace a certain level of difficulty and complexity, to reject the superficial or straightforward. The gaps and how to "repair" them should not be clean and apparent; that is what enriches a narrative and our experience of it.

Engagements: Exemplary text

Quentin Tarantino's film *Pulp Fiction* uses gaps in both time and knowledge, and I think this makes the movie fun; it gives us pleasure. But the result is also a narrative that raises some surprising ethical themes, and that asks us to feel empathy for some pretty vicious characters in surprising ways. The story is told in three chapters—"Vincent Vega and Marsellus Wallace's Wife," "The Gold Watch," and "The Bonnie Situation"—and is structured around the interactions generated by a network of hit men, drug dealers, and assorted underworld types. You wouldn't necessarily expect that a film revolving around such vicious characters would prompt ethical themes, but a great deal depends on how Tarantino chose to structure and order the plot elements.

The main characters are Vincent Vega and Jules Winnfield (John Travolta and Samuel L. Jackson), who are hit men for Marsellus Wallace (Ving Rhames), an imposing figure engaged in criminal activities (some specified, some not). Vincent and Jules are also responsible for recovering a mysterious suitcase, contents unknown (every time it's opened it emits a golden light), and returning it to Marsellus. Marsellus is married to Mia (Uma Thurman); one of Marsellus' specified criminal activities is fixing a boxing match, paying Butch (Bruce Willis) to take a dive. The film begins and ends, is framed, with a scene in a diner, where two petty criminals Pumpkin (Tim Roth) and Honey Bunny (Amanda Plummer) are robbing the customers. The stories created by these interactions are told achronologically, out of order, with gaps in between some of the events where things might be happening that we do not see and which are not reported. The narrative does progress in a way that makes sense to the viewer, as the viewer is able to put the pieces together and reach an

Table 4.2 Plot structure and chronology of *Pulp Fiction*

Events as presented	Events in chronological order
Pumpkin and Honey Bunny begin their robbery of the diner; opening credits roll.	Vincent and Jules arrive at the apartment of a group of dealers trying to double-cross Marsellus; Vincent and Jules kill them, and take the mysterious suitcase.
"Vincent Vega and Marsellus Wallace's Wife": Vincent and Jules arrive at the apartment of a group of dealers trying to double-cross Marsellus; Vincent and Jules kill them, and take the mysterious suitcase.	Vincent and Jules finishing executing the double-crossers. But then one surprises them by coming out of the bathroom with a gun; he shoots, misses, and is in turn shot by Vincent and Jules. Jules believes the shots missing them is a "miracle" and has an epiphany leading to a sense of redemption.
Vincent and Jules bring the suitcase to the bar where Marsellus is meeting with Butch to fix the fight. Vincent also goes to buy some heroin.	Vincent and Jules take their informant, who has survived the bloodbath in the apartment, out to their car to get away, but then accidentally shoot him in the head while driving. They have to take the car to their friend Jimmy for help removing the evidence of this, and they have to finish the job before Jimmy's wife Bonnie comes home from the night shift at the hospital where she is a nurse.
Vincent takes Mia Wallace out to dinner. She accidentally overdoses on heroin, and **Vincent and the drug dealer from whom he purchased the heroin save her life with an adrenaline shot to the heart.**	Vincent and Jules finish with the car and decide to go to the diner to have breakfast together—as they are eating, Pumpkin and Honey Bunny begin robbing the customers.
"The Gold Watch": Butch double-crosses Marsellus and wins the fight, killing his opponent in the process. He flees because he knows Marsellus is going to try to kill him, and also because he himself has killed a man.	Jules convinces Pumpkin to stop the crime and walk away by sharing the story of his spiritual epiphany and redemption.
Butch meets up with his girlfriend, who was supposed to bring him his prized gold watch; she forgot, so he has to return to his apartment to retrieve it.	Pumpkin and Honey Bunny agree and leave the diner together. Vincent and Jules leave, and Jules goes off to walk the earth in search of greater spiritual understanding after returning the suitcase to Marsellus.

Vincent and Jules bring the suitcase to the bar where Marsellus is meeting with Butch to fix the fight. Vincent then goes to buy some heroin.

Vincent takes Mia Wallace out to dinner. She accidentally overdoses on heroin, and Vincent and the drug dealer from whom he purchased the heroin save her life with an adrenaline shot to the heart.

Butch double-crosses Marsellus and wins the fight, killing his opponent in the process. He flees because he knows Marsellus is going to try to kill him, and also because he himself has killed a man.

Butch meets up with his girlfriend, who was supposed to bring him his prized gold watch; she forgot, so he has to return to his apartment to retrieve it.

In his apartment, he discovers Vincent Vega, who has been sent to kill him. He kills Vincent instead. Then, as Butch is escaping, he runs into Marsellus. The two men chase each other into a pawn shop, where they are assaulted by terrifying hillbillies. Marsellus is raped by one of the hillbillies, but then rescued by Butch. After this, Marsellus lets Butch go, and Butch and his girlfriend escape.

In his apartment, he discovers Vincent Vega, who has been sent to kill him. He kills Vincent instead. Then, as Butch is escaping, he runs into Marsellus. The two men chase each other into a pawn shop, where they are assaulted by terrifying hillbillies. **Marsellus is raped by one of the hillbillies, but then rescued by Butch. After this, Marsellus lets Butch go, and Butch and his girlfriend escape.**

"The Bonnie Situation": The film returns us to the apartment where Vincent and Jules are executing the double-crossers. One surprises them by coming out of the bathroom with a gun; he shoots, misses, and is in turn shot by Vincent and Jules. Jules believes the shots missing them is a "miracle" and has an epiphany leading to a sense of redemption.

Vincent and Jules take their informant, who has survived the bloodbath in the apartment, out to their car to get away, but then accidentally shoot him in the head while driving. They have to take the car to their friend Jimmy for help removing the evidence of this, and they have to finish the job before Jimmy's wife Bonnie comes home from the night shift at the hospital where she is a nurse.

Vincent and Jules finish with the car and decide to go to the diner to have breakfast together—the same diner from the beginning, and as they are eating, Pumpkin and Honey Bunny begin robbing the customers.

Jules convinces Pumpkin to stop the crime and walk away by sharing the story of his spiritual epiphany and redemption. Pumpkin and Honey Bunny agree and leave the diner together. Vincent and Jules leave, and Jules goes off to walk the earth in search of greater spiritual understanding after returning the suitcase to Marsellus.

ultimately satisfying conclusion. The shuffling of plot components means that certain questions are never actually answered, and it also means that our judgment of the characters is directed in ways it might not otherwise have been.

If we look at the events of the narrative in the order presented versus the events rearranged to occur in chronological order, it looks like Table 4.2. (In order to emphasize the resolution of each "chapter," I've bolded those events in the left-hand column.)

Several things become clear in comparing the two versions of the structure of *Pulp Fiction*. First of all, by looking at the "resolution" of each "chapter," and then considering each in the context of the film as a whole, we can see that Tarantino has chosen the device of the "chapter" in order to underscore his characters' abilities to reason ethically, and the consequences of that reasoning. Vincent makes the decision to save Mia's life—and more importantly, he convinces the drug dealer, who keeps insisting "it's not my problem," to behave in an ethical manner by helping. Butch makes the decision to rescue Marsellus, the man who is trying to kill him. Jules makes the decision to talk Pumpkin and Honey Bunny out of robbing, and possibly murdering, the diner customers, and also sets them off on what we might read as a path to their own redemption. Each resolution illuminates the characters' realization that they are in relationship with and obligated to other people, and they act accordingly.

Shuffling and reshuffling the plot elements also alters our experience of cause and effect, especially by revealing instances where characters' carelessness leads to dire consequences: Mia's mistaking Vincent's heroin for cocaine and snorting it, resulting in her near-death, Butch's girlfriend's carelessness in forgetting to bring the watch, resulting in the death of Vincent Vega. While it is true that Vincent is a terrible person, by the time of his death we have come to like him. We have seen him dance with Mia (the famous "twist" scene in Jack Rabbit Slim's), and we have seen him save her life. If his death were to occur when in the film it is supposed to, chronologically, it would, perhaps, be unsatisfactory. We would feel we have been robbed of a character we have come to like, or have barely gotten to know. Because of Tarantino's choices, however, Vincent dies in the middle of the film, and essentially returns from the dead for the final third of the movie, in "The Bonnie Situation," and we get to see how the rest of his relationship with Jules plays out. Finally, the choice to create gaps through the use of an achronological structure means the end of the film is given to Jules and his redemption, not Butch and his escape. Butch becomes a minor character with a moment of nobility, while Jules becomes the hero. Tarantino's choices show us the importance of ending, the weight that an ending carries in relation to the overall plot and the progression towards resolution. Jules is given a dynamism at the end that makes us appreciate and believe in his epiphany, especially as we have grown to like him.

Narrative and empathy

In our consideration of character we have addressed the ways readers develop relationships with character; the ways constellations of traits permit entry into a storyworld and "mind-reading"; and the ways they can function mimetically in order to foster ethical responses and judgments on the part of the reader. You may recall our discussion in Chapter 2 of Blakey Vermeule's claims about character, and the ways literary texts activate certain cognitive processes that enable us to recognize, understand, and have emotional responses to character. One such response is empathy, and the study of empathy and narrative has been affected by cognitive science in ways similar to other areas of narrative studies. Thus age-old questions about how we enter into an empathetic relationship with characters, and what narrative can do to foster empathy in readers, are being considered from new perspectives.

Important work on this issue has been done by Suzanne Keen. While it is true that narrative acts have effects on readers which lead them to make judgments and have responses (including ethical responses and emotional responses), those rhetorical strategies do not have the same effect on every reader. Perhaps there is a purpose to a particular rhetorical act—certainly there is—but whether that purpose is achieved and has the desired impact on a reader is a tricky thing. Different readers will have different capacities for experiencing empathy, for ethical reasoning, for their ability to relate to characters. Likewise, the constellation of traits that generates a sense that one can relate to a character might work in one reader but not another. The context of an audience matters; time and place and moment in history and socio-cultural position do as well, as do a number of other factors that affect the level of control an author can exert on a reader's response (Keen 214). The type of text matters, too; we are perhaps more likely to feel empathy for a character in a graphic novel or a film because the image of the human face is so powerful. Finally, whether we have ourselves experienced what a character is going through makes a difference. Will it be harder for me to empathize with a character who has lost a parent because I have not gone through a similar experience? Or am I just human and so I can recognize loss and respond accordingly?

Keen defines three kinds of empathy in narrative. The first, *bounded strategic empathy*, works from a position of "mutuality," where the reader recognizes a shared experience. The second, *ambassadorial strategic empathy*, uses an "ambassador," a representative to the reader for a chosen group whose job is to cultivate empathy. The third, *broadcast strategic empathy*, "emphasiz[es] common vulnerabilities and hopes through universalizing representations" (215). Let's take the novel *Herzog*, by Saul Bellow, which to my mind uses all three strategies. First, I experience empathy for the main character, Herzog, because he is an academic; I am also an academic, and this experience of mutuality enables me to recognize a shared experience. However, I am not a middle-aged Jewish man going through a terrible mid-life crisis, so there is less of a sense of mutuality there; on the other hand, the largely epistolary feature of the novel—the story unfolds through the writing of letters—allows me to have access to Herzog's mind, and the use of flashbacks tells me something about his past. He thus becomes an "ambassador," and through my empathy with him I can empathize with the situation as a whole and who he is as a "person" beyond his commonality with me. Finally, I see in Herzog a figure that resonates thematically with feelings of loss, of anger, and in this way I see his representation as connecting with universal ideas and vulnerabilities.

A number of narrative devices we have defined and examined over the course of this book all work to generate narrative empathy: character, situation, perspective. Yet these can also be sites of empathic inaccuracy (Keen 223). If we accept that the creation of empathy happens through rhetorical acts, performed through the deliberate choice of certain narrative strategies (which we certainly might after reading about James Phelan's ideas above), then we have to consider what happens when the rhetorical purpose of creating empathy is not achieved—when the communicative act breaks down. In this case, there is a gap between the author's empathy in being able to imagine the character and situation, and the reader's empathy in having the appropriate (or hoped-for) response. The relationship between teller and audience breaks down. This might be a fault of the narrative, but it might also be a fruitful instance for investigating more closely how the rhetorical strategies of narrative work, and what happens when they fail.

Conclusion

Our thinking about narrative ethics helps us make a good case for why stories matter, and why the kind of humanistic inquiry into how stories do their work is still so necessary. Throughout the course of this book, we have talked about narrative as the making, experiencing, and sharing of stories. We have a deeply human need to tell others about what it's like to be in the world from our own highly individualized perspectives. We hope that maybe the people on the other end of the telling learn something from our stories. But we are also deeply attracted to the *art* of storytelling, the ways its structures—its art— help us shape meaning in the world, even help us create entirely new worlds and immerse ourselves within them. So, the next time you look up from a book and can't believe how much time has passed; the next time your friend tells you about her day; the next time you're at a funeral listening to a eulogy or a wedding listening to how the couple met; the next time you hear politicians talk about "changing the narrative"; the next time you're at the doctor's office or posting on Tumblr or reading a comic book or crying in the movie theater—the next time you're doing any of these completely human things, remember: *stories matter*. And it is the matter of stories that make us who we are.

Works cited

Abbott, H. Porter. *The Cambridge Introduction to Narrative*. 2nd ed. New York: Cambridge UP, 2008. Print.

——. *Real Mysteries: Narrative and the Unknowable*. Columbus: Ohio State UP, 2013. Print.

Alber, Jan and Fludernik, Monika, ed. *Postclassical Narratology: Approaches and Analyses*. Columbus: Ohio State UP, 2010. Print.

Altes, Liesbeth Korthals. "Ethical Turn." *The Routledge Encyclopedia of Narrative Theory*. Ed. David Herman, Manfred Jahn, and Marie-Laure Ryan. New York: Routledge, 2005. 142–46. Print.

Aristotle. *Nicomachean Ethics. The Complete Works of Aristotle*. Vol. 2. Trans. W. D. Ross. Ed. Jonathan Barnes. Princeton, NJ: Princeton UP, 1984. 1729–1867. Print.

——. *Rhetoric. The Complete Works of Aristotle*. Vol. 2. Trans. W. D. Ross. Ed. Jonathan Barnes. Princeton, NJ: Princeton UP, 1984. 2152–2251. Print.

Booth, Wayne. *The Rhetoric of Fiction*. 2nd ed. Chicago: U of Chicago P, 1983. Print.

Cavell, Stanley. *Pursuits of Happiness: The Hollywood Comedy of Remarriage*. Cambridge, MA: Harvard UP, 1984. Print.

Charon, Rita. "Narrative Medicine: Attention, Representation, Affiliation." *Narrative* 13 (2005): 261–270. Print.

Derrida, Jacques. *On Hospitality*. Trans. Rachel Bowlby. Redwood City, CA: Stanford UP, 2000. Print.

Herman, David, ed. *Narratologies: New Perspectives on Narrative Analysis*. Columbus: Ohio State UP, 1999. Print.

——. "Directions in Cognitive Narratology." *Postclassical Narratology: Approaches and Analyses*. Ed. Jan Alber and Monika Fludernik. Columbus: Ohio State UP, 2010. 137–162. Print.

Iser, Wolfgang. *The Implied Reader: Patterns of Communication in Prose Fiction from Bunyan to Beckett*. Baltimore, MD: Johns Hopkins UP, 1974. Print.

Keen, Suzanne. "A Theory of Narrative Empathy." *Narrative* 14 (2006): 207–36. Print.

Kreiswirth, Martin. "Narrative Turn in the Humanities." *The Routledge Encyclopedia of Narrative Theory*. Ed. David Herman, Manfred Jahn, and Marie-Laure Ryan. New York: Routledge, 2005. 377–382. Print.

Levinas, Emmanuel. *Time and the Other*. Trans. Richard Cohen. Pittsburgh, PA: Duquesne UP, 1990. Print.

Newton, Adam Zachary. *Narrative Ethics*. Cambridge, MA: Harvard UP, 1995. Print.

Nussbaum, Martha. *Love's Knowledge*. New York: Oxford UP, 1990. Print.

——. *Poetic Justice: The Literary Imagination and Public Life*. Boston: Beacon Press, 1995. Print.

Palmer, Alan. *Fictional Minds*. Lincoln: U of Nebraska P, 2004. Print.

Phelan, James. "Rhetoric/Ethics." *Cambridge Companion to Narrative*. Ed. David Herman. New York: Cambridge UP, 2007. 203–16. Print.

——. "Imagining a Sequel to *The Rhetoric of Fiction*; Or, A Dialogue on Dialogue." *Comparative Critical Studies* 7 (2010): 243–55. Print.

Spolsky, Ellen. *Gaps in Nature: Literary Interpretation and the Modular Mind*. Albany: SUNY Press, 1993. Print.

Sternberg, Meir. *Expositional Modes and Temporal Ordering in Fiction*. Baltimore, MD: Johns Hopkins UP, 1978. Print.

Exemplary texts

The 40-Year-Old Virgin. Dir. Judd Apatow. Perf. Steve Carell and Catherine Keener. Universal, 2006. Film.

Albee, Edward. *Who's Afraid of Virginia Woolf?* New York: NAL, 2006. Print.

Austen, Jane. *Sense and Sensibility*. New York: Penguin, New York, 2003. Print.

The Awful Truth. Dir. Leo McCarey. Perf. Irene Dunne and Cary Grant. Columbia, 1937. Film.

Bellow, Saul. *Herzog*. New York: Penguin, 2003. Print.

Cunningham, Michael. *The Hours*. New York: Picador, 2000. Print.

Ferber, Edna. *Fanny Herself*. Urbana-Champagne: U of Illinois P, 2001. Kindle file.

Flynn, Gillian. *Gone Girl*. New York: Broadway Books, 2014. Print.

Freud, Sigmund. "Fragment of an Analysis of a Case of Hysteria ("Dora")." *The Freud Reader*. Ed. Peter Gay. New York: Norton, 1989. 172–238. Print.

Household, Geoffrey. *Rogue Male*. New York: NYRB Classics, 2007. Print.

McEwan, Ian. *On Chesil Beach*. New York: Anchor, 2008. Print.

Nabokov, Vladimir. *Lolita*. New York: Vintage, 1989. Print.

Pulp Fiction. Dir. Quentin Tarantino. Perf. John Travolta, Samuel L. Jackson, Ving Rhames, Uma Thurman, Bruce Willis. Miramax, 1994. Film.

Shteyngart, Gary. *Absurdistan*. New York: Random House, 2007. Print.

Woolf, Virginia. "The Mark on the Wall." *The Complete Shorter Fiction of Virginia Woolf*. Ed. Susan Dick. New York: Harcourt, 1989. Print.

——. *Mrs. Dalloway*. New York: Harcourt Brace Jovanovich, 1990. Print.

Recommended further reading

Booth, Wayne. *The Company We Keep: An Ethics of Fiction*. Berkeley: U of California P, 1989. Print.

Gibson, Andrew. *Postmodernity, Ethics, and the Novel: From Leavis to Levinas*. New York: Routledge, 1999. Print.

Keen, Suzanne. *Empathy and the Novel*. New York: Oxford UP, 2010. Print.

Phelan, James. *Experiencing Fiction: Judgments, Progressions, and the Rhetorical Theory of Narrative*. Columbus: Ohio State UP, 2007. Print.

——. *Living to Tell About It: A Rhetoric and Ethics of Character Narration*. Ithaca, NY: Cornell UP, 2005. Print.

Robbins, Jill. *Altered Reading: Levinas and Literature*. Chicago: U of Chicago P, 1999. Print.

Engagements: Interview with Adam Zachary Newton

Adam Zachary Newton is University Professor and Ronald P. Stanton Chair in Literature and Humanities at Yeshiva University with teaching and research interests in the ethics of reading, narrative poetics, literary theory/criticism, hermeneutics, and Jewish Studies. Dr. Newton's publications include *Narrative Ethics* (Harvard, 1995), *Facing Black and Jew: Literature as Public Space in Twentieth-Century America* (Cambridge, 1998), *The Fence and the Neighbor: Emmanuel Levinas, Yeshayahu Leibowitz, and Israel Among the Nations* (SUNY, 2001), *The Elsewhere: On Belonging at a Near Distance—Reading Literary Memoir from East Central Europe and the Levant* (Wisconsin, 2005), *To Make the Hands Impure: Art, Ethical Adventure, the Difficult and the Holy* (Fordham, 2015), and his work in progress, *Jewish Studies as Counterlife: A Report to the Academy* (Fordham, 2017).

How would you describe your approach to narrative
studies and/or narrative theory?

As one of six presentations in the Contemporary Narrative Theory plenary at the 2015 ISSN conference, mine bore the subtitle, "Notes from an Outlier in the Meta-Narratological Enterprise." What did I mean, exactly? By way of elaboration here, I would describe my approach to narrative studies as an informal supplement (minority report?) to the four regnant models of post-classical narrative theory outlined in *The Core Concepts and Critical Debates* volume (Ohio State University Press, 2012): rhetorical, feminist (one among several such contextualist paradigms), cognitivist, and anti-mimetic. Cutting athwart all four in different ways and stopping short of both an holistic account *and* a formal theory, my own work on narrative represents what might be called a performative intervention or a critical poetics—more pragmatics than grammar, if you will. As such, it is in keeping with an evolving focus on the ethics of reading that has become the organizing category for my work subsequent to *Narrative Ethics* (Harvard, 1993).

As to that particular book-title (for which, when composing the 1990–1992 dissertation on which it was based, the few phrasal antecedents were confined to essays in philosophy related to the work of Paul Ricoeur): the entry for "narrative ethics" on the online *Living Handbook of Narratology* defines it thus:

> Narrative ethics explores the intersections between the domain of stories and storytelling and that of moral values. Narrative ethics regards moral values as an integral part of stories and storytelling because narratives themselves implicitly or explicitly ask the question, 'How should one think, judge, and act—as author, narrator, character, or audience—for the greater good?'

This is not a, however, a definition to which my deployment of the phrase corresponds. If anything, my work in *Narrative Ethics* and thereafter has sought to decenter both the question *and the normative discourse* of moral values, in line with ethical philosophies that could all be said to stage projects of decentering: decentering knowledge (Stanley Cavell), decentering (by "dialogizing") speech and discourse (M. M. Bakhtin), decentering (or "altering") the ethical subject (Emmanuel Levinas). In my work, "ethics" signifies not the abstract, notional matter of values (narrative or otherwise) but the almost material pressure of some force exerted by some Other: another person, the act of telling of a story or of listening to a story, the witnessing, transmission, legacy, *Nachträglichkeit* of a story, the palpable friction between stories, the recapitulation or re-enactment of and by story, the story as an embodied thing. I especially admire Geoffrey Harpham's formulation from *Shadows of Ethics* (Duke, 1999): "Ethics is where thought itself experiences an obligation to form a relation with its other—not only other thoughts but other-*than*-thought .... Ethics does not solve problems, it structures them."

If for Levinas and likewise, ethics signifies a kind of refracting optics (thus he will write, "the experience of morality does not proceed from this vision, it *consummates* this vision"), one might call this embodied account of reading, ethics-as-haptics, since among its various entailments are: force, (im)mobilization, impression, after-effect, touch. Nothing in it, however, necessarily or sufficiently aims at "the greater good," which marks the divergence of my thinking from a normative line of narrative theory predicated on a set of meta-normative "ethical" principles. On this model of reading as an event, ethics empties as much as it fills, undoes as much as does, is both transitive and intransitive, the stuff of affects as much as effects, and in my most recent work, a being-touched while touching.

Constellated at the meta-level of narratology and its own "beyond," I would have to situate my particular concerns on what the great Polish-Jewish original Bruno Schulz called a "branch track," relative to the high-speed network on which the twenty-first century Narratological Maglev travels, with its still-trending instrumentalities of "new media and narrative logics, new technologies and emergent methodologies" (Herman, *Narratologies*) in what has been dubbed postclassical narratology's second phase (Alber and Fludernik). Thus, I might take Fludernik's four organizing paramaters with which readers construe an unfolding narrative—*Telling, Viewing, Acting, and Experiencing*—and grow it into a pentad. The quasi-formal, fifth element I would add—albeit as an intervention that leaves the stricter bounds of narratology behind—is: *Holding*, an ethical figure for what my most recent work calls "the book-in-hand." Or, recasting the subtitle of a recent essay by David Herman about transmediality and cognitivism, I would replace the last member of the triad, "Triangulating Stories, Media, and the Mind," with *Hand*—another figure for an embodied ethics of reading. Herman's exemplary text in that essay, "Directions in Cognitive Narratology," is Blake's lyric poem "The Poison Tree," for whose "cognitive economy" he focuses particularly on the word "see" with its various perceptual entailments, and on the poem's "multimodal staging of discourse practices" and its framing conventions of "emotionology." If only for the contrast *and* the Romanticist synergy, I would revisit the famous Coleridge poem [*The Rime of the Ancient Mariner*] I discussed in *Narrative Ethics* back in the day. "*He holds him with his skinny hand/ Hold off! unhand me, grey-beard loon!'/ He holds him with his glittering eye*": for me, the ethics in these verses are recorded in the nouns and verbs, the acts, the commands of "unhand" and "hold"— perhaps not coincidentally an action intimately and mechanically bound up with the act of reading itself, even as embodied in the state-of-the-art form we now conventionally refer to as "*hand-held* devices" or "*touch-screens*" (which, however, as film critic David Thomson puts it, render touch as a "fraud and a tragic, uncrossed threshold"). For me, as well, the least compelling moment in Coleridge's famous poem and its internal narrative is the apothegmic stanza and its moralizing formula, which, while it may indeed construct an ideologically necessary link between moral values, stories, and storytelling by proposing how to think, judge, and act for the greater good constitutes an instance of meta-normative "branding," whose artificial moralizing closure sidesteps the specifically narrative energies the poem has left unbound. Ethics, by my alternate reckoning, is also about books' own material situation: as hand(l)ed, and with a wish, perhaps—or at least a forcing of the possibility, like Wedding Guest in the clutches of Mariner—to be "unhanded."

Describe your most recent project. What prompted your interest?
What were you hoping to achieve? What questions or ideas
in the field do you see it responding to?

In programmatically direct engagement with these notions of hand(l)ed and unhanded, my most recent book (2015) is entitled *To Make the Hands Impure: Art, Ethical Adventure, the Difficult and the Holy.* Although it returns to the troika of Levinas–Bakhtin–Cavell for certain philosophical underpinnings, its focus is not on narrative per se. Rather, it configures a range of examples—Henry Darger's fiction, the September 11th memorial, rabbinic discussions of ritual "impurity and purity," Martin Scorsese's *Hugo*, Conrad's *Nostromo*, the poetics of touch (Merleau Ponty, Nancy, Derrida, Chrétien), worship in a Havana synagogue—all of which, in some way, stage, model, or problematize an ethics of reading. Across the divide customarily separating sacred and secular reading practices, the book situates its inquiry on the corporeal plane Levinas calls "the sensible." The axial point—what Harpham would call the *hub or matrix* that is ethics—is the embodied situation of "the book in hand." The organizing question, refracted by a number of these optics, is a deceptively simple one, but for me, the most (quite literally) pressing one: what does it mean to handle—that is, become responsible for, the book—any book—that lies in our hands? A "live" version of these ideas was presented at the 2015 ISSN [International Society for the Study of Narrative] conference, where I focused on putatively "unreadable" works by Henry Darger and Arthur Crew Inman.

That presentation concluded with a reframed definition of "the ethics of reading": neither the stuff of content or intent, but rather something on the order of material, tactile pressure, reading as contact and embodiment. Think of the fourteenth century Vernon manuscript, which requires two people to turn over the pages and a separate table to accommodate its size. Ethics, in this sense, has to do with books' own material situation: as *handled*, and thus especially in the Darger example, with a kind of exorbitant care in some ratio to its demand—a demand on our time and consciousness and readerly energy, certainly but also as an object that solicits custodianship.

I ended by taking the liberty of waking the sleeping metaphor in the title given to the online "Living Handbook of Narratology"—that is the word "handbook," which so conveniently fuses embodied personhood to embodied writing. As you can see, whatever questions this book may be responding to lie somewhat outside or supplementary to the field—although I would like to identify that place, in Levinasian–Bakhtinian–Cavellian fashion, as lying exactly *on its border.*

What scholars and texts have influenced your approach?

I've been drawn to (or have configured) a conversation between an account of narrative particulars on the one hand, and philosophical projects like those of Levinas, Cavell, and Bakhtin. While my interest in the specifically narrative implications of such projects most certainly falls under postclassical narratological headings like *experientiality* (Fluderdnik) or *voices and worlds* (Marie-Laure Ryan), it more closely resembles a genre of philosophical poetics on display in Judith Butler's *Giving an Account of Oneself* (2003) or Adriana Cavarero's *Relating Narratives: Storytelling and Selfhood* (2000) and *For More Than One Voice: Toward a Philosophy of Vocal Expression* (2005), and also the more pragmatically oriented "handbook" by Derek Attridge, *The Singularity of Literature* (2011). I would therefore also distinguish it from the uses of the ethical in the field-dominant rhetorical-communicative model in both its American and German-Scandinavian versions, as well an older strain of Anglo-American "ethical criticism."

What do you see as big questions confronting the field? Where's the cutting edge? What are the trends?

Inasmuch as a "boutique strategy company that solves thorny and difficult but fascinating problems" recently advertised for a "freelance narratologist," one such edge may be the seam between academic research and the corporate world. Within the boundaries of the former, though, I think it's fair to say that mind-oriented (Herman), biocultural (Easterlin), and evolutionary-critical (Gottschall) trends meet at the cutting edge right now. Transmedial and transgeneric studies of "platform" (Ryan) and comparatavist- cross-cultural (Helff) paradigms would also qualify as framing some of the field's "big questions." Quite possibly its biggest question is what enduringly fascinated Einstein: the promise of a UFT (unified field theory) for what's now acknowledged as a *plurality* of postclassical narratologies, formal and contextualist alike—some still shaped by regional-national contours of a particular "school" or language community, others by their attention to disciplinary practices, still others with respect to medium, system, or assemblage. In response to a question from the *Amsterdam International Electronic Journal for Cultural Narratology* (No. 6, Autumn 2010/Autumn 2011) about theoretical horizons ahead, David Herman wisely rejoined, "it is difficult to make predictions about the future development of a field undergoing such rapid expansion and transformation," while nevertheless identifying three particular trends: (1) globalized studies as the "necessary complement" to the transmedial; (2) the distinctive character of literary narrative; (3) a multimodal account of story. To these, one might add continuing developments in newly developed subfields like narrative medicine, where, for instance (as responses to a 2015 query on "rape narratives and the rhetoric of assault and survival" explained), the plotlines of traumatic accounts and the neurobiology of trauma converge. But as the last two and obviously still classical elements in Herman's list suggest, and given the current picture in the world away of theoretical physics, where theories general relativity and quantum mechanics remain to be fully coordinated and where gravity itself still awaits successful inclusion in a theory of everything, narrative's UFT beckons from just beyond the horizon. (I note only coincidentally that "the beyond" also marks the region assigned by Levinas to ethics and ethical experience.)

What are you working on next?

Actually, I've exchanged a concern with narrativity on a theoretical-textual plane with something closer to home: a quasi-memoir that doubles as a manifesto of sorts. Its working title is *Jewish Studies as Counterlife: A Report to the Academy*. Its focus is the transdisciplinary, cross-cultural academic pursuit known as Jewish Studies. I want to reflect on its situatedness and also its displacing or decentering properties in regard to topics, fields, practices, major disciplines, and satellite fields—as a special instance of a modern intellectual pursuit both with and against the grain. Both lever (in Derrida's special sense of *mochlos*), and sometimes shadowy supplement, academic Jewish Studies lives, in part, a kind of prosthetic life, hinged or grafted onto practices both academically "prior" (e.g., history of religion, philology) and immediately contemporary (area studies). In asking how its leverage might be utilized for redirected force, the project looks to one source of mechanical load or resistance in particular—the mass of verbiage across a range of venues (scholarly journals, institutional reports and white-papers, general interest books, and the public press) accumulating around the humanities, frequently depicted in a state of decline or crisis. As we know from our middle-school training in trigonometry and geometry, triangulation "is the process of determining the location of a point by measuring angles to it from known points at either end of a fixed baseline, rather than measuring distances to the point directly (trilateration)." Transposed to the non-mathematical, this book, likewise, seeks to locate a set of coordinates in the twenty-first century university (whatever eventually becomes of it)—the point at which Jewish Studies, the humanities, and my own particular academic sojourn meet. In short, one more, very possibly quixotic, sally to the borderline.

Engagements: Interview with Suzanne Keen

Suzanne Keen writes about narrative empathy and the impact of immersion reading. Her affective and cognitive studies combine expertise in the novel and narrative theory with interests in neuroscience, developmental and social psychology, and emotion science. Her books include *Thomas Hardy's Brains, Empathy and the Novel, Romances of the Archive in Contemporary British Fiction, Victorian Renovations of the Novel*, and a volume of poetry. Co-editor of *Contemporary Women's Writing*, she has guest edited special issues of *Poetics Today* and *Style*. She serves as Thomas H. Broadus Professor of English and Dean of the College at Washington and Lee University.

How would you describe your approach to narrative studies and/or narrative theory?

I work in the broad tradition of rhetorical narratology. That means I am concerned not only with texts and forms, but also with what narrative artists do and how readers, the co-creators, participate in narrative transactions. As with many rhetorical narrative theorists (Wayne Booth, James Phelan), this work often has an ethical dimension. An empirically minded feminist, I try to practice an intersectional narratology attentive to multiple intersecting axes of identity—primarily as this would concern readers and their various responses. While I am very interested in the description and analysis of narrative techniques, all of my own interpretive work about narrative literature has involved historical contexts. So even in work that others recognize as part of the newer affective angle of cognitive literary studies, I remain committed to the particularities of history and context. I have also made forays into interdisciplinary scholarship, reading and engaging with developmental psychology and social neuroscience.

Describe your most recent project. What prompted your interest? What were you hoping to achieve? What questions or ideas in the field do you see it responding to?

My most recent book is *Thomas Hardy's Brains: Psychology, Neurology, and Hardy's Imagination* (2014). I have been reading Hardy since I was 16 years old and teaching his work for many years, so when I began to learn about embodied cognition and the science of affect, I often thought of Hardy. I thought (and later confirmed) that Hardy didn't know Freud's work, but I wondered whether he had ever heard of Phineas Gage, whose dramatic life story and personality change after a serious brain injury seemed like it could have been written by Hardy! I turned to Hardy's letters, his self-ghosted biography, and most importantly his reading journals and notebooks to discover what he knew about the field we now call psychology. Most scholars have focused on Hardy's interest in science and philosophy, but there was a significant gap concerning psychology.

In this book I ended up examining the imagery of brains and nerves that Hardy used, showing that he knew the psychology of his own time—from the high Victorian period into the 1920s. By tracing what Hardy read and wrote, I showed how Hardy's representations of minds, the will, and consciousness (and nescience—what Hardy called the self-unknowing) revealed his knowledge of Victorian brain science and Victorian medical neurology. My specific narrative theoretical interest in this book focused on the unusual techniques Hardy used to represent fictional consciousness in his fiction. Hardy employs psycho-narration a lot more and narrated monologue (free indirect discourse) a lot less than his Victorian novelist peers. He often comments on what his characters can't know or don't think about. I believe that his technical choices were motivated by and demonstrate his understanding of monist philosophy and materialist brain science.

I saw this book as an opportunity to see whether—and how—changing understandings of affect and cognition had been registered by an alert humanist who was reading the science of his own day. *Thomas Hardy's Brains* participates in the ongoing conversation about contextual cognitive literary study, using not only the tools of narrative and poetic analysis, but also old-fashioned examination of sources and influences.

What scholars and texts have influenced your approach?

Alan Richardson's work on the Romantic poets, *British Romanticism and the Science of the Mind* (2001), profoundly influenced my search through Hardy's poetry and fiction for neurological imagery. I was inspired in that quest by Lisa Zunshine's commitment to a contextualist, historicist cognitive literary studies.

My narrative theory runs in a channel fed by many tributaries: Wayne C. Booth, Dorrit Cohn, Gérard Genette, Meir Sternberg, Monika Fludernik, Alan Palmer, Peter Rabinowitz, Brian Richardson, James Phelan, Robyn Warhol, and Susan Lanser are some of the many theorists whose work has informed my thinking. That list is just a sampler.

In my work on narrative empathy, I am most indebted to the science of empathy developed by Nancy Eisenberg, Martin Hoffman, Keith Oatley, Peter Goldie, William Ickes, Jean Decety, Tania Singer, and many other neuroscientists, psychologists, and cognitive scientists with an interest in affect. I read with interest everything that comes out of the Raymond Mar lab and the Dan Johnson lab.

In literary empathy studies my closest interlocutors are Patrick Colm Hogan, Blakey Vermeule, Fritz Breithaupt, and Vera Nünning. To a great degree the participants in the current conversation shape my work—always dialogic, always trying to find the next question within the current propositions about narrative empathy.

What do you see as big questions confronting the field? Where's the cutting edge? What are the trends?

Narrative theory in the future should be transmedial in its attentions. It has shaken off the shackles of a narrow canon. Following the lead of Brian Richardson and other unnatural narratologists, narrative theorists in the future will be emboldened to consider exceptional texts in a range of media. Theorists will be more cautious about proposing taxonomies of form that operate within a confined range of high-brow texts.

Narrative theory's understanding of "the reader" will further open up to understanding diverse readers, viewers, and participants in co-creation.

Narrative theorists will continue to collaborate with scholars in neighboring disciplines. Thanks to the narrative turn, distant neighborhoods in the empirical disciplines seem a lot closer to home than they used to.

What are you working on next?

I am thinking and writing about immersion reading of fiction (sometimes called transportation). I am interested in how immersion in a fictional world encourages experiences of narrative empathy.

Index